Early Childhood Education and Development in Poor Villages of Indonesia

DIRECTIONS IN DEVELOPMENT
Human Development

Early Childhood Education and Development in Poor Villages of Indonesia

Strong Foundations, Later Success

Amer Hasan, Marilou Hyson, and Mae Chu Chang, Editors

THE WORLD BANK
Washington, D.C.

Contents

Figures

Tables

Foreword

Indonesia's economic progress over the past decade has been remarkable. One of the 20 largest economies in the world, Indonesia has a growing middle class, almost 100 percent enrollment in primary school, and improved health outcomes. However, many Indonesian children are not sharing in this progress. The prevalence of moderate to severe stunting continues to be high, threatening children's brain development and their long-term behavioral and cognitive well-being. Many poor children drop out of school at the end of the primary grades, and those who remain in school have notably low academic achievement.

Like many other countries, Indonesia has turned to early childhood education and development (ECED) as a promising strategy to address these problems. Research from developed and developing countries is clear: Children who participate in well-conceived ECED programs are more socially and emotionally competent, develop higher language and cognitive abilities during early childhood, and tend to have greater academic success when they enter school than children who are not enrolled in such programs. Ensuring positive child development, therefore, not only is the right thing to do for the sake of the next generation, but also is an investment in a country's future workforce and capacity to thrive economically and as a society.

A major manifestation of Indonesia's early childhood priorities has been the government's design and implementation of a project funded by the World Bank and the Dutch government, initiated in 2007 and now nearing completion. The government and the World Bank agreed that this project would aim to improve poor children's overall development and readiness for further education within a sustainable quality ECED system. Key components included the establishment of services in more than 6,000 communities through a participatory planning process; support for the country's development of a system to ensure continued ECED quality in the future; and the establishment of effective program management, monitoring, and evaluation. As of 2012, more than 500,000 children have received ECED services through the project.

Early Childhood Education and Development in Poor Villages of Indonesia: Strong Foundations, Later Success documents the background, implementation, and preliminary impact evaluation results of this project. The impact evaluation is based on a sample of more than 6,000 children in two age cohorts, living in 310 poor villages across Indonesia.

http://dx.doi.org/10.1596/978-0-8213-9836-4

Although many countries share Indonesia's intention to improve early development, several features of this book make its publication especially valuable:

- Indonesia is an example of a country that has begun to achieve middle-income status, yet persistent poverty continues to affect its children's well-being. Countries in similar situations will find this book an excellent source of insight.
- The book offers readers unusually rich data on all aspects of health and development in a sample of poor young children, collected with internationally validated measures (often including multiple measures of the same construct), as well as household information, information about parenting practices including feeding patterns, parent questionnaires, and data on the prevalence and distribution of ECED services.
- The book features a detailed description of a community-driven development approach to designing and implementing village ECED services.
- The impact evaluation used a randomized design. To date, few impact evaluations of ECED projects have been conducted with a large sample, with multiple measures, and with data from more than one point in time.

To a great extent, the strength of this report is attributable to the large, multidisciplinary team of government officials, World Bank staff, and consultants who have helped the government to design, implement, and evaluate this project since 2007 and who have contributed to the chapters that follow. The team's collective expertise in economics, child development, policy analysis, and program evaluation has resulted in a contribution that goes well beyond the sum of its parts.

The publication of *Early Childhood Education and Development in Poor Villages of Indonesia: Strong Foundations, Later Success* is timely for the government of Indonesia as it embarks on an accelerated scale-up of early childhood services in villages across the country. It is also timely for others within and outside of the World Bank, who are interested in improving the positive effects of interventions in the early years. The book's final chapter, which discusses the insights gained and lessons learned from this project, will be a useful resource for researchers in early childhood development and program evaluation, policy makers within and beyond Indonesia, early childhood service providers, and advocates for quality early childhood services.

I hope this book will serve to reaffirm the great potential of early childhood services and systems to improve the path of development for the poorest and most vulnerable children.

Tamar Manuelyan Atinc
Vice President and Head of Network (2010–2013)
Human Development Network
The World Bank

Acknowledgments

Early Childhood Education and Development in Poor Villages of Indonesia: Strong Foundations, Later Success is the result of a collaborative effort that brought together a team of professionals from within and outside of the World Bank. The report was prepared under the guidance of Luis Benveniste and Mae Chu Chang by a team led by Amer Hasan (all World Bank). Team members included Hafid I. Alatas (World Bank), Sally Brinkman (Telethon Institute for Child Health Research, University of Western Australia and University of Adelaide), Titie Hadiyati (World Bank), Djoko Hartono (World Bank), Marilou Hyson (World Bank and University of Pennsylvania), Haeil Jung (Indiana University), Angela Kinnell (Telethon Institute for Child Health Research, University of Western Australia and University of Adelaide), Menno Pradhan (Amsterdam Institute for International Development, VU University Amsterdam and the University of Amsterdam), and Rosfita Roesli (World Bank).

The production of this report was generously supported by the Dutch Education Support Program, which is funded by the Government of the Kingdom of the Netherlands. It should be noted that while inputs of various officials have been incorporated into the report, the policy recommendations in this document do not necessarily reflect the policies of the Government of Indonesia or the Government of the Kingdom of the Netherlands.

Sally Brinkman, Menno Pradhan, and Angela Kinnell were supported by an Australian Government AusAID Development Research Awards Scheme grant (ADRA0800261).

The report was improved by detailed feedback from three principal reviewers: Mary Eming Young (Harvard University), F. Halsey Rogers (World Bank), and Michelle J. Neuman (World Bank). Helpful comments were also received from Cristobal Ridao-Cano, Samer Al-Samarrai, Joppe De Ree, Susiana Iskandar (all World Bank), and participants at the Australian National University Indonesia Working Group seminar. Carolyn Goldinger served as the editor. Yvonne Armanto Ramali produced the illustrations and graphics. Mayla Safuro and Husnul Rizal provided excellent research assistance. Megha Kapoor, Isti Rahayuni, Ade Sonya Oktaviane, and Gatot Bayu Surya Ningnagara (all World Bank) were instrumental in the production of the final report.

The analyses presented in these pages would not have been possible without the data collection and quality assurance efforts of Amanda Beatty, Dedy Junaedi, Amelia Maika, Elan Satriawan, and the field teams.

Although the writing of this report has been a collective effort, the principal authors of the chapters are as follows (listed alphabetically):

- Chapter 1: Sally Brinkman, Marilou Hyson, and Angela Kinnell
- Chapter 2: Sally Brinkman, Amer Hasan, Marilou Hyson, and Angela Kinnell
- Chapter 3:
  Section 1: Hafid Alatas, Titie Hadiyati, Djoko Hartono, and Rosfita Roesli
  Section 2: Amer Hasan, Haeil Jung, and Menno Pradhan
- Chapter 4: Mae Chu Chang, Amer Hasan, and Marilou Hyson.

About the Authors

Hafid I. Alatas holds a master's degree in development practice from the University of Queensland, Australia. He is a consultant with the Education Unit of the Human Development Department in the East Asia and Pacific Region at the World Bank.

Sally Brinkman is a social epidemiologist at the Telethon Institute for Child Health Research and holds adjunct positions with the University of Western Australia and the University of Adelaide. Sally brings internationally recognized epidemiological skills particularly in relation to monitoring of child development and early education. She has a commitment to practical, pragmatic, and translatable research.

Mae Chu Chang is a lead education specialist at the World Bank and heads the Human Development Sector of the World Bank in Indonesia. She has worked intensively to help governments develop comprehensive education reform strategies and provide technical advice and financial support in countries in the Middle East, East Asia, and South Asia. Dr. Chang also manages a research program that has produced about 100 titles covering a wide range of topics in education, including early childhood development, basic education and teacher development, and higher education and skills development.

Titie Hadiyati is co-task team leader on the implementation of the Indonesia Early Childhood Education and Development Project. She holds degrees in civil engineering and education evaluation.

Djoko Hartono holds a PhD in demography from the Australian National University. He is a consultant on monitoring and evaluation with the Education Unit of the Human Development Department in the East Asia and Pacific Region at the World Bank.

Amer Hasan holds a PhD in public policy from the University of Chicago, Harris School of Public Policy Studies. He is an economist with the Education Unit of the Human Development Department in the East Asia and Pacific Region at the World Bank.

Marilou Hyson holds a PhD in child development and early childhood education. She is a consultant for the World Bank and other organizations in early child development and education and an adjunct faculty member in the Graduate School of Education at the University of Pennsylvania from Bryn Mawr College.

Haeil Jung is an assistant professor at the School of Public and Environmental Affairs at Indiana University. His research focuses on social policy and program evaluation.

Angela Kinnell is a research fellow at the Telethon Institute for Child Health Research and holds adjunct positions with the University of Western Australia and the University of Adelaide. She has a PhD in psychology from the University of Adelaide. Angela's research examines the factors contributing to child health, development, and well-being.

Menno Pradhan is a professor of project and program evaluation for international development at the VU University Amsterdam and the University of Amsterdam. He is also a fellow of the Tinbergen Institute and the Amsterdam Institute for International Development.

Rosfita Roesli is an education specialist with the Human Development Department of the World Bank Office, Jakarta, and one of the task team leaders of the Early Childhood Education and Development Project. She holds a master of arts degree in development studies from the University of Leeds, United Kingdom.

Abbreviations

BAPPENAS	Agency for National Development Planning Board
BCCT	Beyond Centers and Circle Time
BKB	*Bina Keluarga Balita* (toddler family groups)
BKKBN	National Family Planning Board
BMI	body mass index
BPS	*Badan Pusat Statistik* (Bureau of Statistics)
BSNP	National Education Standards Board
CDD	community-driven development
CDW	child development worker
CPICU	Central Project Implementing and Coordinating Unit
DCCS	Dimensional Change Card Sort
EAP	East Asia and Pacific
ECCD	early childhood care and development
ECCE	early childhood care and education
ECD	early childhood development
ECEC	early childhood education and care
ECED	early childhood education and development
EDI	Early Development Instrument
EFA	Education for All
HDI	Human Development Index
HI ECD	Holistic Integrated ECD
KB	*Kelompok Bermain* (playgroup)
LSAC	Longitudinal Study of Australian Children
M and E	monitoring and evaluation
MDGs	Millennium Development Goals
MoEC	Ministry of Education and Culture (formerly Ministry of National Education)
MoHA	Ministry of Home Affairs
MoNE	Ministry of National Education

MoRA	Ministry of Religious Affairs
MoU	memorandum of understanding
NEST	national early childhood specialist team
OLS	ordinary least squares
PAUD	*Pendidikan Anak Usia Dini* (Early Childhood Directorate)
PISA	Programme for International Student Assessment
PKK	*Pemberdayaan dan Kesejahteraan Keluarga* (Family Empowerment and Welfare) or women's association
PLN	*Perusahaan Listrik Negara* (State Electricity Company)
PODES	*Potensi Desa* (Survey of Village Potential)
Pos-PAUD	*Pos Pendidikan Anak Usia Dini* (ECED posts)
Posyandu	*Pos Pelayanan Terpadu* (village health posts)
RA	*Raudhotul Atfal* (Islamic kindergarten)
RENSTRA	*Rencana Strategis* (Indonesia's strategic plan)
RKM	*Rencana Kegiatan Masyarakat* (community grant proposal)
SDQ	Strengths and Difficulties Questionnaire
SES	socioeconomic status
SMA	*Sekolah Menengah Atas* (senior secondary school)
SPS	*Satuan PAUD Sejenis* (other early childhood units)
SUSENAS	National Socioeconomic Household Survey
TK	*Taman Kanak-kanak* (kindergarten)
TPA	*Taman Penitipan Anak* (child care centers)
TPK	*Tim Pengelola Kegiatan* (activities management team)
TPQ	*Taman Pendidikan Quran* (Islamic kindergarten)
UNICEF	United Nations Children's Fund

Overview

Influenced by the condition of young children within its own country and by the pattern of international evidence about the value of early childhood education and development (ECED), the government of Indonesia has implemented policies and programs that prioritize the early years of children's lives. The first critical step was taken in 2001, when a new directorate dedicated to early childhood was established within the Ministry of Education and Culture. Its early advocacy within and beyond the government influenced policy development, put additional resources into community ECED services, and created strategies to raise Indonesian awareness about the importance of the early years. The second critical step was taken when early childhood education was included in a succession of key policy documents—the National Education System Law No. 20 in 2003 and the Ministry of Education and Culture's Strategic Plan (*Rencana Strategis* or RENSTRA) in 2004.

In 2007, the government of Indonesia launched a project that seeks to improve the school readiness of young children in the nation's poor rural communities through early childhood services. A year later, the need to consider ECED services holistically—across sectors and developmental domains—was recognized through the government's issuance of an ambitious policy strategy and guidelines. The development of national standards for ECED by the National Education Standards Board (BSNP) in 2009 situated early childhood education as the first level of the country's education system.

One lingering barrier to better-coordinated ECED service provision was removed when the "formal" and "nonformal" directorates were merged into one unit in 2010 with responsibility for all ECED activities. In addition, the initiation of the first-ever ECED census in 2011 has begun to provide researchers and policy makers with essential data and will continue to inform ECED decisions in the future.

These milestones of progress are very similar to those of other countries that have worked hard to bring early childhood education onto the national policy agenda. Despite such progress, the major challenges that Indonesia faces today are also akin to those faced by many other middle- and low-income countries.

Enrollment in ECED services is an example. A 4-year-old child from among the richest 20 percent of the country has a 40 percent probability of enrolling in ECED services. In contrast, a 4-year-old child from among the poorest 20 percent of the country has only a 16 percent probability of ever enrolling in ECED services. For the most part, ECED services are privately provided in multiple formats intended to cater to distinct age groups, and several different government ministries regulate the services. These arrangements underscore the continuing challenges in coordinating services and ensuring high quality across service providers.

Against such a background, this book uses Indonesian data to answer five questions with significance for research, policy, and practice within and beyond Indonesia:

1. What does global evidence tell us about the importance of ECED, and what policies and programs has Indonesia implemented to promote ECED?
2. What is the pattern of development among young children in poor villages in Indonesia, and how is that development linked with their families' characteristics and the ECED services typically available to them?
3. What were the processes and challenges of implementing a community-driven ECED project across 50 poor districts in Indonesia?
4. What can be learned from the short-term results of a randomized evaluation of the project's impact on children's development?
5. What insights can be derived from this body of research to inform future policies and practices in Indonesia and beyond?

The experiences and research results discussed in this book are especially relevant for the following:

• Researchers in early childhood development and program evaluation
• Policy makers within and outside of Indonesia
• Providers of early childhood services
• Professional development providers
• Advocates for quality early childhood services.

Early Childhood Research and Indonesia's Young Children

Since the economic crisis of 1997, Indonesia has experienced economic growth, reduced poverty, and made progress toward many of the Millennium Development Goals (MDGs). For poor families, however, national economic improvements have brought only modest gains in health and education. Poverty and the lack of related opportunities continue to challenge the development, school readiness, and educational progress of many of Indonesia's children, which is the subject of chapter 1. The incidence of children whose growth is stunted remains high even in comparison to countries of similar wealth. Poor children in Indonesia are less likely to be enrolled in preschool programs, less likely to continue their education into junior and senior secondary school, and (if they stay in school) less likely to perform well academically than their better-off peers.

International evidence underscores the importance of the early years and the value of early intervention as a tool to mitigate the negative effects of poverty on children's short- and long-term outcomes. It is clear that children's development—including their physical well-being and motor development, language and literacy development, cognitive development, general knowledge, social and emotional development, and executive functions—is the product of multiple interconnected influences, from family environments to the availability of community supports to broad national policies and economic resources. These circles of influence (figure O.1) form the organizing framework of this book.

Poverty challenges this development at all levels, yet in both developed and developing countries research has shown the benefits of ECED services for a child's short- and long-term health and development, as well as economic benefits to society from investing in ECED. Research also shows that the most

Figure O.1 Circles of Influence on a Child's Development

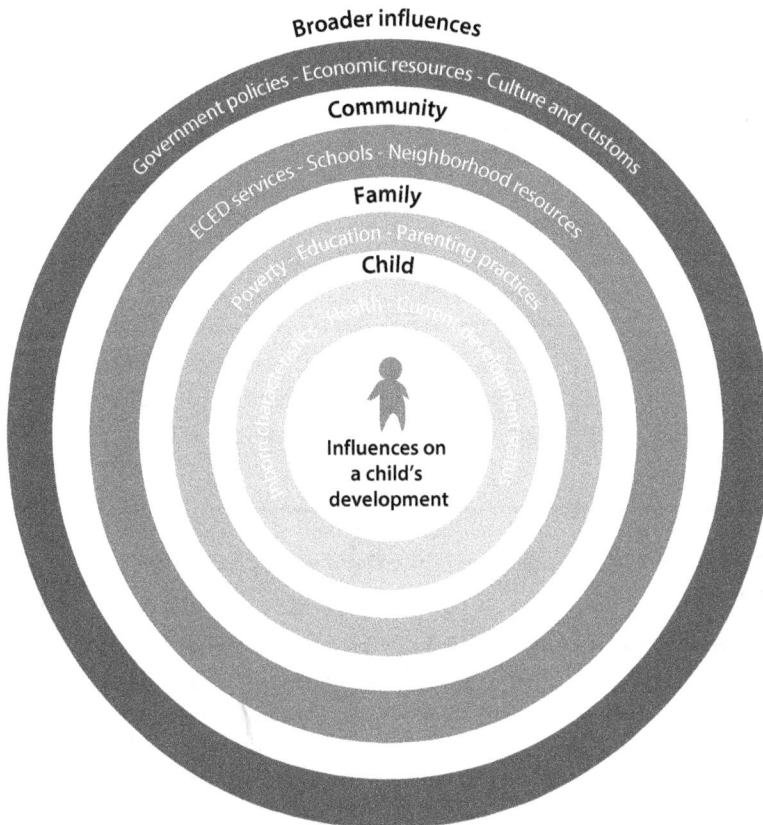

Source: Adapted from Bronfenbrenner 1979.
Note: ECED = early childhood education and development.

Early Childhood Education and Development in Poor Villages of Indonesia •
http://dx.doi.org/10.1596/978-0-8213-9836-4

effective services begin at birth, involve families, target the poorest children, are sufficiently intensive and long-lasting, and are holistic: they include health, nutrition, and parenting in addition to education.

This evidence has influenced significant government attention to ECED policies and services in Indonesia. As a result, the government has taken steps to strengthen the policy environment for ECED. These steps include the establishment of an early childhood directorate, making ECED a priority in national planning documents, and the creation of national ECED standards. With support from the World Bank and other development partners, the government has provided new early childhood services in 6,000 poor communities across 50 districts in the country. The lessons from this experience are the focus of this book.

Young Children in Indonesia's Low-Income Rural Communities: How Are They Doing and What Do They Need?

ECED initiatives have been part of the Indonesian policy agenda for several years. As a consequence, data on ECED enrollment are available, although different sources have chosen various definitions of what constitutes enrollment in ECED. In contrast to the enrollment information, very little information exists on child development outcomes. This book fills a critical gap in knowledge through a variety of child assessments carried out in 2009 and 2010 (box O.1).

These assessments—some of which were being used in Indonesia for the first time—are discussed in chapter 2. They include measurements of each child's height and weight; the Early Development Instrument (EDI), an assessment of five dimensions of school readiness (Janus and Offord 2007); the Strengths and Difficulties Questionnaire (SDQ), assessing social and emotional development (Goodman 1997); the Dimensional Change Card Sort (DCCS) task, which assesses executive function skills (Zelazo 2006); and various other tasks to assess children's abilities across a number of domains, performed directly by the child or, if necessary, reported by the child's mother (adapted from Office of Population Studies 2005). Taken together, these measures provide information about chil-

---

Box O.1 Data on Child Development Are Detailed but Not Nationally Representative

The data describe the development of a sample of children residing in 310 poor villages across nine districts in Indonesia, using a battery of internationally validated measures in multiple domains, from physical health and well-being to cognitive development. Two age cohorts were assessed: in 2009, when the children were ages 1 and 4, and in 2010, when they were 2 and 5. These nine districts are a subset of the 50 districts involved in an ongoing project that provided expanded access to early childhood education and development services for children from birth to age 6.

---

dren's progress across all of the key domains of development considered important for children's school readiness.

Children's Development Shows Strengths but also Areas of Concern

In physical development, this sample of rural children in poor villages showed high rates of stunted growth, wasting, and being underweight for age. The percentage of children with these growth problems declines somewhat with age, but remains high in relation to children in other countries and is consistent with national statistics for Indonesia.

In the domain of language, cognitive, and conceptual development, on average, children in this sample have not gained foundational, age-appropriate school readiness skills in literacy, math, and other aspects of cognitive problem-solving. As reported by their mothers, the children do not seem to have much interest in these domains. Children do improve in their cognitive and conceptual development as they get older, but their competencies in this domain remain low compared with children of the same age in other settings. Additionally, children's conceptual development, as reflected in their ability to draw detailed pictures of humans and houses, was limited at age 4 but improved considerably by age 5. Wide variations in children's abilities were noted.

Assessment of children's executive function skills indicated that children in this sample seem to be developing their abilities to plan and manage their thinking and behavior at about the same rate as children in other countries.

With respect to communication and general knowledge, children performed better in these areas than in the more school-related domain of cognitive and conceptual development. In general, they were reported to speak clearly and to express their wants and needs to others. Children in this sample are able to play imaginatively, tell stories, and show understanding of the everyday world around them.

In social and emotional development, in most respects children in this sample are doing well. Mothers describe their children as independent and cooperative, and they report few behavior problems or examples of emotional difficulties. In addition, children show slight improvements in prosocial behavior—being helpful and concerned about others.

On Average, Home Environments Are Missing Opportunities to Promote Positive Development

Daily Activities

Many everyday opportunities to support development appear to be missing in the home environments of children in this sample. Parents of the vast majority of these children never read books to their children or tell them stories, activities that predict children's later competence in language and literacy. About one-quarter of mothers in these rural villages report that their children never play outdoors, and 17 percent of 4-year-olds never draw or scribble at home. Moreover, the children living in the greatest poverty are the least likely to have these experiences.

Mothers' Feeding Practices

Like mothers in other parts of Indonesia, this sample of mothers does not breast-feed for as long as recommended. Children's daily diets as reported by mothers include snacks more often than they include vegetables or milk.

Parenting Practices

Because higher quality parenting is associated with better developmental out-comes, a 24-item parenting practices interview assessed mothers' (or other pri-mary caregivers') warmth, consistency, and hostility in relation to their children. Mothers of older and younger children reported using similar practices, with wide variations across parents in their child-rearing techniques.

Access to Affordable ECED Services in Poor Villages Has Been Limited

Because these data were collected before project services were available, information was gained about the kinds of ECED services available in typical villages. Only one-third of the subvillages in this study had any kind of playgroup or kindergarten. As in Indonesia as a whole, kindergartens typically serve children ages 4 and up and are privately run, placing them out of reach of most of the poorest families. The most common kind of ECED service was the village health post, usually a volunteer-run, once-a-month service primarily tracking children's physical growth and well-being.

On Average, Children from the Least-Educated and Poorest Families Are Making the Least Developmental Progress

Although the villages in this sample were generally poor, it was possible to look at children's development in relation to levels of parental education and poverty. Taken as a whole, these results show that even in low-income communities, the poorest children and the children with the least-educated parents tend to do less well in many aspects of their early development.

Beyond the Family: Children Living in Poorer Districts and Poorer Communities within Districts Are Developing Less Well

Children's developmental vulnerability scores on one of the major measures used in this study—the EDI—were compared across the sample of districts. Because these districts were selected for their high levels of poverty, it is not surprising that on average the children's vulnerability scores were also high. Within districts, however, there was evidence of socioeconomic disparity—that is, those children living in the poorest households have the greatest developmental vulnerability, especially in the language and cognitive skills domain.

Putting It Together: Both Positive Parenting and Children's ECED Enrollment Contribute to Positive Development

Taking into account the developmental patterns and home environment charac-teristics summarized above, chapter 2 considers whether two potential influ-ences in children's environments—parenting practices within the family and enrollment in ECED services—can improve children's development. The analyses suggest that more stimulating home environments and more access to ECED services are beneficial for children. Both predict differences in children's development even when controlling for other child, household, and village characteristics. This message is encouraging, as these two influences are especially amenable to change through practical strategies.

Providing and Evaluating Services for Low-Income Young Children

These kinds of concerns about the current and future development of the nation's young children prompted the government of Indonesia to develop an ECED project that included both the implementation of ECED services in nearly 3,000 villages across 50 low-income districts and the development of a sustainable quality ECED system. Chapter 3 describes the rationale for and implementation and evaluation of the project, focusing especially on impacts on child development outcomes in the short run from a midline evaluation.

The ECED Project: Background and Implementation

The project's development objective is to improve poor children's overall development and readiness for further education within a sustainable quality ECED system. The project's goals are:

1. To increase integrated ECED service delivery through community-driven mechanisms in targeted poor communities
2. To develop a sustainable system for ECED quality
3. To establish effective program management, monitoring, and evaluation.

Project activities have included the government's ECED policy development and capacity-building efforts at the central and local levels, raising awareness about the importance of ECED within villages, training community members to serve as ECED teachers, and the monitoring and evaluation of project activities.

A Participatory Planning Process Established Community-Based ECED Services

The ECED project used a step-by-step process to identify target districts and communities within those districts, based on objective criteria including district poverty rates and level of district and village commitment to ECED. Using a community-driven development process (CDD) similar to that employed in a number of other projects within and beyond Indonesia, trained local facilitators helped village members identify their ECED needs and prepare proposals for small grants to meet those needs. Most communities used their resources to establish center-based playgroups in existing renovated facilities, primarily serving children ages 3–5, with some satellite services in surrounding areas. Staffed by teachers selected from the community and trained through the ECED project, these centers typically operate at least 3 days a week, usually in 2-hour sessions a day. To date, these centers have served more than 500,000 children.

Villages Selected Local Individuals to Be Trained as ECED Personnel

Villages used objective criteria to identify two local individuals as potential ECED personnel for each site. In response to the realities of typical education levels in project villages, a minimum requirement of secondary school completion was set, with additional criteria including an interest in young children and commitment to ECED.

Training used a cascade approach, with modules developed by a National Early Childhood Specialist Team (NEST). After their own training, they in turn provided 500 hours of training to approximately 200 district and provincial master trainers. These trainers then provided 200 hours of training to the future teachers and child development workers (CDWs), in two blocks of 100 hours each, prior to the village personnel beginning their work with children and families.

Impact Evaluation Results at the Midline

We report results from an ongoing impact evaluation, using both experimental and nonexperimental analyses, of the short-term effects on ECED enrollment and on children's development.

The impact evaluation design relies on the fact that the project was implemented in phases. The ECED project's impact evaluation uses data from two cohorts of children that were studied first in 2009 (baseline) and then again in 2010 (midline). The younger cohort of children were a year old when they were first studied (baseline) and 2 years old when they were studied a second time (midline). The older cohort was 4 years old in 2009 and 5 years old in 2010.

Villages with project-supported services experienced a positive impact on ECED enrollment. The impact analyses show that the ECED project had a clear, statistically significant positive effect on enrollment in ECED services in project villages (including but not limited to enrollment in those services provided by the project). This effect was notable for both cohorts of children. Short-run effects were largest. As children grew older and villages had project-supported ECED services in place for a longer period of time, the impact on enrollment became smaller.

The most positive impacts are on the development outcomes of the most disadvantaged children. We find clear positive and statistically significant effects for children from poorer families, for girls, and for children who were not enrolled at baseline and live in a village with ECED project services. Noteworthy positive results are seen in the domain of language and cognitive development— the domain in which children had been most vulnerable when assessed at baseline. These results emerge when comparing villages with nine months of exposure to the project to villages without project services.

In contrast, the data show only limited impacts on the development of a typical child living in villages where project-supported ECED services had been put in place. Most of the estimates for such a child are in the positive direction, but are not statistically significant. This finding is as expected and underscores the importance of a targeted approach to the provision of ECED services.

No impacts have been seen on nutrition outcomes or parenting practices. At midline there was no impact of having the ECED project in villages on parents' use of more positive parenting practices or on children's nutritional indicators. This is true both for the younger and older cohorts in the sample.

Insights from Indonesia: Implications for Policy and Practice

With a broad vision for the importance of early childhood services, many countries, Indonesia among them, are moving forward on a number of ambitious initiatives. Chapter 4 draws upon the preceding chapters to highlight insights about Indonesian children's development and about the ECED project's planning, implementation, and midline evaluation, linking these insights to emerging ECED priorities. Four such priorities are discussed, placing each within one of the circles of influence that have been the organizational framework of the book throughout.

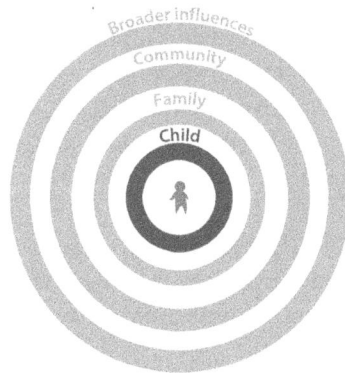

The Influence of Children's Current Characteristics

An effort to obtain valid assessments of young children's health and development must be made so that the results can inform the focus of ECED interventions. With a large sample of two age cohorts of children in poor rural villages, extensive data were available from a set of internationally validated assessments of children's development, collected before project services were implemented. The data indicated that:

1. Information on children's developmental strengths—not just their vulnerabilities—is a useful basis for planning interventions.
2. Assessing children's development holistically can identify areas of risk or vulnerability in more than one domain, suggesting priorities for intervention. Examples include widespread vulnerabilities in children's EDI scores in the language and cognitive domain, together with high levels of stunted growth.

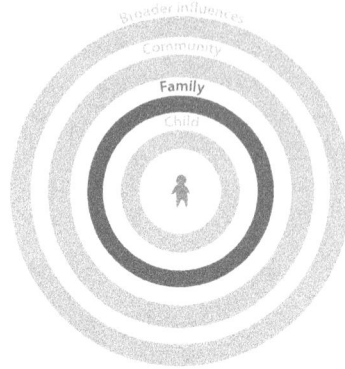

Family Influences

A key role exists for families and family-focused interventions in promoting positive outcomes for children. Family-focused ECED has become a priority in many countries. Data on parenting practices and household characteristics from this study yielded a number of helpful insights.

1. Even for children not enrolled in an ECED program, parents' education and home practices predicted their development, strongly suggesting that parenting should be a priority in government programs and policies.
2. In general, parents in poor villages are eager, motivated supporters of ECED for their children, making them a valuable resource in expanding ECED services.
3. In the absence of explicitly family-focused interventions, it is unlikely that improvements in parenting practices or home environments will be seen—and in this ECED project, such interventions have only recently begun to be observed.
4. Information about home environments and parenting practices is useful in identifying specific targets for family support, such as low incidences of book-reading and storytelling or shorter than optimal periods of breastfeeding.

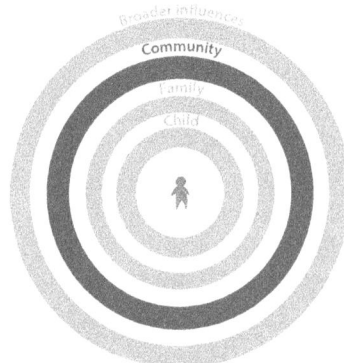

Community Influences: Community-Based ECED Services

A focus on providing comprehensive, community-based ECED services across age groups and sectors can facilitate holistic development. The lack of accessible, affordable ECED services continues to challenge the holistic development of poor children in Indonesia and elsewhere. Insights from the data and implementation experiences described in this book suggest the following:

1. Enrollment in ECED services fosters children's development, especially children from the poorest environments, suggesting that some targeting of services to areas most in need may be effective.
2. Data on village-level enrollment patterns by age provide practical insights because regulations about which services should be attended by which age children do not always fit with local preferences and realities.
3. Communities are ready and willing to engage in a well-facilitated planning process to identify their own ECED needs, but long-term impact may be enhanced through greater involvement of the influential village head or other leadership figure.
4. It is important to locate services in places convenient for families, especially the poorest.
5. Even when lacking a high level of education, teachers selected from rural villages can, with adequate training, serve as motivated ECED personnel.
6. Center-based ECED programs that are organized to serve preschool-aged children have great difficulty meeting the needs of infants, toddlers, and their families. Other approaches to providing holistic services—such as using the village health posts as a base—may be more effective for the youngest children.

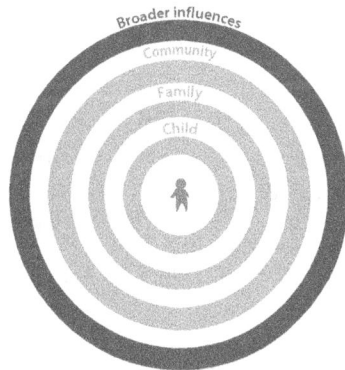

Broader Influences: Policies, Systems, and Resources

Policies, systems, and resources that contribute to long-term sustainability of quality ECED services are needed. Improved outcomes for young children will not be sustained by simply establishing additional ECED programs in communities. Comprehensive policies, systems, and resources are essential supports for sustainability and long-term impact. Although this book's primary focus is the evaluation of community-based services and their effects on children's development, a number of insights may be relevant to this broader purpose.

1. Government commitment to ECED is essential. Participation in this project required evidence of district commitment, such as establishing ECED units within district education offices and including ECED within the district's strategic plan. Such commitments build capacity, contribute to sustainability, and provide models for other poor districts that may be planning ECED initiatives.
2. The presence of significant disparities in children's developmental progress across and within districts suggests that governments should consider targeting areas most in need, while at the same time moving toward universal access.
3. National policies are needed to promote holistic integrated services for young children and their families, addressing common barriers created by the separation of ECED functions into separate ministries and directorates.
4. A cost-effective practical system of supports is needed for current and future ECED personnel. As originally designed, the project's training system would be difficult to scale up and would need more systematic follow-up, coaching, and supervision. Government efforts to implement a variety of in-service activities such as teacher cluster groups and internships may yield promising directions for the future.
5. Quality assurance systems for ECED at all levels are essential. Neither the project's training nor the teachers' classroom practices were systematically evaluated, making it difficult to identify areas for improvement or factors that might mediate the impacts on child outcomes.
6. Monitoring and evaluation efforts are vital if interventions such as these are to be continuously improved. Two lessons emerge from the Indonesian experience. First, program evaluation design needs to be sensitive to program implementation realities. Designs that are robust and immune to foreseeable changes in project implementation timelines are preferable to designs that are easily compromised by routine changes in those timelines. Second, once a design has been agreed upon, project implementation needs to make certain that the design is followed to ensure the quality of the evaluation.

Bibliography

Bronfenbrenner, U. 1979. *The Ecology of Human Development.* Cambridge, MA: Harvard University Press.

Goodman, R. 1997. "The Strengths and Difficulties Questionnaire: A Research Note." *Journal of Child Psychology and Psychiatry* 38 (5): 581–86. doi:10.1111/j.1469-7610.1997.tb01545.x.

Janus, M., and D. Offord. 2007. "Development and Psychometric Properties of the Early Development Instrument (EDI): A Measure of Children's School Readiness." *Canadian Journal of Behavioural Science* 39: 1–22.

Office of Population Studies. 2005. *A Study of the Effects of Early Childhood Interventions on Children's Physiological, Cognitive and Social Development.* Cebu City, Philippines: Office of Population Studies, University of San Carlos.

Zelazo, P. D. 2006. "The Dimensional Change Card Sort (DCCS): A Method of Assessing Executive Function in Children." *Nature Protocols* 1 (1): 297–301. doi:10.1038/ nprot.2006.46.

CHAPTER 1

Early Childhood Research and Indonesia's Young Children

This chapter assesses what global evidence tells us about the importance of early childhood education and development (ECED) and documents some of the policies and programs Indonesia has implemented to promote ECED. Despite economic progress and reductions in poverty, inequalities remain for Indonesia's children and families. Poverty challenges the holistic development and school readiness of many of the country's children. Research on early childhood development suggests ways to address these inequalities and change the trajectory of poor children's development.

In the years from birth to age 6, children develop essential competencies and skills in every area of development, and one of the largest influences on child development is poverty. Poor children are significantly more likely to experience negative outcomes, starting early in life and continuing into adulthood. ECED services can improve outcomes for all children, particularly for those living in poverty. Research has demonstrated the benefits of ECED services for a child's short- and long-term health and development, as well as the social and private economic benefits from investing in ECED. This evidence has prompted an international focus on establishing and expanding ECED services, especially for the poorest children.

Since the economic crisis of 1997, Indonesia's government has made major advances in its policies and investments in ECED. Illustrating these advances and real-world challenges, this book reports on how a sample of rural children in Indonesia is developing. It describes the rationale, implementation, and effects of a community-driven government project supported by the World Bank to increase access to ECED services in poor villages and offers recommendations for future early childhood policies and practices in Indonesia and beyond.

The Indonesian Environment for Children's Development

Indonesia is the world's fourth most populous country, with more than 238 million people living in an archipelago of over 17,000 islands. Recovering from the global financial crisis, Indonesia has experienced economic growth, reduced poverty, and made continued progress toward many of the Millennium Development Goals (MDGs). For example, Indonesia has already met and surpassed projected reductions in the number of underweight children under 5 years of age to below 18 percent and is on track to meeting its targets for reducing overall child mortality and the targets for achieving universal basic education.

Figure 1.1 shows that although clear progress has been made on reducing poverty rates, inequality has persisted, with the result that many children and families have not shared in these gains. More than 30 million Indonesians live below the poverty line (US$2 per day), and half of all households are clustered around the poverty line. Of the poor, 65 percent currently live in rural areas. For these families, national economic improvements have brought only modest gains in health and education, putting children's development at risk and threatening national progress.

Unequal experiences for Indonesia's richer and poorer children and their parents begin early in their lives and are compounded as they get older. The improvement in skilled birth attendance has been impressive, but the poor continue to lag behind in the prevention of maternal deaths and infant mortality. Disparities also exist across provinces, economic quintiles, and education levels (World Bank 2008).

Maternal mortality has fallen from 340 to 220 deaths per 100,000 live births (between 2000 and 2010) in Indonesia, but it remains far above the 2010 average rate of 83 per 100,000 for all developing countries in the East Asia and Pacific (EAP) region. Likewise, between 2000 and 2010 the mortality rates for children under 5 years of age have fallen from 54 to 35, and the infant mortality from 38 to 27, per 1,000 births, but the rates remain far

Figure 1.1 Progress in Poverty Reduction Has Not Been Accompanied by Progress in Inequality Reduction

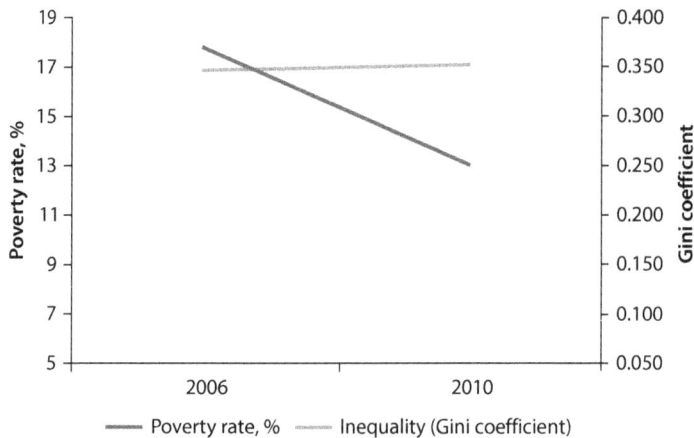

Source: Calculations using SUSENAS 2006, 2010 databases.

above the average for all developing countries in the EAP region in 2010, which stood at 24 and 20, respectively. Births attended by skilled health staff, rates of immunization, and rates of access to improved sanitation facilities also remain behind the region's developing country average. Furthermore, an estimated 42 percent of rural households have children whose growth is stunted, putting these children at risk for long-term cognitive deficits, emotional and behavioral problems, and low school achievement.

Another area of continuing disparity is education. For example, enrollment rates in early childhood programs such as playgroups and kindergartens have been rising in Indonesia, but disparities persist between the rich and the poor (figure 1.2).

A notable achievement for Indonesia is that primary school enrollment is now near 100 percent for boys and girls of all income levels. As children move through the primary years, however, the enrollment disparities seen in ECED services re-emerge. Educational attainment profiles reveal that almost all children from all segments of society start primary schooling, but children from poorer households and children from rural areas have more difficulty progressing from lower levels of education to higher levels. Only 55 percent of rural children make it to junior secondary school, and less than a quarter enroll in senior secondary. In contrast, 80 percent of urban children make it to junior secondary school, and almost two-thirds enroll in senior secondary. When these data are disaggregated further, and we explore how the richest and poorest quintiles in urban and rural areas compare to each other, the differences are even more stark (figure 1.3).

Figure 1.2 Enrollment Rates in ECED Are Rising for All Socioeconomic Groups, but Disparities Persist

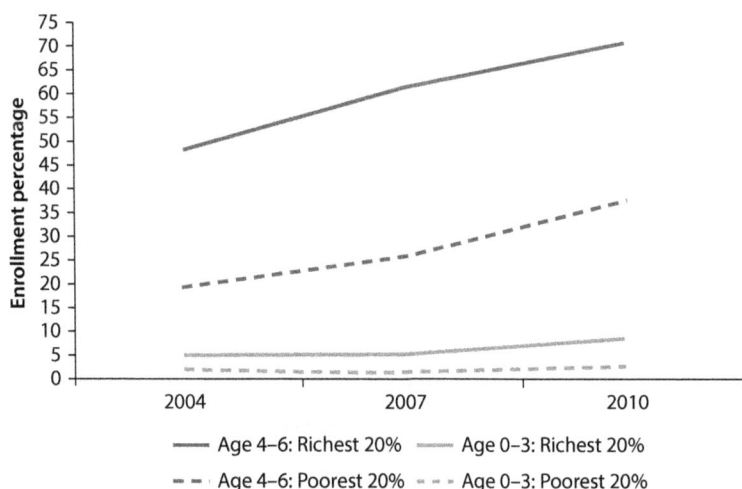

Source: Calculated using BPS 2005, 2008, 2011, SUSENAS 2004, 2007, 2010 databases.
Note: ECED = early childhood education and development. Enrollment of 0–2 year-olds was assumed to be zero in 2004 as the enrollment question was only asked of 3–6 year-olds. In 2007 and 2010, the question was asked of all children 0–6 years old.

Early Childhood Education and Development in Poor Villages of Indonesia •
http://dx.doi.org/10.1596/978-0-8213-9836-4

Figure 1.3 Virtually All Children Enroll in Primary School, but Children from Poorer Households and Rural Households Have Difficulties Progressing from Lower to Higher Levels

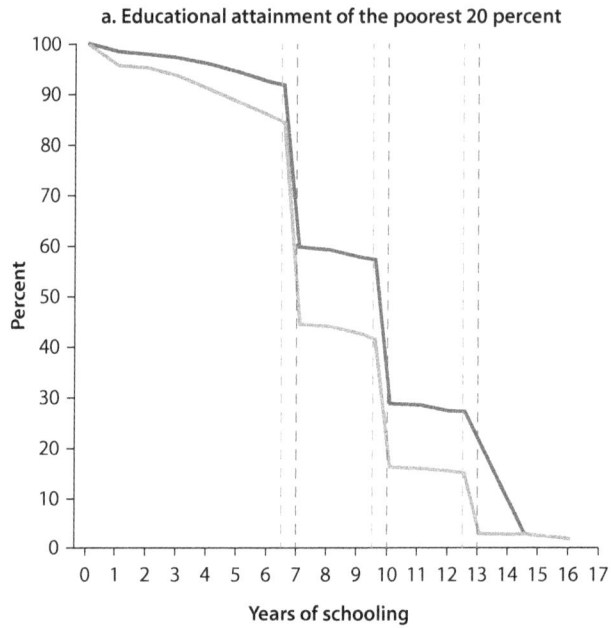

a. Educational attainment of the poorest 20 percent

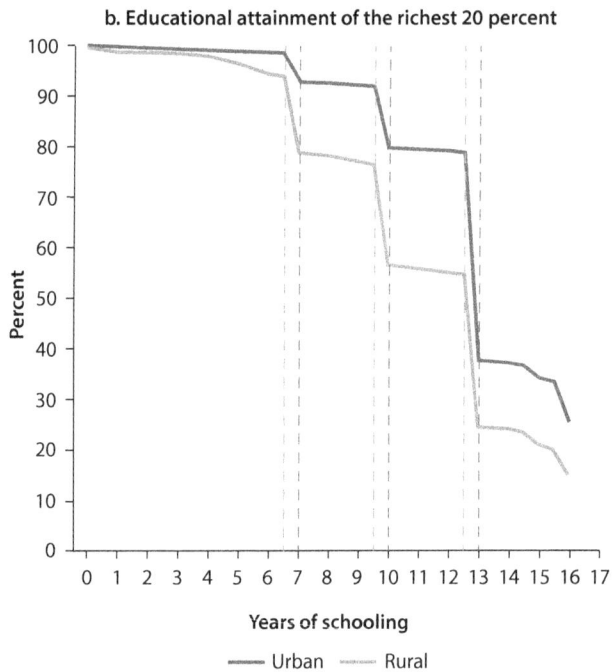

b. Educational attainment of the richest 20 percent

Urban ——— Rural

Source: Calculations using BPS 2011, SUSENAS 2010 database.

Finally, results from the 2009 Programme for International Student Assessment (PISA) find Indonesia near the bottom of 65 countries: 57th in reading, 63rd in math, and 62nd in science (OECD 2009, 2010). PISA tests 15- and 16-year-old students. Disaggregating the data for Indonesia by wealth reveals that even among the subset of children that manage to stay in school until age 15 or 16, poorer children perform worse than richer children (figure 1.4). In 2009, the Organisation for Economic Co-operation and Development (OECD) average score on reading was 493 points with a standard deviation of 93 points. Research has shown that, controlling for differences in socioeconomic background, Indonesian students who had attended preprimary school for more than a year scored an average of 30 points higher than those who had not (OECD 2011). The difference amounts to roughly half of the gap between the richest and poorest 10 percent in 2009 shown in figure 1.4, suggesting that a greater focus on the early years may help to narrow Indonesia's achievement gaps.

These data show a picture of Indonesia as a country where many children are not sharing in the benefits of progress that, on average, has greatly improved the environment for children's development. For Indonesia, as for other developing countries, research indicates that an emphasis on the early childhood years, and on early childhood services, will help reduce disparities related to poverty and other risks to positive development. We turn now to international evidence about the importance of development from birth to age 6 and the value of services that support that development.

Figure 1.4 Learning Levels Are Lower for Indonesian Children from Poorer Socioeconomic Backgrounds

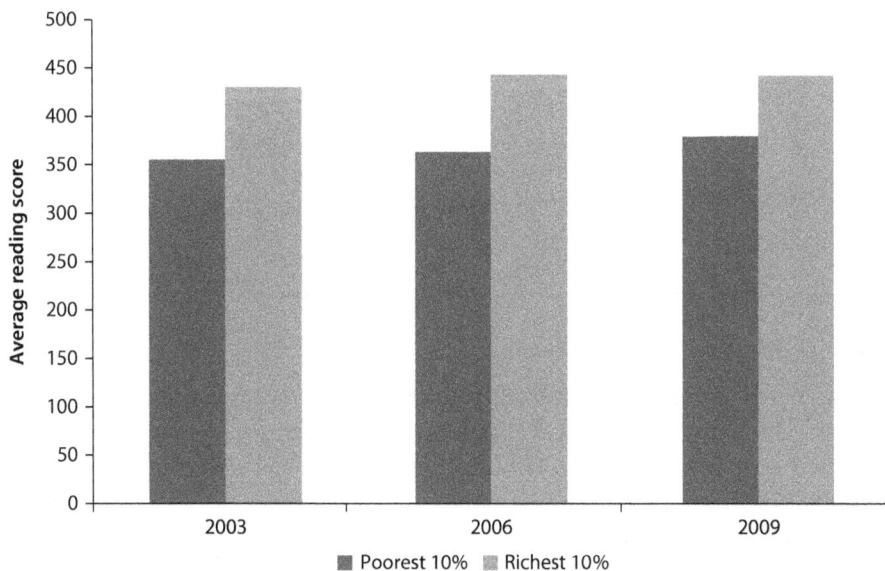

Source: Calculations using OECD (PISA) 2003, 2006, 2009 data.

Early Childhood Education and Development in Poor Villages of Indonesia •
http://dx.doi.org/10.1596/978-0-8213-9836-4

Early Childhood Development: Dramatic Changes, Lifelong Impact

In Indonesia and many other countries, early childhood is considered to extend from the prenatal period through 6 years of age. During this period the central nervous system, brain cells, and neural pathways are established, laying the foundations for a child's future trajectory or pathway through life (Irwin, Siddiqi, and Hertzman 2007). Although children's later experiences can still change that pathway, development in early childhood may affect health, behavior, and learning outcomes for years to come (Grantham-McGregor et al. 2007; Irwin, Siddiqi, and Hertzman 2007; Mustard 2007). Compelling evidence from the health sector indicates that chronic life-threatening conditions such as diabetes and heart disease are influenced by adverse environmental influences beginning in the prenatal period (Barker 1990; Halfon and Hochstein 2002). If children's early learning and holistic development are promoted, then their later years are likely to be far more healthy, engaged, productive, and successful. A key message for policy makers and practitioners in Indonesia and elsewhere is "skill begets skill" and "motivation begets motivation" (Heckman 2008, p. 290).

The Components of Child Development

Young children's development is influenced by multiple factors or "circles of influence," encompassing their immediate families' circumstances, the availability of resources in their communities, and broad policies that promote or, at times, restrict their developmental opportunities. We begin with a close look at the components or key domains of children's development. In effect, these components define the outcomes that Indonesia and other countries aim for in ECED. Each is important for children's overall well-being and school readiness (box 1.1), and each depends on an intersection of positive or negative influences.

In the early years, with supportive environments children typically become more competent in the following areas.

- Physical well-being and motor development. Development of the brain and central nervous system; growth of the body; learning to stand, walk, run, using hands and fingers in skilled ways (Forget-Dubois et al. 2007; Mustard 2002; Shonkoff and Phillips 2000).

Box 1.1 What Is School Readiness?

School readiness involves more than just children. School readiness, in the broadest sense, is about children, families, early environments, schools, and communities. Children are not innately "ready" or "not ready" for school. Their skills and development are strongly influenced by their families and through their interactions with other people and environments before coming to school.

Source: Maxwell and Clifford 2004, 42.

- Language and literacy development. Speaking, listening, understanding (Hoff and Shatz 2007); beginning to connect letters, sounds, and words; beginning to write (Neuman and Dickinson 2002).
- Cognitive development. Reasoning, thinking, problem-solving (Goswami 2010).
- General knowledge. Understanding of everyday places, people, and events, including basic knowledge of math and science (NEGP 1995).
- Social and emotional development. Learning to cooperate, make friends, and be a friend (Dunn 2004; Zins et al. 2004); developing secure relationships; understanding others' feelings; understanding and expressing one's own feelings (Hyson 2004; Raver 2002).
- Executive function skills. Self-regulation: planning and carrying out plans; controlling how one moves, feels, and thinks; remembering details; handling tasks in persistent, flexible ways (Shonkoff and Phillips 2000; Zelazo, Carlson, and Kesek 2008).

Progress in all of these components is necessary to help children develop well and be ready to make the most of the opportunities provided by formal schooling. Later in this book we describe how a sample of Indonesian children was assessed in each of these areas and how services were implemented to improve their holistic development.

A Closer Look at Influences on Child Development

Even among children of exactly the same age, we often see great differences in development, with some children far ahead of what we might expect and others far behind. Almost all children become more skilled as they get older (especially in their physical development), and children are also born with some characteristics that are influenced by their heredity. However, how children develop is strongly influenced by factors in their environments—the experiences and opportunities available to them (Shonkoff and Phillips 2000). Urie Bronfenbrenner's ecological systems theory of human development, an adapted version of which is illustrated in figure 1.5, elaborates on these "circles of influence" (Bronfenbrenner 1979). Examples include:

1. An individual child's current characteristics, innate temperament, and health problems, such as the presence of stunting or the presence of disabilities or developmental delays. These characteristics do not determine development, but can affect the impact of other influences.
2. Family influences, such as parenting practices or parents' income and education.
3. Community influences, including the presence and characteristics of services such as ECED programs or health monitoring and the social networks that may exist in a community.

Figure 1.5 Circles of Influence on a Child's Development

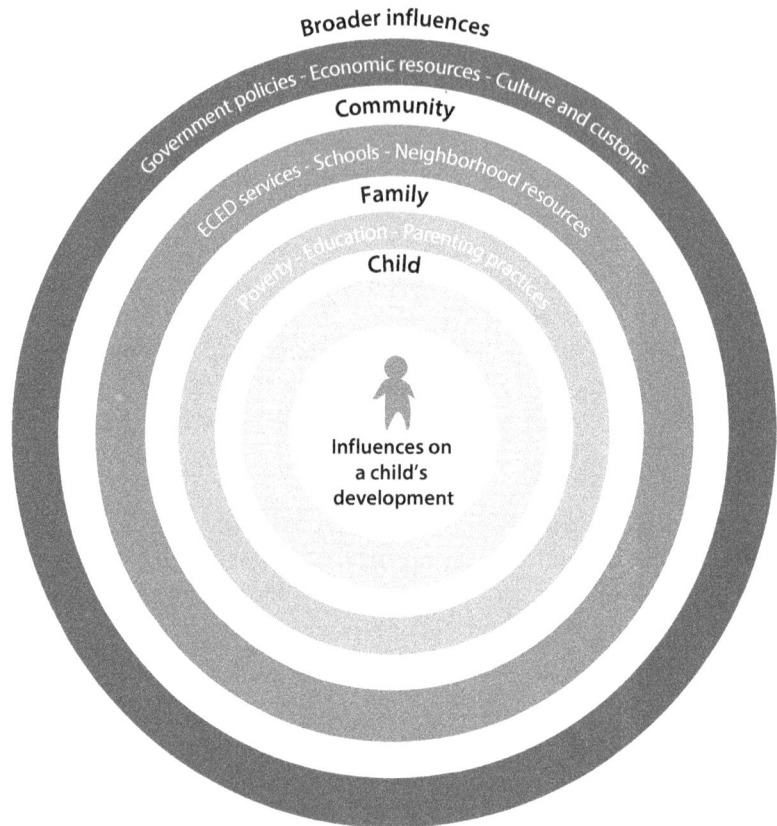

Source: Adapted from Bronfenbrenner 1979.
Note: ECED = early childhood education and development.

4. Broader influences from government policies, economic resources, and cultural traditions, which may create conditions that support or hinder children's development.

Subsequent chapters describe how Indonesia has attempted to increase the potential of these influences to change the trajectory of development for poor children.

Family and Community Influences: Environments and Experiences That Support Early Development

Research has identified a relatively small number of developmental essentials— environments and experiences that should be part of each child's daily life within their family and community. Each of these essentials can have a powerful influence on children's health, development, and learning, yet each can be difficult to find in the environments of children who live in poor communities.

An Environment That Provides the Foundation for Good Health and Nutrition

From the prenatal period onward, children who are healthy and well-nourished develop better in all respects (Grantham-McGregor et al. 2007). Good prenatal care, breastfeeding, community monitoring of children's health and nutrition status, and other healthy practices prevent malnutrition and stunting—serious conditions that can affect brain development in ways that have long-term consequences for learning and behavior.

Warm, Responsive Relationships with Caring Adults

In every culture, babies and young children usually develop close affectionate relationships with parents or other caregivers. The security gained from such relationships at home and in their communities encourages children to explore their environment and develop into confident learners. Yet some children do not have the benefit of those relationships either because of harsh, neglectful, or abusive parenting or a lack of community support for parents who live in highly stressful conditions. The cumulative effects of these factors can create for young children what Jack Shonkoff and colleagues call "toxic stress," which can have lasting detrimental effects on brain development and physical and mental health (Shonkoff and Garner 2012).

Opportunities to Have Stimulating, Interesting, Challenging Experiences, to Learn about the World through Play and Exploration

Play, especially make-believe play supported and guided by adults, is young children's way of making sense of their experiences. It is important that children are able to use all of their senses in the early years (UNESCO 2007), looking, touching, and hearing the wonders of the world around them. Children do not need expensive toys, but language, cognitive, and social development are harmed if young children are not able to explore and play (Bodrova and Leong 2010; Singer, Golinkoff, and Hirsh-Pasek 2006).

An Environment with Many Opportunities to Hear and Use Language and to Explore Books, Stories, and Other Literacy Materials

An environment rich in language sets the foundation for later development (UNESCO 2007). Even if families do not know how to read and write, it is possible for them to give children an environment rich in the foundations of language and literacy. Talking, singing, and telling stories with children are activities that support their vocabulary development and encourage more complex language use (Hart and Risley 1995). Young children who look at books together with their families, teachers, or other adults are more likely to be ready to read when they enter school than children who miss out on such experiences (Neuman and Dickinson 2002).

Early Childhood Education and Development in Poor Villages of Indonesia •
http://dx.doi.org/10.1596/978-0-8213-9836-4

Opportunities to Practice Self-Regulation and Build Executive Function Skills
From infancy onward, children's family and community environments must offer opportunities for children to gradually gain physical, emotional, and cognitive self-control and to practice the planning skills that are a core part of the brain's executive functions (box 1.2). All children can develop executive function skills, but children who have not had the opportunity to gain these competencies are at risk for many later academic, social, and emotional difficulties (Bronson 2000; Zelazo et al. 2003).

Broader Influences: Poverty and Child Development

To develop well, children need to be provided with developmental essentials at home and within their communities. For many children, however, poverty stands in the way of positive development (Alderman 2011; UNICEF 2012; Yoshikawa, Aber, and Beardslee 2012). More than 200 million children under age 5, most of them living in developing countries, fail to reach their developmental potential because of poverty and its associated risks, including malnutrition, iodine and iron deficiency, malaria, diarrhea, HIV/AIDS, inadequate cognitive and language stimulation, violence, and their mothers' depression (Engle et al. 2007; Engle et al. 2011; Walker et al. 2007).

Unfortunately, evidence of the harmful effects of poverty on children's development is abundant. Low-income young children's health status is often low, and they are likely to have poorer cognitive development (Naudeau et al. 2011). As they get older, poor children in every country are the most at risk of not being ready to begin school and not being successful in school, and as a result are at risk of long-term negative outcomes such as dropping out of school and unemployment.

Box 1.2 What Are Executive Function Skills?

Executive function skills are a group of cognitive abilities that help people control and regulate other aspects of their behavior. Executive function skills help children as well as adults to do the following:

- Plan
- Keep track of things
- Organize themselves
- Wait to speak or act
- Manage their emotions and behavior
- Pay attention

As children get older, their brains gradually develop these executive functions, but early experiences also help children gain these skills. Without them, children's later cognitive and socio-emotional development may be hampered.

Across each circle of influence, poverty impacts children's development. Even before children are born, inadequate nutrition can create the likelihood of stunting, with long-term irreversible effects. Although poor families have many strengths and, often, remarkable resilience in the face of challenges (Orthner, Jones-Sanpei, and Williamson 2004; Valladares and Moore 2009), they lack essential material resources. Low levels of education and limited community support may also restrict parents' knowledge about some important aspects of child development and parenting (Schady, Galiani, and Portela Souza 2006). In Indonesia and elsewhere, poor communities are the least likely to have ECED services that are accessible and affordable. And many countries' governments—including Indonesia's until recently—have yet to create policies and programs targeted at the poor.

The adverse results of growing up in poverty can affect more than the lives of individual poor children and their families. These outcomes also diminish a country's ability to produce better-educated, more capable citizens and thereby to improve the long-term economic outlook for all.

Creating More Positive Influences on Poor Children's Development through ECED Services

ECED Services—Many Types

ECED services have become an important way to change the pathway of development for young children.[1] Provided under many auspices and settings, these services can promote all aspects of young children's development and learning. Preferably, services for young children should be integrated, holistic programs that "nurture all aspects of children's development—physical, social, emotional, language, and cognitive" (Irwin, Siddiqi, and Hertzman 2007, 28). More often, however, the programs specialize, with some primarily focused on health and nutrition, while others are primarily education-focused—often because of government agencies' defined mandates, separating what might be integrated service delivery into specialized and sometimes disconnected components. Whatever their focus, ECED services may be delivered in many settings: group or center-based programs (such as preschools, kindergartens, child care centers), home-based child care programs, home visiting or parent education and support programs, and maternal-child health posts. Many other service options and delivery systems are also possible under the large ECED umbrella (UNESCO 2007).

Such services are especially valuable for young children and families who live in poverty. We have already seen that poor children's development is seriously at risk, in Indonesia as elsewhere. ECED services can create additional opportunities for those children and their families, using community support to strengthen and supplement the resources available for low-income children's positive development.

Figure 1.6 Access to ECED Services Is Difficult for Poor Children and Their Families

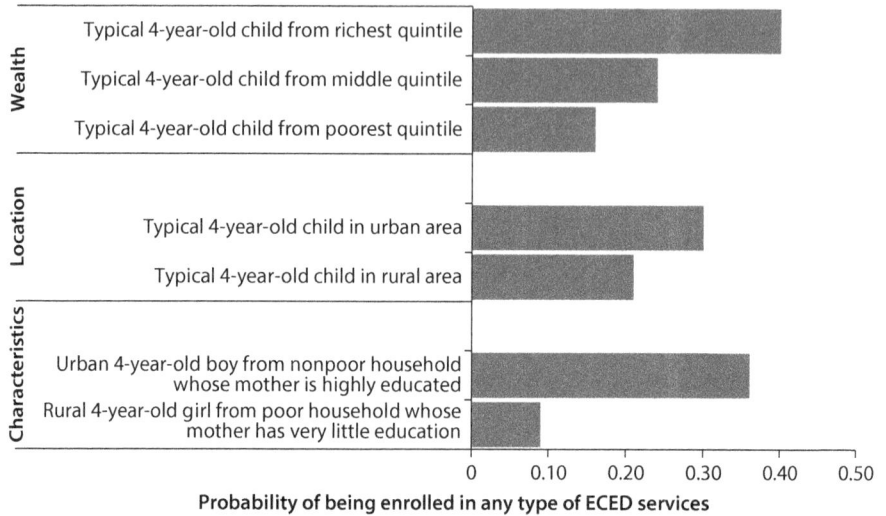

Source: Calculations using BPS 2011, SUSENAS 2010 database.
Note: ECED = early childhood education and development.

ECED Services—Unequal Access

In developed and developing countries around the world, the access to ECED services is not always equal. Better-off families know about and can afford to pay for kindergarten or other programs, while poor children, especially in rural communities, are the least likely to receive these services (UNESCO 2007). Figure 1.6 shows that Indonesia is no exception. If a child's family is wealthier, better-educated, and urban, the child is far more likely to have ECED experiences than if the opposite is the case. As a result of these accumulated disparities, by the time they begin school, poor children are already far behind in essential areas of development and school readiness. Yet it is these children—the most vulnerable, disadvantaged children in society—who stand to benefit the most from ECED services (Irwin, Siddiqi, and Hertzman 2007; Vargas-Barón 2005).

Positive Effects of ECED Services

Indonesia has taken seriously the research message that providing ECED services to young children and their families—especially those who live in poverty—can have positive, long-term benefits. The benefits include (1) short-term benefits to young children's health and development; (2) more positive academic, behavioral, and employment outcomes as children move into adolescence and adulthood; and (3) economic benefits to society.

Short-Term Health and Development Benefits

Research in developed and developing countries has identified many immediate benefits for the health, school readiness, and overall well-being of children who receive ECED services. As summarized in reports from the World Bank, such as Alderman (2011); Alderman and King (2006); Naudeau et al. (2010); and Save the Children Foundation (2012), and a recent meta-analysis of data from 37 countries (Nores and Barnett 2010), the short-term benefits for children typically include:

- Reduced prevalence of stunting
- Improved nutritional status
- Improved cognitive development and other school readiness skills
- Improved socio-emotional development and reduced behavior problems

Longer-Term Outcomes as Children Grow into Adulthood

Only a few studies have been able to track longer-term outcomes, comparing poor children who participated in ECED services with those who did not. The comparisons included either those receiving no services or, more frequently, those who received whatever other services may have been available in their communities. These longitudinal studies—some following former ECED program participants up to age 40—show fairly consistent results: Children who were enrolled in these programs have better outcomes. A report by the Ounce of Prevention Fund (2012) explored and summarized many studies of the long-term effects of early intervention programs for children living in poverty in the United States. The report concluded that early childhood interventions make a huge difference. Without high-quality ECED services, as compared to better-off children, poor children were, on average:

- 25 percent more likely to drop out of school
- 40 percent more likely to become a teen parent
- 50 percent more likely to be placed in special education
- 60 percent more likely to never attend college
- 70 percent more likely to be arrested for a violent crime

In reviewing international research, Naudeau et al. (2010) and GTZ (2009) have identified similar patterns of benefits as those summarized in the Ounce of Prevention Fund report, again drawing primarily on studies in developed countries. Although they are much needed, similar long-term, well-controlled studies have not yet been conducted in settings within developing countries.

Economic Benefits to Society

For policy makers, including those in Indonesia, a pressing question is whether resources should be invested in the early years or in other alternatives. Persuasive evidence exists that the greatest return on any investment in human capital comes when governments or others make investments in the early years, rather than waiting to intervene until children are older (Heckman 2006). Figure 1.7 shows economist James Heckman's depiction of probable returns

Early Childhood Education and Development in Poor Villages of Indonesia •
http://dx.doi.org/10.1596/978-0-8213-9836-4

Figure 1.7 Early Investments Have the Highest Returns

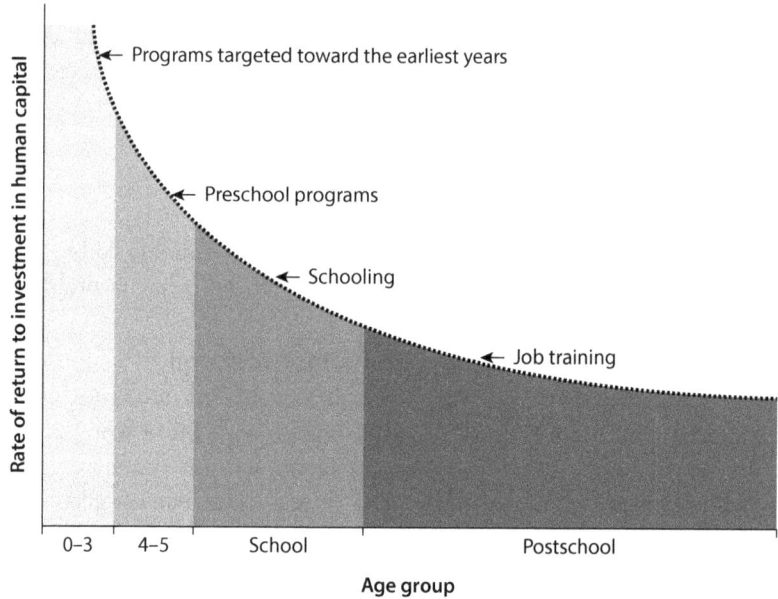

Source: Heckman 2008.

to investments directed towards various age groups. This depiction reinforces the belief that returns on early investment are higher in part because during the first few years of life the brain is developing rapidly and therefore investments at this stage have higher returns. The returns on these early investments are likely to be greatest if services are targeted to the poorest, most at-risk children and if the investments begin as early as possible. Cost-benefit analyses of a number of early childhood intervention projects, such as Belfield et al. (2006) and Reynolds et al. (2001), have found similar long-term patterns: early investments prevent later, more costly expenses to society. If a child has to spend extra years in school because she has failed a grade, or if a child's future earning potential is reduced because he did not complete his education, society ultimately pays the cost.

Features of Effective Early Childhood Interventions

As countries like Indonesia plan and implement ECED services in light of this evidence, they will need to keep some caveats in mind. The reality is that not every ECED program can produce significant benefits for children, families, and society. The ECED interventions upon which most of the longitudinal data and cost-benefit analyses have been based were implemented in developed countries with extensive resources. All were of very high quality, with high levels of teachers' qualifications, intensive training and supervision, and well-designed and well-implemented curricula. Although all ECED services do not have to reach this high standard to produce good results, they must have certain key features.

Patrice Engle and colleagues' 2007 review of ECED interventions in developing countries shows that effective interventions need to succeed at several tasks. First, they should make it a priority to provide services for the youngest children, including birth to age 3, often through parent-focused interventions. (Approximately half of the countries of the world lack an official ECED program for the youngest children [UNESCO 2007; Vargas-Barón 2005], and even when such programs are available, the enrollment rate is less than 20 percent [Britto, Yoshikawa, and Boller 2011].) Second, they should target the most disadvantaged children, as research repeatedly shows the greatest impact for such children, and yet these children have the least access to services. Third, the programs should last long enough and be of high enough intensity to make a difference. Fourth, the programs should integrate a holistic range of services: education, health, nutrition, and family support.

International Efforts on ECED

The evidence concerning the importance of the early years and the benefits of early childhood services has prompted extensive international efforts to develop ECED policies and expand access to ECED services, especially for children living in poverty. ECED is recognized as a right for every child and has been ratified as part of the United Nations (UN) Convention on the Rights of the Child by some 193 states worldwide, including developed and developing countries (United Nations 2010). The early childhood period and ECED services are also emphasized in the UN's MDGs, particularly as a tool for reducing poverty throughout the world and achieving improved child health and primary school completion (UNESCO 2007). The Dakar Framework for Action (UNESCO 2000) includes early childhood care and education as a goal of Education for All (EFA), emphasizing the need to expand and improve comprehensive services in the early years, especially for vulnerable children (UNESCO 2007).

Indonesia and ECED: Milestones of Progress

Influenced by the condition of poor children within its own country and by the pattern of international evidence about the value of ECED, for more than a decade the government of Indonesia has implemented policies and programs that prioritize the early years. The upper half of figure 1.8 highlights some of these milestones.

The first critical step was taken in 2001, when a new directorate dedicated to early childhood was established within the Ministry of Education and Culture. Its early advocacy within and beyond the government influenced policy development, put additional resources into community ECED services, and created strategies to raise Indonesian awareness about the importance of the early years. The United Nations Children's Fund (UNICEF) initiated integrated health service clinics for mothers and children (*Taman Posyandus*) as part of their Smart

Figure 1.8 ECED Milestones in Indonesia Generally and Under the Current ECED Project

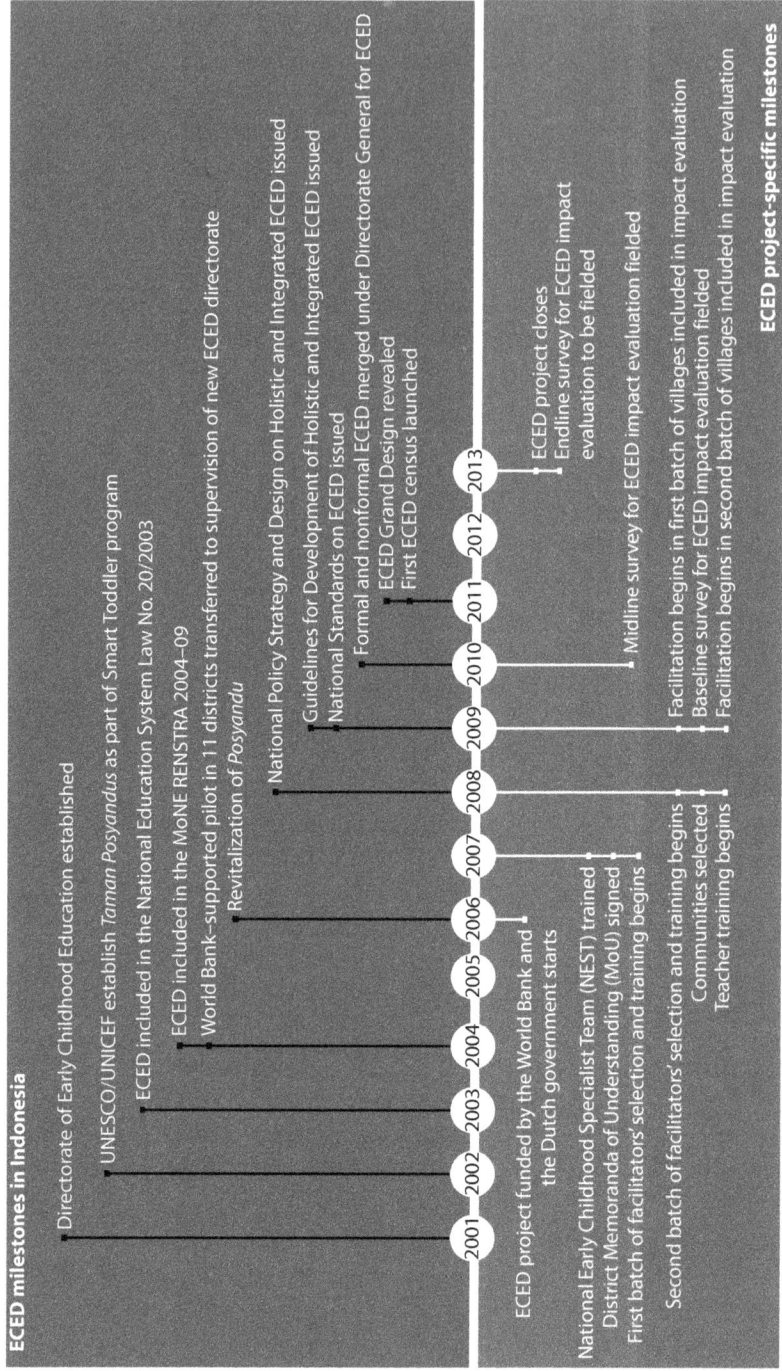

ECED milestones in Indonesia

- 2001 — Directorate of Early Childhood Education established
- 2002 — UNESCO/UNICEF establish *Taman Posyandu* as part of Smart Toddler program
- 2003 — ECED included in the National Education System Law No. 20/2003
- 2004 — ECED included in the MoNE RENSTRA 2004–09
- 2006 — World Bank–supported pilot in 11 districts transferred to supervision of new ECED directorate
- 2006 — Revitalization of *Posyandu*
- 2008 — National Policy Strategy and Design on Holistic and Integrated ECED issued
- 2009 — Guidelines for Development of Holistic and Integrated ECED issued
- 2009 — National Standards on ECED issued
- 2010 — Formal and nonformal ECED merged under Directorate General for ECED
- 2011 — ECED Grand Design revealed
- 2011 — First ECED census launched

ECED project-specific milestones

- ECED project funded by the World Bank and the Dutch government starts
- National Early Childhood Specialist Team (NEST) trained
- District Memoranda of Understanding (MoU) signed
- First batch of facilitators' selection and training begins
- Second batch of facilitators' selection and training begins
- Communities selected
- Teacher training begins
- Midline survey for ECED impact evaluation fielded
- Facilitation begins in first batch of villages included in impact evaluation
- Baseline survey for ECED impact evaluation fielded
- Facilitation begins in second batch of villages included in impact evaluation
- ECED project closes
- Endline survey for ECED impact evaluation to be fielded

Note: ECED = early childhood education and development; MoNE = Ministry of National Education; UNESCO/UNICEF = United Nations Educational, Scientific, and Cultural Organization/ United Nations Children's Fund.

Toddler program (*Balita Cerdas*), one component of the government's initiatives to support early childhood.

The second critical step was taken when early childhood education was included in a succession of key policy documents: the National Education System Law No. 20 in 2003 and the Ministry of Education and Culture's Strategic Plan (*Rencana Strategis* or RENSTRA) in 2004.

In the context of these institutional and policy changes, a pilot project covering 12 districts (box 1.3), which had begun under the purview of the Directorate of Community Education, was transferred to the supervision of the newly formed Directorate of Early Childhood Education. The pilot project established new ECED services in poor villages. It previewed and provided key lessons that were subsequently incorporated into a larger-scale project initiated in 2006 and described in this book. The bottom half of figure 1.8 highlights project-specific milestones.

More recently, the need to consider ECED services holistically, across sectors and developmental domains, was recognized through the government's issuance of an ambitious policy strategy and accompanying guidelines in 2008. The development of national standards for ECED by the National Education Standards Board (BSNP) in 2009 situated early childhood education as the first level of the country's education system.

A lingering barrier to coordinated ECED service provision was removed when the "formal" and "nonformal" directorates were merged into one unit in 2010 with responsibility for all ECED activities. Finally, the initiation of the first-ever ECED census in 2011 has begun to provide researchers and policy makers with essential data and will continue to inform ECED decisions in the future.

Box 1.3 Highlights of the ECED Pilot Project, 1997–2005

What was provided?

- Six hundred newly constructed Early Childhood Education and Development (ECED) centers in 12 districts in four provinces
- Services for children ages 4–6
- Teachers with minimum 2 years of postsecondary education and ECED specialization

What were the effects?

- Evaluation followed progress of 235 children who attended the centers, compared with randomly selected children from the same communities, who did not attend (statistically accounting for selection bias: the possibility that families of those who attended were more motivated).
- Children who attended the new ECED centers for 2 years had higher school readiness scores than those who did not attend.
- Greater impact on the most disadvantaged children living in poorer districts was observed.
- Greater impact on children whose parents had less education was observed.

Source: World Bank 2006.

Early Childhood Education and Development in Poor Villages of Indonesia •
http://dx.doi.org/10.1596/978-0-8213-9836-4

What This Book Provides

This book tells the story of Indonesia's efforts to change the trajectory of development for poor children. Many countries have similar aims, but several aspects of what is reported here are especially valuable and perhaps unique.

Indonesia has characteristics that make its story of special interest. Indonesia is an example of a country that has begun to emerge into middle-income status, yet with persistent poverty and stark inequalities affecting young children's development. Most studies of ECED interventions have been conducted at one of two demographic extremes: either in rich countries such as the United States or in countries with much higher levels of poverty than exist in Indonesia. Indonesia's story thus makes a new contribution with considerable relevance for similarly situated countries.

An unusually rich set of data was collected for this study. The study offers data on all aspects of health and development in a sample of young rural children, collected with internationally validated measures (often including multiple measures of the same construct), as well as household information, information about parenting practices including feeding patterns, parent questionnaires, and data on the prevalence and distribution of ECED services.

The key components of the ECED project combined direct service delivery with broad policy and systems goals. From the start, the ECED project aimed not only to support service provision, but also to support the development of national standards, build national and district capacity, and encourage the establishment of a system of ECED quality assurance—efforts that are still in process. The book focuses primarily on the services themselves and their association with child outcomes, but the project's broad scope is relatively rare and is highlighted in the last chapter.

The use of a community-driven development approach to ECED services was a key ingredient for success. The ECED project empowered village members to identify their own needs, find local teachers, and guide the implementation of services with district commitment and support. This kind of approach seems to have promise for creating sustainable services responsive to local needs.

A large sample of rural children and families was studied at two points in time, 1 year apart. The data reported here are based on a sample of more than 6,000 Indonesian children living in 310 poor villages, including two age cohorts (1-year-olds and 4-year-olds when data were first collected on their development in 2009).

The impact evaluation used a randomized design to judge the effect of the project. Few such analyses have been done with such a large sample, with multiple measures, and with more than one data point. These design features allow a high level of confidence in the reported results.

That this is not yet the project's final evaluation provides an opportunity to use the lessons learned in further research, policies, and practices. The final word has not yet been said about the children, families, and interventions that are being studied: data for the ECED project's endline evaluation will be collected in early 2013. However, what is being learned from the project's baseline data and from this midline evaluation will help to inform the project's further implementation and the government's broader ECED initiatives.

Note

1. Services for young children and their families are referred to by many names. ECED— early childhood education and development—is the term used in Indonesia by the World Bank and government, so that acronym is used throughout this report. The equivalent term in Bahasa Indonesia is PAUD (*Pendidikan Anak Usia Dini*, Early Childhood Directorate). Other names commonly used include Early Childhood Development (ECD), Early Childhood Care and Education (ECCE), Early Childhood Care and Development (ECCD), and Early Childhood Education and Care (ECEC).

Bibliography

Alderman, H. 2011. *No Small Matter: The Impact of Poverty, Shocks, and Human Capital Investments in Early Childhood Development*. Washington, DC: World Bank.

Alderman, H., and E. King. 2006. *Investing in Early Childhood Development*. Washington, DC: World Bank.

Barker, D. J. 1990. "The Fetal and Infant Origins of Adult Disease." *British Medical Journal* 301 (6761): 1111.

Belfield, C., M. Nores, W. S. Barnett, and L. J. Schweinhart. 2006. "The High/Scope Perry Preschool Program: Cost-benefit Analysis Using Data from the Age-40 Follow Up." *Journal of Human Resources* 41 (1): 162–90.

Bodrova, E., and D. Leong. 2010. *Curriculum and Play in Early Child Development*. Montreal, Canada: Centre of Excellence for Early Childhood Development and Strategic Knowledge Cluster on Early Child Development.

Britto, P. R., H. Yoshikawa, and K. Boller. 2011. "Quality of Early Childhood Development Programs in Global Contexts: Rationale for Investment, Conceptual Framework and Implications for Equity." *Social Policy Report* 25 (2): 1–23.

Bronfenbrenner, U. 1979. *The Ecology of Human Development*. Cambridge, MA: Harvard University Press.

Bronson, M. B. 2000. *Self-Regulation in Early Childhood: Nature and Nurture*. New York: Guilford Press.

Dunn, J. 2004. *Children's Friendships: The Beginnings of Intimacy*. Oxford, U.K.: Blackwell.

Engle, P. L., M. M. Black, J. R. Behrman, M. Cabral de Mello, P. J. Gertler, L. Kapiriri, R. Martorell, and M. E. Young. 2007. "Strategies to Avoid the Loss of Developmental Potential in More Than 200 Million Children in the Developing World." *The Lancet* 369 (9557): 229–42.

Engle, P. L., L. C. H. Fernald, H. Alderman, J. R. Behrman, C. O'Gara, A. Yousafzai, N. Ulkuer, I. Ertem, and S. Iltus. 2011. "Strategies for Reducing Inequalities and Improving Developmental Outcomes for Young Children in Low-Income and Middle-Income Countries." *The Lancet* 378 (9799): 1339–53.

Forget-Dubois, N., J. P. Lemelin, M. Boivin, G. Dionne, J. R. Séguin, F. Vitaro, and R. E. Tremblay. 2007. "Predicting Early School Achievement with the EDI:

A Longitudinal Population-Based Study." *Early Education and Development* 18 (3): 405–26. doi:10.1080/10409280701610796.

Goswami, U. 2010. *The Wiley-Blackwell Handbook of Childhood Cognitive Development.* 2nd ed. Oxford, U.K.: Blackwell.

Grantham-McGregor, S., Y. B. Cheung, S. Cueto, P. Glewwe, L. Richter, and B. Strupp. 2007. "Developmental Potential in the First 5 Years for Children in Developing Countries." *The Lancet* 369 (9555): 60–70. doi:10.1016/S0140-6736(07)60032-4.

GTZ (Deutsche Gesellschaft für Technische Zusammenarbeit). 2009. *Getting the Basics Right: The Contribution of Early Childhood Development to Quality, Equity and Efficiency in Education.* Eschborn, Germany: GTZ.

Halfon, N., and M. Hochstein. 2002. "Life Course Health Development: An Integrated Framework for Developing Health, Policy and Research." *Milbank Quarterly* 80 (3): 433–79.

Hart, B., and T. R. Risley. 1995. *Meaningful Differences in the Everyday Experience of Young American Children.* Baltimore, MD: Paul H. Brookes.

Heckman, J. 2006. "Skill Formation and the Economics of Investing in Disadvantaged Children." *Science* 312 (5782): 1900–2.

———. 2008. "Schools, Skills, and Synapses." *Economic Inquiry* 46 (3): 289–324.

Hoff, E., and M. Shatz. 2007. *Blackwell Handbook of Language Development.* Oxford, U.K.: Blackwell.

Hyson, M. C. 2004. *The Emotional Development of Young Children: Building an Emotion-Centered Curriculum.* 2nd ed. New York: Teacher College Press.

Irwin, L. G., A. Siddiqi, and C. Hertzman. 2007. *Early Child Development: A Powerful Equalizer.* Final Report for the World Health Organization's Commission of the Social Determinants of Health, Human Early Learning Partnership, Vancouver, Canada.

Maxwell, K., and R. Clifford. 2004. "Research in Review: School Readiness Assessment." *Young Children* 59 (1): 42–46.

Mustard, J. F. 2002. "Early Child Development and the Brain—the Base for Health, Learning and Behaviour Throughout Life." In *From Early Child Development to Human Development: Investing in Our Children's Future,* edited by M. E. Young, 23–62. Washington, DC: World Bank.

———. 2007. "Experience-Based Brain Development: Scientific Underpinnings of the Importance of Early Child Development in a Global World." In *Early Child Development from Measurement to Action,* edited by M. E. Young and L. M. Richardson, 43–84. Washington, DC: World Bank.

Naudeau, S., N. Kataoka, A. Valerio, M. J. Neuman, and L. K. Elder. 2010. *Investing in Young Children: An Early Childhood Development Guide for Policy Dialogue and Project Preparation.* Washington, DC: World Bank.

Naudeau, S., S. Martinez, P. Premand, and D. Filmer. 2011. "Cognitive Development among Young Children in Low-Income Countries." In *No Small Matter: The Impact of Poverty, Shocks, and Human Capital Investments in Early Childhood Development,* edited by H. Alderman, 9–50. Washington, DC: World Bank.

NEGP (National Education Goals Panel). 1995. *Reconsidering Children's Early Development and Learning: Toward Shared Beliefs and Vocabulary.* Washington, DC: NEGP.

Neuman, S., and D. Dickinson. 2002. *Handbook of Early Literacy Research.* New York: Guilford Press.

Nores, M., and W. S. Barnett. 2010. "Benefits of Early Childhood Interventions across the World: (Under) Investing in the Very Young." *Economics of Education Review* 29 (2): 271–82.

OECD (Organisation for Economic Co-operation and Development). 2003. PISA (Programme for International Student Assessment) Database 2003. http://pisa2003.acer.edu.au/.

———. 2006. PISA (Programme for International Student Assessment) Database 2006. http://pisa2006.acer.edu.au/.

———. 2009. PISA (Programme for International Student Assessment) Database 2009. http://pisa2009.acer.edu.au/.

———. 2010. *PISA 2009 Results: What Students Know and Can Do, Student Performance in Reading, Mathematics, and Science.* Vol. 1. http://dx.doi.org/10.1787/9789264091450-en.

———. 2011. "Does Participation in Pre-primary Education Translate into Better Learning Outcomes at School?" *PISA (Programme for International Student Assessment) in Focus.* http://www.oecd.org/pisa/pisaproducts/pisa2009/47034256.pdf.

Orthner, D. K., H. Jones-Sanpei, and S. Williamson. 2004. "The Resilience and Strengths of Low-income Families." *Family Relations* 53: 15967.

Ounce of Prevention Fund. 2012. "Why Investments in Early Childhood Work." http://www.ounceofprevention.org/about/why-early-childhood-investments-work.php.

Raver, C. C. 2002. "Emotions Matter: Making the Case for the Role of Young Children's Emotional Development for Early School Readiness." *Social Policy Report* 16 (3): 3–19.

Reynolds, A. J., J. A. Temple, D. L. Robertson, and E. A. Mann. 2001. "Age 21 Cost-Benefit Analysis of the Title I Chicago Child-Parent Center Program." http://www.waisman.wisc.edu/cls/cbaexecsum4.html.

Save the Children International. 2012. *Laying the Foundations: Early Childhood Care and Development.* Save the Children International, London. http://www.savethechildren.org/atf/cf/%7B9def2ebe-10ae-432c-9bd0-df91d2eba74a%7D/ECCD_ADVOCACY_BRIEF_200412_FINAL.PDF.

Schady, N. R., S. S. Galiani, and A. P. Souza. 2006. "Early Childhood Development in Latin America and the Caribbean." *Economia* 6 (2): 185–225.

Shonkoff, J. P., and A. S. Garner. 2012. "The Lifelong Effects of Early Childhood Adversity and Toxic Stress." *Pediatrics* 129 (1): 232–46.

Shonkoff, J. P., and D. A. Phillips. 2000. *From Neurons to Neighborhoods: The Science of Early Childhood Development.* Washington, DC: National Academy Press.

Singer, D., R. M. Golinkoff, and K. Hirsh-Pasek. 2006. *Play-Learning: How Play Motivates and Enhances Children's Cognitive and Social-emotional Growth.* New York: Oxford University Press.

SUSENAS (National Socioeconomic Survey). Various years. Jakarta: Central Board of Statistics of Indonesia.

UNESCO (United Nations Educational, Scientific, and Cultural Organization). 2000. *The Dakar Framework for Action.* Paris: UNESCO.

———. 2007. *Strong Foundations: Early Childhood Care and Education.* Education for All, Global Monitoring Report. http://unesdoc.unesco.org/images/0014/001477/147785E.pdf.

UNICEF (United Nations Children's Fund). 2012. *Inequities in Early Child Development: What the Data Say*. New York: UNICEF.

United Nations. 2010. *Status of the Convention on the Rights of the Child*. Report of the Secretary-General. New York: United Nations.

Valladares, S., and K. A. Moore. 2009. *The Strengths of Poor Families*. Research Brief, Child Trends, Washington, DC. http://www.childtrends.org/Files/Child_Trends-2009_5_14_RB_poorfamstrengths.pdf.

Vargas-Barón, E. 2005. *Planning Policies for Early Childhood Development: Guidelines for Action*. UNESCO, UNICEF and ADEA.

Walker, S. P., T. D. Wachs, J. M. Gardner, B. Lozoff, G. A. Wasserman, E. Pollitt, and J. A. Carter. 2007. "Child Development: Risk Factors for Adverse Outcomes in Developing Countries." *The Lancet* 369 (9556): 145–57.

World Bank. 2006. *Early Childhood Education and Development in Indonesia: An Investment for a Better Life*. Jakarta: World Bank.

———. 2008. "Health Sector Review." http://go.worldbank.org/NQUJ9JFSS0.

Yoshikawa, H., J. L. Aber, and W. R. Beardslee. 2012. "The Effects of Poverty on the Mental, Emotional, and Behavioral Health of Children and Youth: Implications for Prevention." *American Psychologist* 67 (4): 272–84. doi:10.1037/a0028015.

Zelazo, P. D., S. M. Carlson, and A. Kesek. 2008. *The Development of Executive Function in Childhood*. 2nd ed. Cambridge, MA: MIT Press.

Zelazo, P. D., U. Müller, D. Frye, S. Marcovitch, G. Argitis, J. Boseovski, J. K. Chiang, D. Hogwanishkul, B. V. Schuster, A. Sutherland, and S. M. Carlson. 2003. "The Development of Executive Function in Early Childhood." *Monographs of the Society for Research in Child Development* 68 (3): 1–151. doi:10.2307/1166202.

Zins, J. E., R. P. Weissberg, M. C. Wang, and H. Walberg. 2004. *Building Academic Success on Social and Emotional Learning: What Does the Research Say?* New York: Teachers College Press.

CHAPTER 2

Young Children in Indonesia's Low-Income Rural Communities: How Are They Doing and What Do They Need?

This chapter describes the development of young children in a sample of poor rural communities across Indonesia. It links their developmental trajectories with the characteristics of their families, the parenting practices they are exposed to, and the typical early childhood education and development (ECED) services available to them. Using a number of different sources of data, including data on several measures of child development employed for the first time in Indonesia, the chapter offers new evidence about the development of poor children in each of the domains important for comprehensive school readiness. We also describe characteristics of young children's families and the kinds of ECED services available in their communities. The chapter shows how various child, family, and community characteristics may lead to differences in children's development. We show that even when looking only at districts that have similar levels of poverty, disparities in child development are apparent. The chapter concludes by assessing the relative importance of parenting practices and ECED service enrollment for improving child outcomes and reducing inequalities in children's development.

Using Internationally Validated Measures to Learn More about the Development of Young Children from Families Living in Poverty

Chapter 1 noted that despite Indonesia's substantial progress toward middle-income status, wide disparities exist between poor and better-off children and that these disparities affect poor children's progress through primary and secondary education and their academic success. International research strongly suggests that to remedy this situation, focused attention must be paid to the early years. Positive development from birth to age 6 lays the foundation for the future, but poverty puts young children at risk of inadequate development and negative outcomes. Evidence from developed and developing countries repeatedly documents the ways that ECED services can support the health, development, and school readiness of poor vulnerable young children.

To expand and improve such services within Indonesia, more in-depth information is urgently needed about the current development of the nation's young children, the key characteristics of their families, and the ECED services that have been available in their communities. Gathering this information requires the use of internationally validated measures of children's development in multiple domains, as well as measures of their families' beliefs and parenting practices. In this chapter we describe the developmental trajectories of a sample of children residing in 310 villages across nine districts in Indonesia. These data draw from the ongoing impact evaluation discussed in greater detail in chapter 3. The nature of the data is described in box 2.1. Details on these and other data sources are in appendix 1.

Using these data, in this chapter we:

1. Describe the development of children in our sample, beginning with statistics on the percentage of children who are stunted, wasting, or underweight,

---

Box 2.1 Measuring Child Development in a Rural Sample

The 310 villages that are part of the early childhood education and development (ECED) project study are located in nine districts. These districts were selected on the basis of a composite score that assigned weights to district poverty rates, Human Development Index (HDI) rankings, gross enrollment rates, remoteness, border location, and commitment to ECED. Within these districts, priority villages were identified on the basis of poverty rates and size of the birth to age 6 population. Therefore, not all children in the sample are poor.

In this chapter, we report on the development of two cohorts of children that were assessed, and whose families were interviewed, in 2009 and 2010. The children were 1 year old and 4 years old in 2009, when their development was measured for the first time using an array of internationally validated measures of development. Because the data are longitudinal, these children were 2 and 5 when these measures were collected again in 2010.

Some aspects of development were assessed by interviewing each child's primary caregiver—usually the mother, but sometimes another family member such as a grandparent. Others assessments of development were based on direct observations or interaction with the children, such as asking them to draw pictures or perform tasks.

Data on parenting beliefs and practices were collected using face-to-face interviews with the child's primary caregiver. Data on availability of ECED services come from interviews with village leaders.

and report results of assessments in physical, socio-emotional, language, cognitive, communication, and general knowledge domains.

2. Describe the characteristics of children's families in our sample, including basic information about their relative wealth or poverty and formal education and their parenting practices at home.

3. Describe the availability of different kinds of ECED services in these communities, such as kindergartens, playgroups, and health posts (*Posyandu*).

4. Present information about the effects of parents' education and relative wealth on children's development.

5. Utilize information from a selection of districts to assess how disparities in children's development may evolve over time and how differences between groups in these districts compare to those found in other settings.

6. Describe how two factors—parenting practices and enrollment in ECED services—predict differences in children's development even after accounting for differences in family income and education, children's ages, sex, and physical condition.

How Well Are Indonesian Children Developing?

Considering how important children's early development is, it is equally important to be able to measure it accurately in each of its many dimensions. In this study, we use a number of measures of child development. Some assess only one aspect, such as language development or socio-emotional development; others are more comprehensive. Some measures are based on descriptions of the child's development by the mother or other family caregiver.[1] Other measures ask the child to do tasks that show his or her development directly. To assess physical growth, we take the child's height and weight. Together, all of these data tell a more complete story of child development in a sample of children from poor rural settings.

We begin by presenting results from measurements of the children's height and weight. The results tell a great deal about obstacles in the path of positive development and set the stage for much of what follows. Next, we describe results from measures of different areas or domains of early development and school readiness. We used the Early Development Instrument (EDI) (Janus and Offord 2007), the Strengths and Difficulties Questionnaire (SDQ) (Goodman 1997), the Dimensional Change Card Sort (DCCS) task (Zelazo 2006), and various tasks to assess children's abilities across a number of domains, performed directly by the child or, if necessary, reported by the mother. Taken together, these measures provide information about children's development across all of the key development domains.[2] To illustrate this comprehensiveness, an overview of how each of these measures is related to each of the major areas of child development is provided in table 2.1. The key features of each of the measures are summarized in box 2.2.

Table 2.2 presents an in-depth view of the measurements.

Early Childhood Education and Development in Poor Villages of Indonesia •
http://dx.doi.org/10.1596/978-0-8213-9836-4

Table 2.1 Child Development Measures and the Developmental Domains to Which They Relate

	Physical	Socio-emotional	Cognitive	Language	Communication	Growth and nutrition
Height and weight measurements	✓	—	—	—	—	✓
Early Development Instrument (EDI)	✓	✓	✓	✓	✓	—
Strengths and Difficulties Questionnaire (SDQ)	—	✓	—	—	—	—
Dimensional Change Card Sort (DCCS) task	—	—	✓	—	—	—
Child ability tasks and mother-rated child skills	✓	✓	✓	✓	—	—
Drawing tasks	—	—	✓	—	—	—
Expressive and receptive language questions	—	—	—	✓	✓	—

Note: — = Not measured.

Box 2.2 How Well Do These Measures Predict Later Development Outcomes?

Predictive validity shows how well a measure predicts later outcomes, either on the same instrument or another related outcome. Several of the child development measures used in this study have evidence of their predictive validity, although for the most part the evidence has not been from developing countries. For example, scores on the Early Development Instrument (EDI) and its domains have been shown to significantly predict children's teacher-rated school achievement one year later,[a] a range of visual-motor, emotional, and cognitive outcomes measured 2 years later,[b] and mathematics and literacy ability, and behavioral outcomes measured 4 years later.[c]

Two studies have found the Strengths and Difficulties Questionnaire (SDQ) to be a good predictor of children's scores on the same instrument one year later.[d] However, SDQ scores at age 4 are poor predictors of mathematics and literacy skills and behavioral outcomes 4 years later.[e] In their 2010 review of the validity evidence for the SDQ, Stone et al. (2010) called for further longitudinal investigation of the SDQ's predictive ability.

There is little published predictive validity evidence regarding the Dimensional Change Card Sort (DCCS). A 2012 thesis reviewing multiple studies of executive function measures has, however, shown that DCCS scores are significant predictors of emergent mathematics, literacy, and vocabulary skills.[f] Additionally, in 2012 an expert panel identified the DCCS as one of a small number of well-validated assessments that have shown associations between executive function scores and later mathematics and literacy achievement.[g]

Although widely used, the Draw-a-Person test also has limited evidence of predictive validity. A 2005 paper suggests that evidence is stronger for the measure's ability to predict cognitive development levels, and to differentiate between typically developing children and those with developmental delays, than for other aspects of development.[h]

---

box continues next page

Box 2.2 How Well Do These Measures Predict Later Development Outcomes? *(continued)*

Given the evidence on the predictive validity of these measures for children's school readiness and the lack of such information in Indonesia, data were collected on young children at multiple points in time to see how development progresses in poor settings. The government has demonstrated its interest in improving children's outcomes in school, and the data from these measures are expected to yield valuable insights into early predictors of later development in the Indonesian context.

Note: a. Forget-Dubois et al. 2007; b. Janus et al. 2007; c. Brinkman, Zubrick, and Silburn, under review; Brinkman et al., under review; d. Hawes and Dadds 2004; Perren et al. 2007; e. Brinkman, Zubrick, and Silburn, under review; f. Duncan 2012; g. Turner et al. 2012; h. Laak et al. 2005.

Table 2.2 A Closer Look at the Child Development Measures

Measure	Objective	Background and uses
Height and weight measurements	To measure children's height and weight by age to determine extent and severity of stunting, wasting, or underweight conditions	Measures of height for age, weight for age and body mass index (BMI) were constructed using these measures to assess stunting, wasting, and long-run nutritional challenges.
Early Development Instrument (EDI) short version[a]	To measure children's school readiness in five major developmental domains: 1. Physical health and well-being 2. Social competence 3. Emotional maturity 4. Language and cognitive development 5. Communication skills and general knowledge	The EDI was developed at the Offord Centre for Child Studies in Canada[b] and has been used extensively in many countries such as the Philippines and Jordan. In some countries, such as Canada and Australia, the EDI is used as a national monitoring tool for all children in their first year of full-time schooling. In Indonesia, a 47-item short version was used instead of the standard 104-item version.
Strengths and Difficulties Questionnaire (SDQ)[c]	To identify possible social and emotional difficulties as shown in reports of emotional symptoms, conduct problems, hyperactivity/inattention, and peer-relation problems; also to identify strengths in prosocial behavior (sharing, helping)	The SDQ[d] is a behavioral checklist designed to be completed by teachers or mothers/family caregivers for children between 3 and 16 years of age. The SDQ uses five scales, each scored from 1 to 10, and made up of five items: emotional symptoms, conduct problems, hyperactivity/inattention, peer relationship problems, and prosocial behavior. In this book, all scales have been coded identically, so that for all scales, the higher the score, the more concern about possible social or emotional difficulties.
Demonstrations of child skills (and mother reports of these skills), drawing on a study conducted by the University of San Carlos Office of Population Studies[e]	To directly observe (or, with younger or reluctant children, to learn from the mother) children's gross and fine motor skills, language, cognitive and socio-emotional development	In one set of questions, children were asked to demonstrate their ability to perform a specified skill. When the child did not want to demonstrate this skill, the mother was asked if the child is usually able to do it. In another set of questions, the mother was asked directly whether their child could perform the activity. For these skills, the child was never asked to do a demonstration.

table continues next page

Early Childhood Education and Development in Poor Villages of Indonesia •
http://dx.doi.org/10.1596/978-0-8213-9836-4

Table 2.2 **A Closer Look at the Child Development Measures** *(continued)*

Measure	Objective	Background and uses
Dimensional Change Card Sort (DCCS)[f]	To measure children's executive function skills	The DCCS task[g] is an executive function test designed for children between 3 and 7 years of age. Children are shown a series of cards with pictures of everyday images. The images are either red or blue in color, and some cards have a border while others do not. Children are asked to sort the cards by either color or shape and then to sort the card using a different dimension (stage 1). Next, children are asked to sort cards with a border by color and those without a border by shape (stage 2).
Drawing tasks (based on the Draw-a-Man test)[g]	To measure children's cognitive skills	Children were asked to draw pictures of both a human figure and a house as a measure of their cognitive skills. The drawings were scored by counting the number of body or house parts included in the drawing. More detailed drawings received higher scores.
Expressive and receptive language tasks	To measure children's ability to use words or to say the names of things and their ability to understand what is said by others	To demonstrate expressive language, children were shown a selection of everyday items and asked to name four of them. For receptive language, the assessor named different body parts, such as "nose," and asked children to point to each of them on their own bodies. Each question was scored according to whether or not the child answered correctly.

Note: a. Janus and Duku 2005; Janus and Offord 2007; Janus et al. 2007; b. Janus and Offord 2007; c. Goodman 1997; Muris, Meesters, and van den Berg 2003; d. Goodman 1997; e. Office of Population Studies 2005; f. Zelazo 2006; Zelazo et al. 2003; g. Frye, Zelazo, and Palfai 1995; Zelazo 2006; h. Goodenough 1954; Harris 1963.

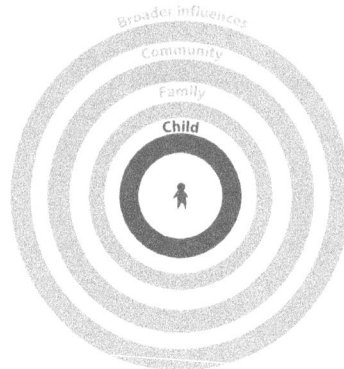

Physical Health: Stunting, Underweight, and Children's Body Mass Index

Children are considered to be stunted if they have low height for their age, underweight if they have low weight for their age, and wasting if they have low weight for their height. These issues remain major concerns in Indonesia because they put overall child development at risk. In this sample, all of the children were measured and weighed by interviewers. We were then able to calculate each child's height for age, weight for age, and body mass index (BMI) for age. The BMI for age calculation is similar to weight for age but is a predictor of a longer-term, and therefore more serious, wasting problem.[3]

This sample of children has high rates of stunting, wasting, and being underweight. Table 2.3 summarizes the percentage of Indonesian children in this sample who are considered to have moderately and severely low height for age (stunting), weight for age (underweight), and BMI for age. As usually defined by researchers, children classified in the moderately stunted/wasted category are more than 2 standard deviations below the mean of an ideally healthy reference population, and children in the severe category are more than 3 standard deviations below the mean of the same reference population. Table 2.3 shows a somewhat smaller percentage of children in the stunted, underweight, and low BMI categories as children get older (age 2 vs. age 1; age 5 vs. age 4). Nevertheless, the overall percentage of children showing these growth problems remains high.

The proportion of children in this sample with moderate levels of stunting and being underweight is similar to that of Indonesia as a whole and very high compared to many other countries. Worse yet, the proportion of children with severe levels of these growth problems is also very high: in a well-nourished population such as the reference group, less than 1 percent of children are expected to be in the severe category. Because stunting is not reversible, these results have serious implications for children's later physical, cognitive, and behavioral development, putting their school success and potential contributions to society seriously at risk.

Table 2.3 Stunting and Underweight Rates Are High by International Standards in 2009 and 2010

		Younger cohort		Older cohort	
		At age 1	At age 2	At age 4	At age 5
Height for age (stunting)	moderate	23.11	24.74	23.70	24.80
	severe	16.70	12.70	9.07	7.58
Weight for age (underweight)	moderate	21.74	24.06	23.14	24.46
	severe	15.45	12.22	8.53	7.34
Body mass index (BMI) for age	moderate	22.79	24.89	23.57	24.79
	severe	16.49	12.80	9.06	7.62
Number of children		2,874–3,036	2,796–2,889	3,114–3,177	3,005–3,061

Source: Calculations using ECED survey data.

Note: Moderate is between 2 and 3 standard deviations below the mean of the British Growth Reference; severe is 3 standard deviations below the mean of the British Growth Reference. The British Growth Reference was developed using data from 17 cross-sectional surveys conducted in the United Kingdom between 1978 and 1993. The Childhood Obesity Working Group of the International Obesity Taskforce recommended the use of BMI cutoff points to categorize children as normal weight, overweight, or obese based on age, sex, and BMI. These cutoff points were developed using large, nationally representative cross-sectional datasets from six countries: Brazil, Great Britain, Hong Kong, the Netherlands, Singapore, and the United States.

Early Childhood Education and Development in Poor Villages of Indonesia •
http://dx.doi.org/10.1596/978-0-8213-9836-4

School Readiness: The Early Development Instrument

The EDI is a comprehensive measure of school readiness and is widely used internationally. First developed by Canadian researchers, the EDI provides a holistic picture of how well children are developing by the time they enter school. It assesses children's school readiness across five developmental domains: (1) physical health and well-being; (2) social competence; (3) emotional maturity; (4) language and cognitive skills; and (5) communication skills and general knowledge. Children who score high on the EDI share certain traits (box 2.3).

Box 2.3 Profiles of Children Who Perform Well on Each of the EDI Domains

Physical health and well-being

Children who perform well on the physical health and well-being domain are usually dressed appropriately for school activities and do not come to school hungry or tired. They are independent, have established a hand preference, and are well-coordinated. Children are physically ready for school each day and have well-developed gross and fine motor skills.

Social competence

Children who perform well on the social competence domain get along well with other children, are cooperative and self-confident. They show respect for others, follow rules, exercise self-control, and take responsibility for their actions. These children work neatly and independently the majority of the time. Children who score high on the social competence domain are able to solve problems, follow instructions, and easily adjust to changes. They are curious about and eager to explore the world around them.

Emotional maturity

Children who score high on the emotional maturity domain demonstrate helping behaviors, often spontaneously. They rarely show signs of anxiousness or aggressive or hyperactive behaviors. They concentrate well, do not have temper tantrums, and are not mean to others.

Language and cognitive skills

Children who perform well on the language and cognitive skills domain possess basic literacy skills (know how to handle a book, can identify letters, know some letter sounds, are aware of rhyming words, and are able to write his or her name). These children are interested in books, mathematics, and numbers, and have good memories. They are able to read and write simple words or sentences. Additionally, these children have basic numeracy skills (can count to 20, recognize numbers and shapes, compare numbers, sort, and classify).

Communication skills and general knowledge

Children who score high on the communication skills and general knowledge domain can communicate effectively with ease, can tell stories and engage in imaginative play, articulate clearly, and show reasonable general knowledge.

Note: EDI = Early Development Instrument.

Table 2.4 Children's EDI Scores Reveal Challenges in Language and Cognitive Skills at Age 4 and Age 5

	Older cohort	
	At age 4 mean (SD)	At age 5 mean (SD)
Physical health and well-being	7.74 (1.11)	8.88 (1.02)
Social competence	7.71 (1.45)	8.31 (1.33)
Emotional maturity	6.57 (1.53)	6.97 (1.49)
Language and cognitive skills	3.14 (2.05)	5.71 (2.67)
Communication skills and general knowledge	9.58 (1.24)	9.66 (1.04)
Number of children	3,250–3,253	3,392–3,393

Source: Calculations using ECED survey data.
Note: Each domain has a maximum score possible of 10. EDI = Early Development Instrument; SD = standard deviation.

With the help of the interviewers, mothers of the older cohort of children in our sample answered the EDI questions twice, first when their children were 4 years old and then again when they were 5.

Table 2.4 shows EDI scores in each domain at age 4 (2009) and age 5 (2010). As expected, children have somewhat higher scores when they are older, as they typically would become more knowledgeable and skilled in most areas even without instruction.

The children in the sample have not gained key readiness skills and interests in early literacy and math. Looking at table 2.4, we see that by far the lowest scores are in the language and cognitive skills domain. The skills in this domain include the more formal elements of language development and skills, such as the ability to read simple sentences and count to 20, interest in learning more about reading and math, and aspects of cognitive problem solving. Internationally, these skills are considered important elements of school readiness, and yet they are not strengths of the children in our sample, at least as reported by their mothers.

In contrast, children in the sample score relatively high in the communication skills and general knowledge domain. As seen in the examples in box 2.3, these skills are more related to a child's ability to use words to tell others what he or she needs, in ways that others in the community may understand.

Compared to Canadian norms, a high percentage of children in the Indonesian sample is "developmentally vulnerable" in one or more domains. As described in box 2.4, the EDI's vulnerability score reflects especially low performance on an EDI domain. The percentage of children who scored low enough to be considered vulnerable in each EDI domain is shown in table 2.5.

Although comparisons of Indonesian scores with other data should be made with caution (see box 2.4), there are reasons to be worried about some aspects of children's performance, while recognizing other areas of strength. The pattern of results in table 2.5 is similar to that in table 2.4. We do see that vulnerability percentages are lower and scores are higher on each domain at age 5 than age 4. These improvements do not necessarily reflect the effects of policy, but that

Box 2.4 What Is Developmental Vulnerability?

A child is classified as developmentally vulnerable on an Early Development Instrument (EDI) domain if he or she scores below the vulnerability cutoff as calculated in Canada, where the EDI was originally developed. On each domain, the cutoff is the score below which 10 percent of Canadian children fell. The proportion of children scored as vulnerable on one or more domains is an indicator of how well or poorly a group of children is developing in that domain.

We should be cautious in applying these vulnerability scores in Indonesia and in comparing the scores to other countries because:

- The scores were based on Canadian norms.
- The number of items on the Indonesian version of the EDI is fewer than other versions (47 vs. 104), so scores may not be directly comparable.
- The Indonesian EDI was completed by mothers instead of teachers, as is usual in other studies; therefore, ratings may be based on different perceptions and sources of information.

Table 2.5 Developmental Vulnerability Declines between Ages 4 and 5, but Almost Two-Thirds of 5-Year Olds Are Vulnerable on One or More EDI Domain

	Older cohort	
	At age 4 percentage vulnerable	At age 5 percentage vulnerable
Physical health and well-being	26.30	5.60
Social competence	9.00	4.40
Emotional maturity	35.80	26.40
Language and cognitive skills	88.00	47.50
Communication skills and general knowledge	1.10	0.40
Proportion vulnerable on one or more domain	93.20	60.90
Number of children	3,253	3,393

Source: Calculations based on Canadian norms.

children naturally improve on some domains as they get older. But the scores and the percentage of children considered developmentally vulnerable are especially poor for two of the five domains: emotional maturity and language and cognitive skills.

On the language and cognitive skills domain, even at age 5 almost half of our sample scored below the cutoff point for developmental vulnerability. In contrast, both Canada and Australia have about 10 percent vulnerability on this domain. Children in other middle-income and developing countries show a range of results on this domain from 10 to 60 percent developmental vulnerability (Brinkman 2009; Centre for Community Child Health and Telethon Institute for Child Health Research 2009; Janus et al. 2007).

On the positive side, we see very low vulnerability (very few children scoring below the Canadian cutoff point) in the domain of communication skills and general knowledge (similar to results in table 2.5). The domains of social competence and (at age 5) physical health and well-being also show low vulnerability. In other words, children in our sample appear to be doing well in these domains of school readiness, both of which primarily emphasize aspects of verbal communication and interaction with peers and adults.

Emotional and Social Problems and Assets: Strengths and Difficulties Questionnaire

In addition to cognitive or academic skills, readiness for school includes social and emotional competence (Raver 2002). The results of the SDQ provide in-depth information on children's social and emotional development. The SDQ measure has been translated into 40 languages and is used in many countries. As described in table 2.2, for this measure mothers were asked about their children's possible behavioral and emotional problems as well as their children's prosocial assets. These questions were asked first when the children were age 4 and then a year later.

Table 2.6 shows children's SDQ scores in both age groups. Typically, the first four scales are coded such that a higher score represents more difficulties and therefore a worse outcome, and the prosocial behavior scale is coded such that a higher score represents fewer difficulties and therefore a more positive outcome. However, for ease of readers' interpretation, in this case all scales have been coded with an identical metric, so that for all scales, the higher the score, the more concern about possible social or emotional difficulties. It is encouraging that on average the children in this sample scored low to middle of the range on each of these scales (maximum score is 10). The average scores are moderate to good and not high enough to cause concern, although individual children may have significant problems in any of these areas. In the second year of data collection, on average children's scores were somewhat better; that is, their mothers said that they had fewer difficulties with behavior and emotions than a year earlier. This is what one would usually expect as children mature, in part because of further development of executive function skills.

Table 2.6 Children Have Fewer Difficulties as They Get Older: SDQ for Children at Ages 4 and 5

SDQ categories	Older cohort	
	At age 4 mean (SD)	At age 5 mean (SD)
Emotional symptoms	3.70 (2.04)	3.55 (2.02)
Conduct problems	3.48 (1.90)	3.41 (1.98)
Hyperactivity/inattention	5.04 (1.31)	4.61 (1.33)
Peer relationship problems	2.60 (1.52)	2.34 (1.53)
Prosocial behavior (reversed)	3.61 (1.90)	3.36 (1.90)
Total difficulties score	14.81 (4.52)	13.90 (4.55)
Number of children	3,243–3,253	3,372–3,393

Source: Calculations using ECED survey data.
Note: Maximum score is 10 on the 5 scales. Total difficulties is the sum of the first 4 scales (maximum score is 40).
SD = standard deviation; SDQ = Strength and Difficulties Questionnaire.

Early Childhood Education and Development in Poor Villages of Indonesia •
http://dx.doi.org/10.1596/978-0-8213-9836-4

Table 2.7 Children's Executive Functions Improve as They Age: DCCS in 2009 and 2010

	Older cohort of children	
	At age 4 percentage	At age 5 percentage
Failed to complete stage 1 (color and shape)	34.82	11.95
Completed stage 1 (color and shape)	49.14	66.48
Completed stage 2 (color, shape, and border)	16.04	21.57
Number of children	2,800	3,222

Source: Calculations using ECED survey data.
Note: DCCS = Dimensional Change Card Sort.

Executive Function Skills: Dimensional Change Card Sort Task

As described in table 2.2, the DCCS task uses a card-sorting game to assess young children's executive function skills—for example, their ability to stop sorting the cards one way (such as by shape) and to shift their attention to sorting on a different dimension (such as by color). Executive function skills are important in children's ability to regulate their own thinking, planning, and behavior, which in turn predicts both academic and social competence in later years. From extensive use of this measure in other countries, researchers find that 3-year-old children are usually unable to complete stage 1 of the task, switching between color and shape, but the majority of 4- and 5-year-olds complete it successfully. International research finds that most 4-year-olds and about half of 5-year-old children are not successful at the more challenging stage 2, where a different sorting rule applies depending on whether a card has a border (Zelazo 2006).

Table 2.7 shows that, at least for stage 1, our sample of rural Indonesian children are at roughly the same level in developing their executive function skills as are children in other countries. We also see that when the same children are assessed a year later (by then, most are age 5), there is some improvement in executive function, evident in the percentage who now are able to be successful at stage 1.

Can You Do This? And This?

It is always valuable to assess children's development using many different measures, not just one. The following measures provided complementary information about several areas of development, using both children's demonstrations and mothers' reports.

Children's Demonstrations of Their Skills

Besides asking mothers about various aspects of their children's development using the EDI and the SDQ, the interviewers asked the children to demonstrate some of these skills directly. These skills included developmental areas similar to those in the EDI—physical (divided into gross motor and fine motor), language, cognitive, and socio-emotional skills—and were assessed through a series of tasks.

Table 2.8 The Younger Children Are Able to Complete the Majority of the Child Tasks Successfully, 2009 and 2010

Tasks	Younger cohort			Older cohort		
	Maximum score	At age 1 mean (SD)	At age 2 mean (SD)	Maximum score	At age 4 mean (SD)	At age 5 mean (SD)
Gross motor	20	13.71 (4.59)	18.00 (1.56)	5	4.90 (0.41)	4.96 (0.22)
Fine motor	12	6.10 (2.32)	10.00 (1.50)	2	1.91 (0.30)	1.96 (0.20)
Language	5	2.95 (1.46)	4.75 (0.52)	26[a]	13.49 (4.32)	21.05 (4.91)
Cognitive	8	4.43 (1.52)	7.00 (1.21)	–	–	–
Socio-emotional	2	1.63 (0.54)	1.45 (0.50)	–	–	–
Number of children		2,851–3,107	2,539–3,185		3,008–3,239	3,382–3,393

Source: Calculations using ECED survey data.
Note: a. Total score for language skills for 4-year-olds can increase beyond 26 in the 2009 data, as children are asked to name as many body parts as they can. SD = standard deviation.

The interviewer began by asking the child to perform the easiest task in a group. For example, gross motor tasks for the 1-year-olds began with them being placed on a table to see if they were able to support themselves with some assistance. For the 4-year-olds, gross motor tasks began with an assessment of whether the child was able to walk upstairs, taking each step with the alternate foot and without holding the handrail. The tasks got progressively more difficult, with the children asked to perform harder and harder tasks until they reached the limit of their ability to perform the tasks.

If the child did not want to perform the task at that time, the mother was asked if the child could usually complete the task. As noted above, in the gross motor example, the tasks requested of the child (or through the child's mother) were quite different for the 1- and 2-year-old cohort and the 4- and 5-year old cohort, and not all of the same categories of development were assessed. From 2009 to 2010, both the younger and older children improved in most of the skill areas in which they were assessed (table 2.8).

Mothers' Reports of Toddlers' Skills

Because the EDI and SDQ are not designed for children under 4, for the 1- and 2-year-olds we relied on mothers' reports of their toddlers' cognitive, socio-emotional, receptive language, and gross motor skills. Questions covering cognitive skills included asking about the child's reaction to sour/bitter/salty food and their ability to intentionally make sounds with toys intended to do so, such as shaking a rattle. Socio-emotional skills included questions about the child's ability to take turns and whether they look happy when carried by someone they know. Receptive language asked whether the child stops crying when they hear soothing music and/or voices and about the child's ability to imitate sounds. Gross motor skills covered whether the child is able to move from a sitting position to a crawling position, walk unassisted despite occasionally falling, and how well coordinated their body

Table 2.9 Mother Ratings of Child Skills for 1- and 2-Year-Olds Are (Too?) High

		Younger cohort	
Skills	Maximum score	Age 1 mean (SD)	Age 2 mean (SD)
Cognitive	6	5.48 (0.72)	5.95 (0.21)
Socio-emotional	6	4.45 (1.00)	4.85 (0.96)
Receptive language	5	4.54 (0.77)	4.80 (0.44)
Gross motor	3	2.53 (0.53)	2.94 (0.25)
Number of children		73–3,079	454–3,175

Source: Calculations using ECED survey data.
Note: The lowest number of responses was for the gross motor skills for both cohorts. Interviewers and mothers may have deemed these questions to be redundant after watching the children demonstrate these same skills in the child tasks section. SD = standard deviation.

movement is. Descriptive statistics for mother-rated child skills (table 2.9) showed that the younger cohort were generally able to perform almost all the tasks. Although there was a small improvement on all skill sets as children got older, it is striking how well all children are reported as doing, suggesting that mothers may be biased and may tend to over-report their child's abilities.

Cognitive and Conceptual Development: Drawing a Human and a House

As another way of assessing children's cognitive abilities, each child was invited to draw two pictures: one a picture of a human being and another one of a house. The child was not told which parts of a person or house he or she should draw. Using a scoring system based on the Goodenough-Harris Draw-A-Man test (Goodenough 1954), each child's drawings were scored by counting the number of different body or house parts in the drawing. The more elaborate or complex a child's drawing was, the higher the score, and the more advanced his or her concepts and ability to represent these in a drawing were thought to be.

Both the younger and older children in this sample were originally asked to do the drawing task. However, because almost none of the 1- and 2-year-olds could attempt anything beyond scribbling (in fact, many babies could not yet hold a pencil), and because this task is usually administered to children over age 3 or 4, we report only the results for the older children here. Table 2.10 shows these results. Scores show that at age 4, the children included relatively few elements in their drawings, especially in the house drawing (an element might include such features as doors, windows, a roof, and so forth). By age 5, children were typically including considerably more elements, suggesting advances in cognitive development. It is important to notice, however, that there were very large standard deviations, indicating a wide range in children's ability to accomplish this task.

Early Childhood Education and Development in Poor Villages of Indonesia •
http://dx.doi.org/10.1596/978-0-8213-9836-4

Table 2.10 Draw a Human and House Tasks Reveal Children's Cognitive Abilities Improve as They Get Older

	Older cohort	
	At age 4 mean (SD)	At age 5 mean (SD)
Draw human	5.17 (5.57)	10.70 (6.12)
Draw house	2.10 (3.46)	7.82 (6.09)
Number of children	2,770–2,793	3,384–3,385

Source: Calculations using ECED survey data.
Note: SD = standard deviation.

Understanding and Using Words: Assessing Receptive and Expressive Language

Because language and communicative development are so important in the early years, and are such important predictors of school readiness, data were collected on children's language competence using a number of different measures, including parts of the EDI as well as mothers' reports of child development and other tasks administered to children in their homes.

In the receptive and expressive language task, children in the younger cohort (age 1 in 2009 and age 2 in 2010) were asked a series of questions to assess both their *expressive language* (ability to use words, say the names of things) and their *receptive language* (ability to understand what is said by others). To demonstrate expressive language, the children were shown a selection of items and asked to name four of them. The items were a bunch of bananas, a chair, some goldfish, a spoon, a television, a chicken, a cat, and a motorbike. For receptive language, the assessor named different body parts, such as "nose," and asked children to point to each of them on their own bodies. Each question was scored according to whether or not the child was able to answer correctly.

As seen in table 2.11, at age 1 fewer than 40 percent of children were able to answer all of the items from the receptive and expressive language questions correctly. As was the case in most other measures, children performed better at age 2 than at age 1: all of the 2-year-olds successfully answered the expressive language questions, and around 85 percent of children were able to answer the receptive language questions correctly.

Putting It All Together: How Are These Children Developing?

Taken together, the evidence from a large set of internationally validated measures clearly points to some areas where this sample of poor children is developing well and to others where challenges persist, even as children get older.

Box 2.5 summarizes what has been learned so far from these two assessments roughly 1 year apart. This summary is for all children we observed—and therefore combines the effects of living in villages where ECED project services had

Early Childhood Education and Development in Poor Villages of Indonesia •
http://dx.doi.org/10.1596/978-0-8213-9836-4

Table 2.11 The Receptive and Expressive Language Questions Are Answered Correctly by Almost All 2-Year-Olds

	Younger cohort	
	At age 1 percentage completing correctly	*At age 2 percentage completing correctly*
Receptive language	37.01	85.33
Expressive language	39.73	100.00
Number of children assessed	2,635–2,645	2,544–3,169

Source: Calculations using ECED survey data.

Box 2.5 How Are the Children Doing? Findings from Assessments of the Development of Indonesian Children in Poor Villages

Physical development

- Children in this sample have high rates of stunted growth, wasting, and being underweight for age.
- The percentage of children with these growth problems declines somewhat with age, but remains very high in relation to children in other countries and is consistent with national statistics for Indonesia.

Cognitive and conceptual development

- On average, children in this sample have not gained key school readiness skills in literacy, math, and other aspects of cognitive problem-solving and do not seem to have much interest in these domains (as reported by their mothers).
- Children improve in their cognitive and conceptual development as they get older, but their competencies in this domain remain low compared with children of the same age in other settings.
- Children's conceptual development, as reflected in their ability to draw detailed pictures of humans and houses, was limited at age 4 but improved considerably by age 5; however, there were wide variations in children's ability.

Executive function skills

- Children in this sample seem to be developing their abilities to plan and manage their thinking and behavior at a similar level as children in other countries.

Communication and general knowledge

- Children's practical communication skills appear strong, including being able to speak clearly and express their wants and needs to others.
- Children are able to play imaginatively, tell stories, and show understanding of the everyday world around them.

box continues next page

Box 2.5 How Are the Children Doing? Findings from Assessments of the Development of Indonesian Children in Poor Villages (continued)

Social and emotional development

- In most respects, children in this sample are doing well in this domain. Mothers report few behavior problems or examples of emotional difficulties.
- According to their mothers, however, children show slight improvements in prosocial behavior—being helpful and concerned about others.

been implemented with the effects of growing older. For this reason, the results should not be read as an estimate of the effect of the project services.

It is evident that despite a number of areas in which development is adequate or even strong, there are points of concern. In the next section, we explore what families may or may not be doing to reinforce positive developmental outcomes for their children.

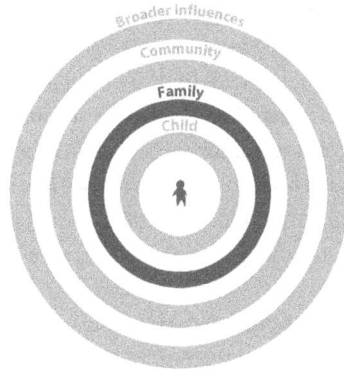

Household Environments and Parenting Practices: Are Families Promoting Positive Child Development?

In chapter 1, we saw that families are a key element in the circles of influence on children's early development. The research is clear: the things that parents—rich or poor—do with their young children every day can affect all aspects of children's health, development, and learning. Whether or not children are enrolled in some kind of ECED program, most children spend a substantial portion of their day at home with their mother or other family caregiver. Therefore, in this section we look within the household to assess whether children in our sample are growing up in environments that are likely to promote positive child development. We focus on two aspects of what parents can influence: daily activities, especially related to language, and children's diets. We will also look at the influence of household wealth on daily activities and diets. Box 2.6 compares the measurement of household

Box 2.6 Measuring Wealth in the ECED Project Sample

Throughout this book, we have referred to children from poor and rich households. Here we explain how a measure of household wealth was constructed for this study. It compares our results with the results one would obtain in a sample representative of rural Indonesia using household per capita expenditure—the measure used for official poverty calculations.

We constructed a measure of household wealth for the sample of children whose developmental outcomes are examined above using information obtained from household interviews on:

- whether households own assets such as bicycles, cell phones, land, and livestock (among others); and
- whether good materials have been used in the construction of the walls, floors, and roofs of the respondents' homes.

This information was then combined using principal components analysis, which reduces a large amount of information into a single asset index. The index was then used to divide households into quintiles of wealth, ranging from poorest to richest. When the index is standardized, the average value of the index is zero and the standard deviation is one. In chapter 3, we use this standardized index to divide the sample into two groups: poor (those with wealth below the mean) and nonpoor households (those with wealth above the mean).

The asset index approach differs from that used in official calculations of poverty in Indonesia, which rely on calculating household per capita expenditures and comparing them with a poverty line. Had enough resources been available, ideally the ECED study would have measured poverty according to the official methodology, but doing so was not feasible. Therefore, poverty was measured using information on asset ownership by households, which is faster to collect.

To assess how comparable these approaches are and to provide a more easily understandable measure of wealth, we compared the results of the asset index approach in the ECED sample with the results of the official approach, using only the rural sample of the 2010 National Socioeconomic Household Survey (SUSENAS). A selected set of characteristics was compared, using places where the two surveys asked comparable questions. Thus, the quintiles shown in the figure B2.6.1 use the asset index approach for the ECED sample and the per capita expenditures approach for the rural sample of the SUSENAS 2010. We then compared the education levels of the heads of households, the rates of asset ownership, and the quality of construction materials used in the home to see if there were substantial differences across the two methods.

The results show that the asset index approach can differentiate between groups in ways that are comparable to what we would obtain if we used the per capita expenditure approach: those in the bottom quintile are far less likely to be highly educated, far less likely to own assets, and less likely to report having good materials used in the construction of their homes when compared to those in the top quintile. Looking across the SUSENAS and ECED samples, average rates of asset ownership and education levels are by and large similar (they are not, obviously, identical).

box continues next page

Early Childhood Education and Development in Poor Villages of Indonesia •
http://dx.doi.org/10.1596/978-0-8213-9836-4

Box 2.6 Measuring Wealth in the ECED Project Sample *(continued)*

Figure B2.6.1 Households in the Rural Sample of the SUSENAS Are Similar to Those in the ECED Sample

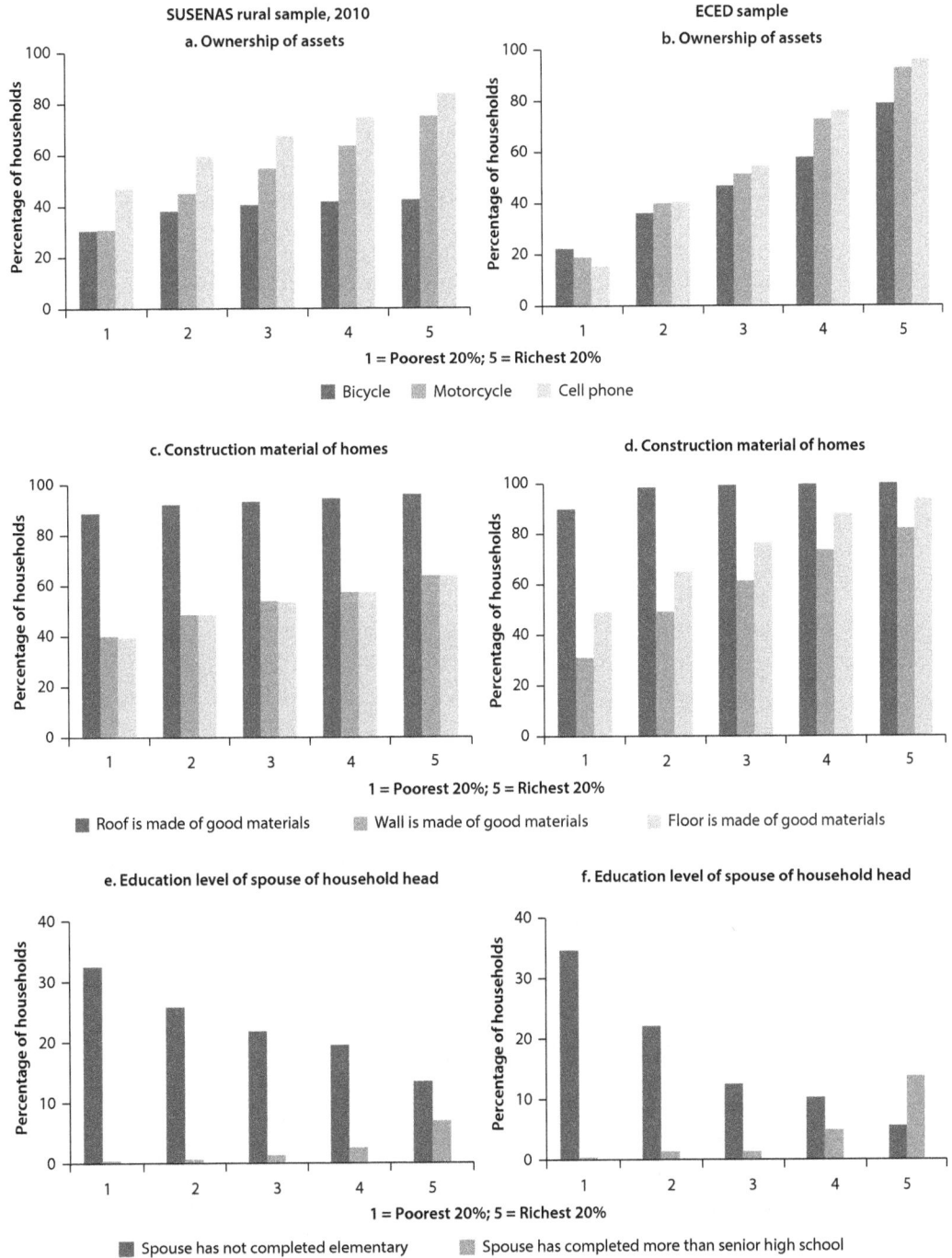

SUSENAS rural sample, 2010
a. Ownership of assets

ECED sample
b. Ownership of assets

1 = Poorest 20%; 5 = Richest 20%

■ Bicycle   ▨ Motorcycle   ▨ Cell phone

c. Construction material of homes

d. Construction material of homes

1 = Poorest 20%; 5 = Richest 20%

■ Roof is made of good materials   ▨ Wall is made of good materials   ▨ Floor is made of good materials

e. Education level of spouse of household head

f. Education level of spouse of household head

1 = Poorest 20%; 5 = Richest 20%

■ Spouse has not completed elementary   ▨ Spouse has completed more than senior high school

Source: Calculations using ECED survey data and rural sample of SUSENAS 2010.

box continues next page

Early Childhood Education and Development in Poor Villages of Indonesia •
http://dx.doi.org/10.1596/978-0-8213-9836-4

Box 2.6 Measuring Wealth in the ECED Project Sample *(continued)*

This comparison, however, does allow us to assert that the bottom quintile in the ECED sample is similar to, if not a bit worse off than, the bottom quintile in the SUSENAS. Likewise, it allows us to assert that the top quintiles appear similar. For simplicity, we note that in the rural sample of the SUSENAS, monthly per capita expenditures in the bottom quintile are roughly US$20 and in the top quintile they are roughly US$76. In the ECED sample, our analysis suggests that the poorest may have monthly per capita expenses lower than US$20 and the richest may have monthly per capita expenses of about US$76.

wealth within the study sample to wealth as measured using a sample representative of rural Indonesia.

Reading Books and Telling Stories

Children whose parents look at and read books with them usually know more words, have better cognitive abilities, are more interested in books, and become better readers in the future (Duursma, Augustyn, and Zuckerman 2008). Book-reading is an important home activity even for children under age 3 (Raikes, Luze, and Brooks-Gunn 2006). Interviewers asked mothers in our sample about books, book-reading, and storytelling. Figure 2.1 shows that the vast majority of the children in the sample are growing up in households where parents never read stories to their children. For many households, this is understandable, as very few report owning any children's books. Two-thirds of children in the poorest quintile grow up in households with no children's books. Even among the highest wealth quintile in our sample, one-third of children have no books.

Even if parents do not own books or are not able to read, storytelling is another valuable way to improve children's receptive and expressive language, starting in infancy and continuing into the preschool years (Tamis-LeMonda and Rodriguez 2009). Yet in our sample very few parents report telling stories to their children, no matter how old they are.

Considering the importance of these activities for child development, the preponderance of such responses is disconcerting and suggests a focus for possible ECED interventions. At the same time, we must avoid blaming families for what they are not doing. Instead, we need to identify and build upon their strengths and resilience in the face of poverty and multiple related challenges.

Children's Everyday Activities at Home: Few Books, Little Play

The developmental essentials in early childhood, described in chapter 1, include many opportunities for children to play, use toys and other materials, and explore their environment. Such opportunities promote children's cognitive, language, socio-emotional, and physical development and help them develop important executive function skills.

In our sample, however, we find that many children seldom engage in these kinds of daily activities. For example, 26 percent of mothers report that

Figure 2.1 Parents Hardly Ever Read to Their Children, nor Do Many of Them Tell Their Children Stories

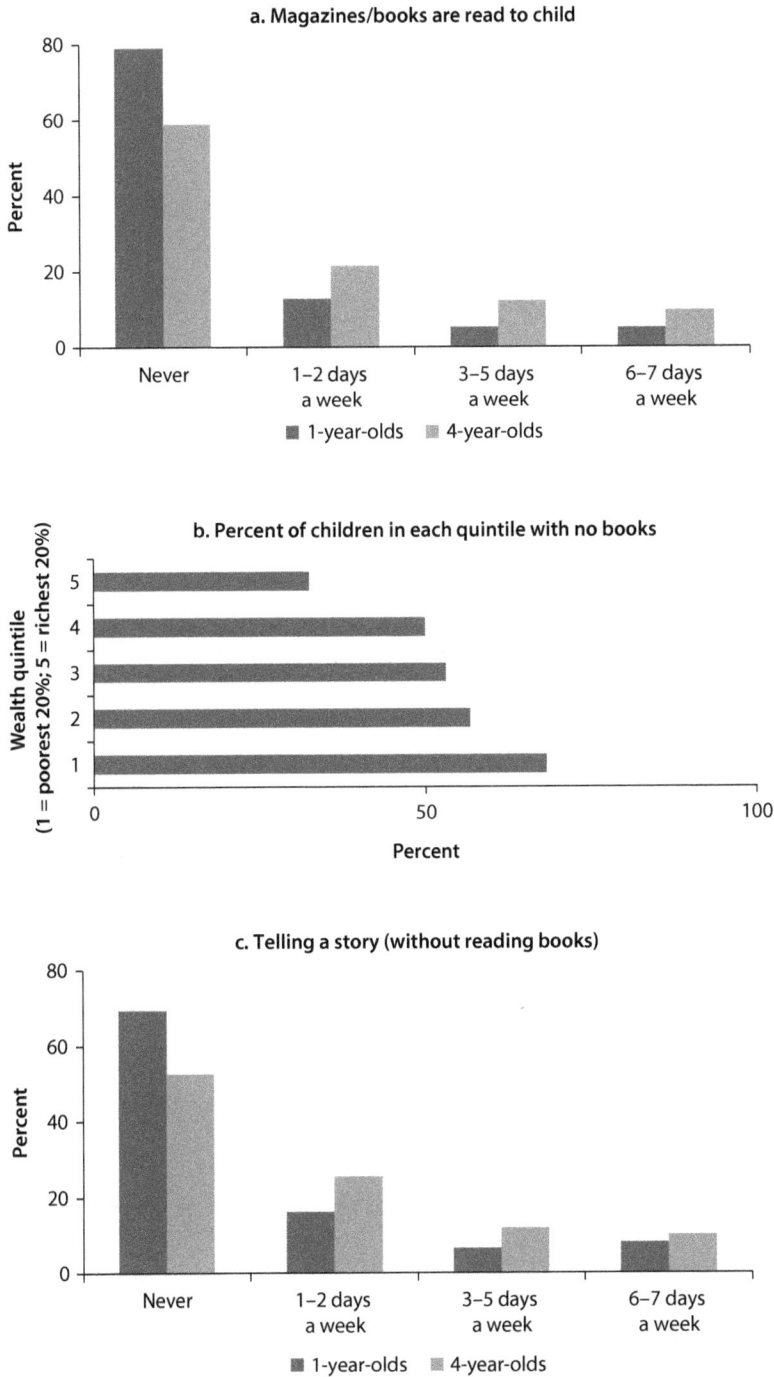

a. Magazines/books are read to child

b. Percent of children in each quintile with no books

c. Telling a story (without reading books)

figure continues next page

Early Childhood Education and Development in Poor Villages of Indonesia •
http://dx.doi.org/10.1596/978-0-8213-9836-4

Figure 2.1 Parents Hardly Ever Read to Their Children, nor Do Many of Them Tell Their Children Stories *(continued)*

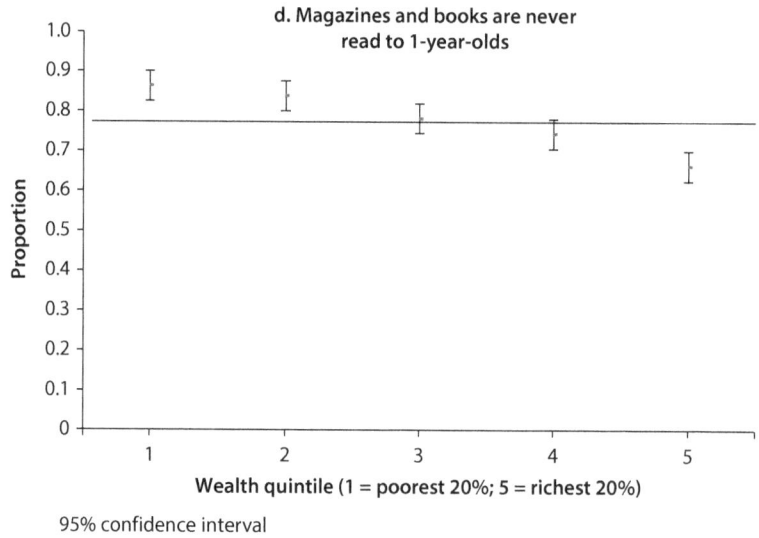

d. Magazines and books are never read to 1-year-olds

95% confidence interval

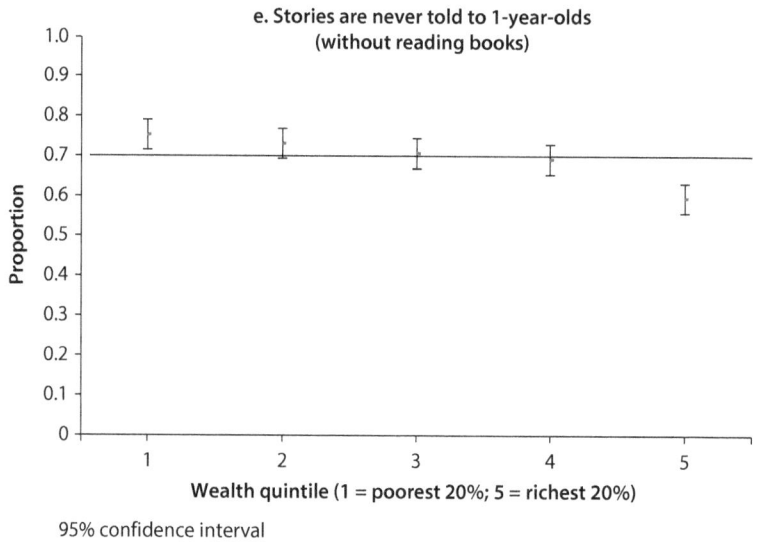

e. Stories are never told to 1-year-olds (without reading books)

95% confidence interval

figure continues next page

Figure 2.1 Parents Hardly Ever Read to Their Children, nor Do Many of Them Tell Their Children Stories *(continued)*

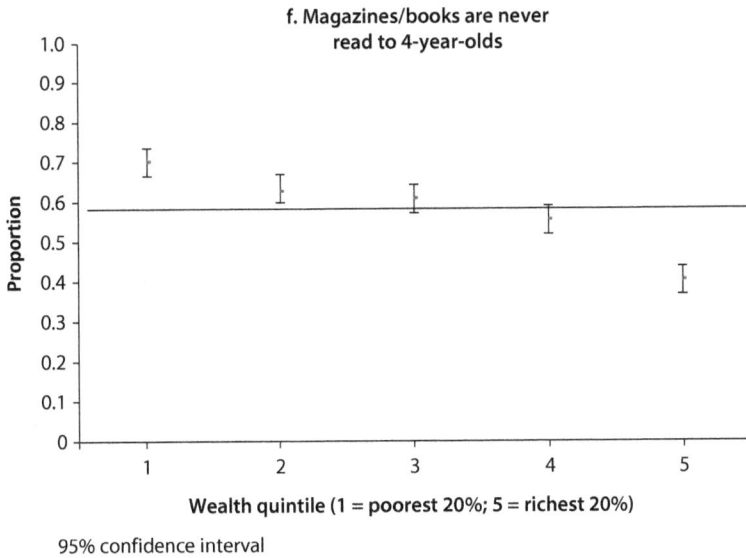

f. Magazines/books are never read to 4-year-olds

95% confidence interval

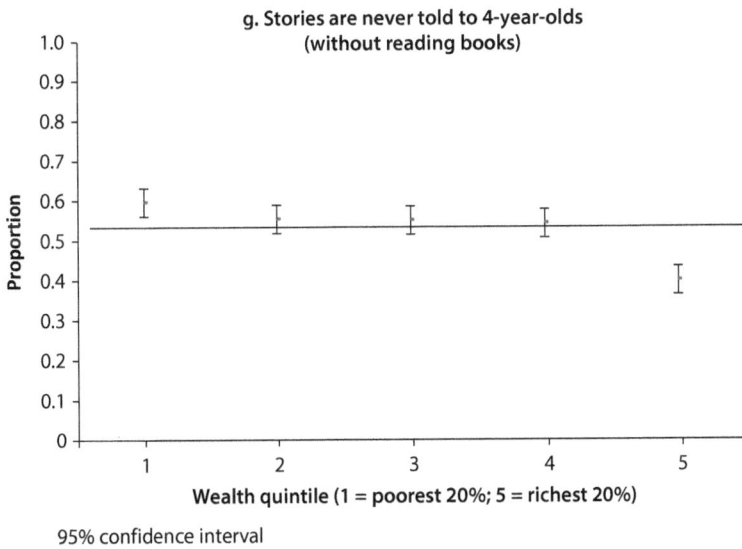

g. Stories are never told to 4-year-olds (without reading books)

95% confidence interval

Source: Calculations using ECED survey data.
Note: Horizontal line shows sample average. For each wealth quintile, the mean and 95 percent confidence interval are shown.

their children (1- and 4-year-olds) never play outdoors (figure 2.2). Given the high percentage of children who are stunted, wasting, or underweight, one wonders if a possible reason is lack of energy. Even indoors, 12 percent of mothers report that their 4-year-old children never play with toys or play indoor games. And 17 percent of mothers of 4-year-olds and 34 percent of mothers of 1-year-olds say that their child never draws or scribbles. In contrast, more than half of all children are involved in everyday household activities at least some time during the week (not shown). Clearly, children's everyday experiences lack many of the elements needed to stimulate development.

Children living in the greatest poverty are the least likely to participate in many of these developmentally positive activities. For example, among

Figure 2.2 Almost a Quarter of Children Are Not Engaged in Typical Activities

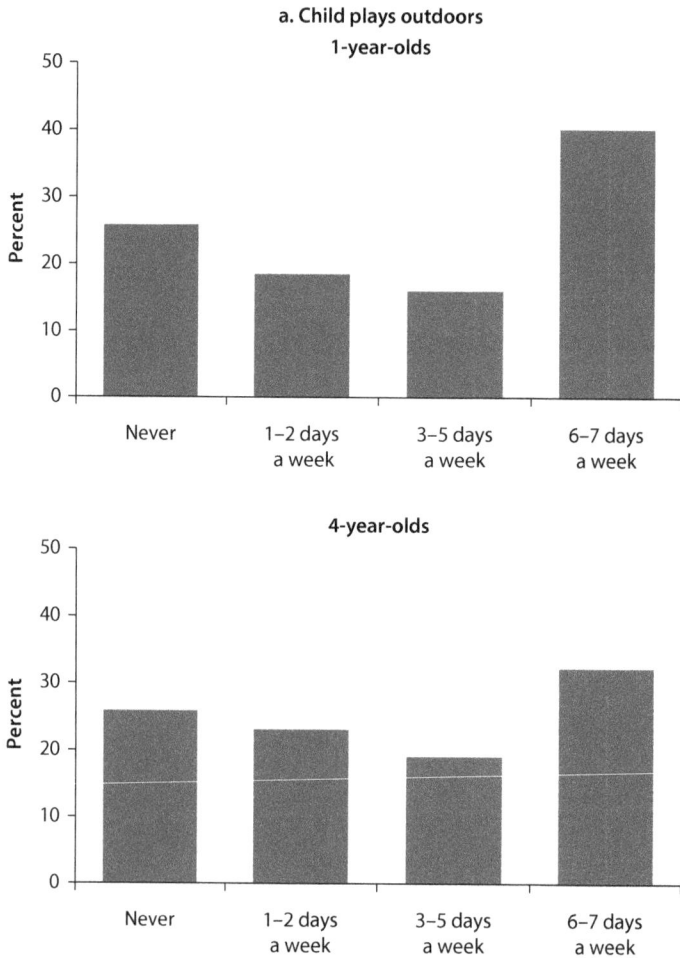

a. Child plays outdoors
1-year-olds

4-year-olds

figure continues next page

Early Childhood Education and Development in Poor Villages of Indonesia •
http://dx.doi.org/10.1596/978-0-8213-9836-4

Figure 2.2 Almost a Quarter of Children Are Not Engaged in Typical Activities *(continued)*

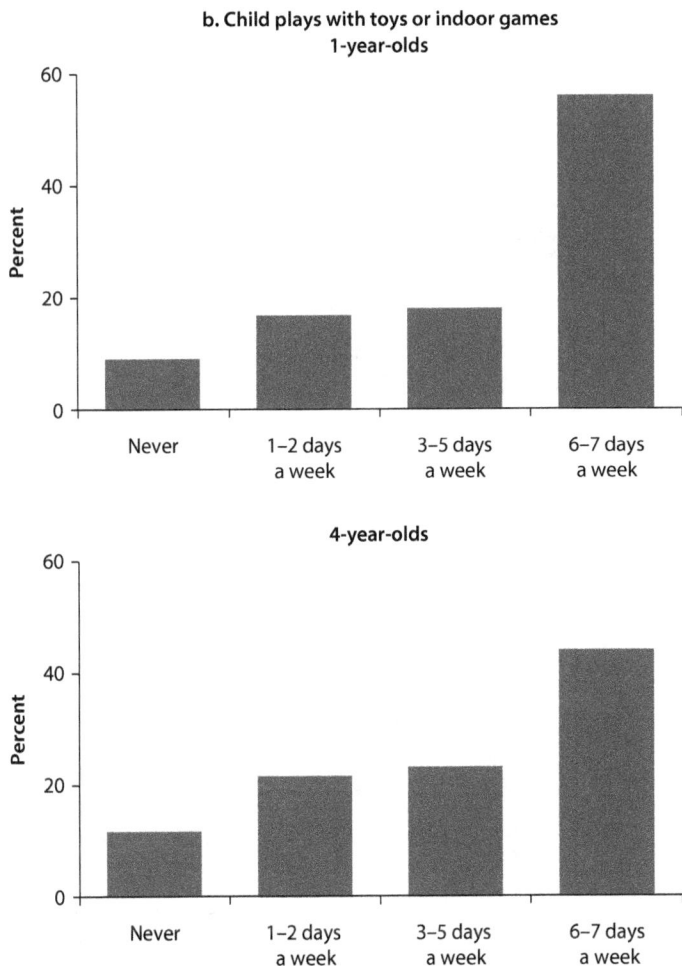

b. Child plays with toys or indoor games
1-year-olds

4-year-olds

figure continues next page

Early Childhood Education and Development in Poor Villages of Indonesia •
http://dx.doi.org/10.1596/978-0-8213-9836-4

Figure 2.2 Almost a Quarter of Children Are Not Engaged in Typical Activities *(continued)*

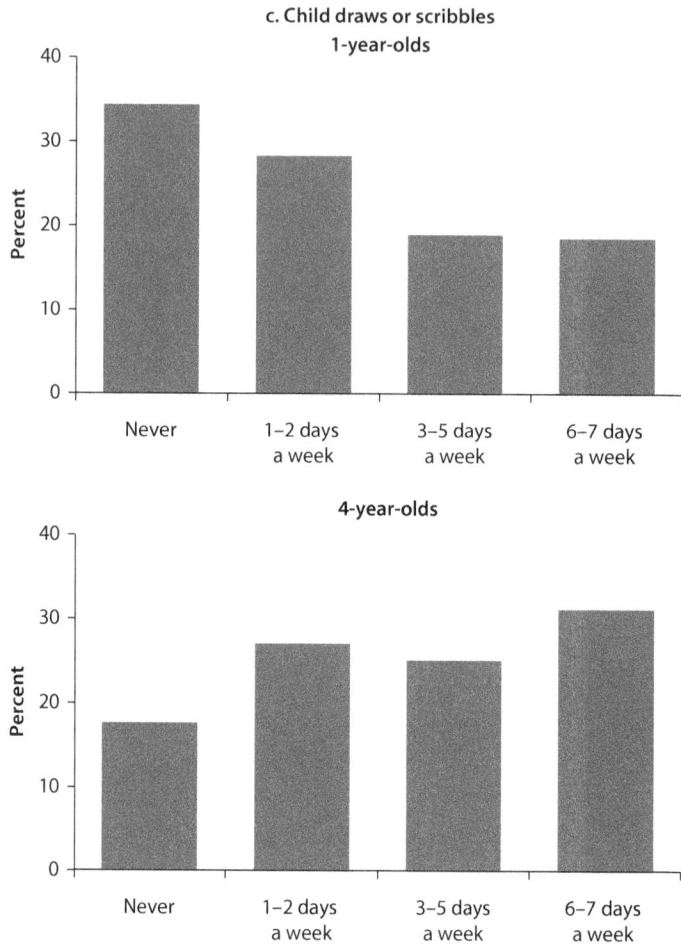

c. Child draws or scribbles
1-year-olds

4-year-olds

figure continues next page

Figure 2.2 Almost a Quarter of Children Are Not Engaged in Typical Activities *(continued)*

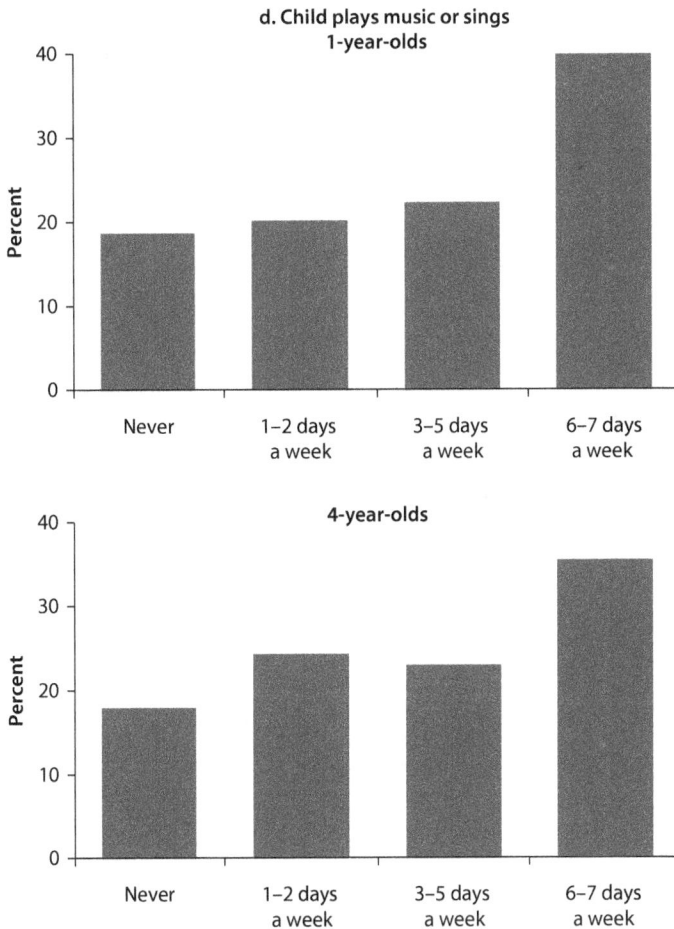

d. Child plays music or sings

1-year-olds

4-year-olds

Source: Calculations using ECED survey data.

1-year-olds, half the children in the bottom (poorest) quintile are reported to never draw or scribble. In the top quintile, only 14 percent are reported to never do so. In the bottom quintile, mothers of 4-year-olds are seven times more likely to say their children never draw or scribble than mothers in the top quintile and three times more likely to say their child never plays music or sings (figure 2.3). Finally, mothers in the bottom quintile are twice as likely to say their children never play outdoors as mothers from the highest quintile for both age groups (not shown).

Feeding the Body and Brain

Another developmental essential is good health and nutrition, starting from prenatal care and continuing throughout childhood. Indonesia has policies to promote breastfeeding, but national statistics show that Indonesian mothers stop breastfeeding earlier and introduce complementary food earlier than

Figure 2.3 Poorer Children Are Less Likely than Richer Children to Participate in Developmentally Positive Activities

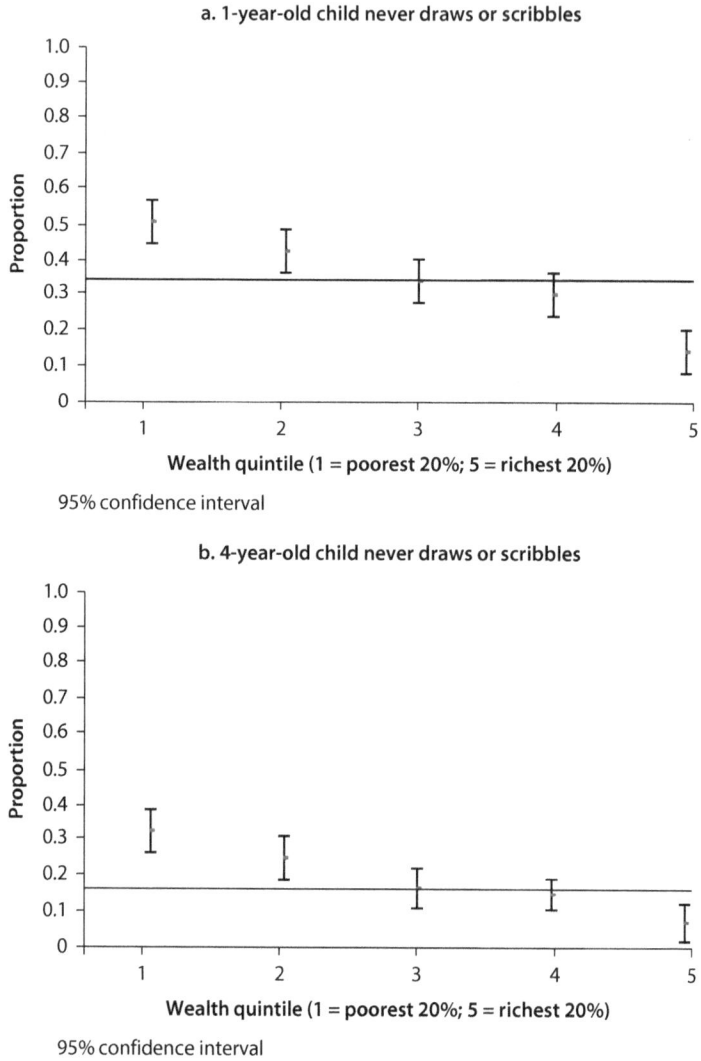

a. 1-year-old child never draws or scribbles

95% confidence interval

b. 4-year-old child never draws or scribbles

95% confidence interval

figure continues next page

Figure 2.3 Poorer Children Are Less Likely than Richer Children to Participate in Developmentally Positive Activities *(continued)*

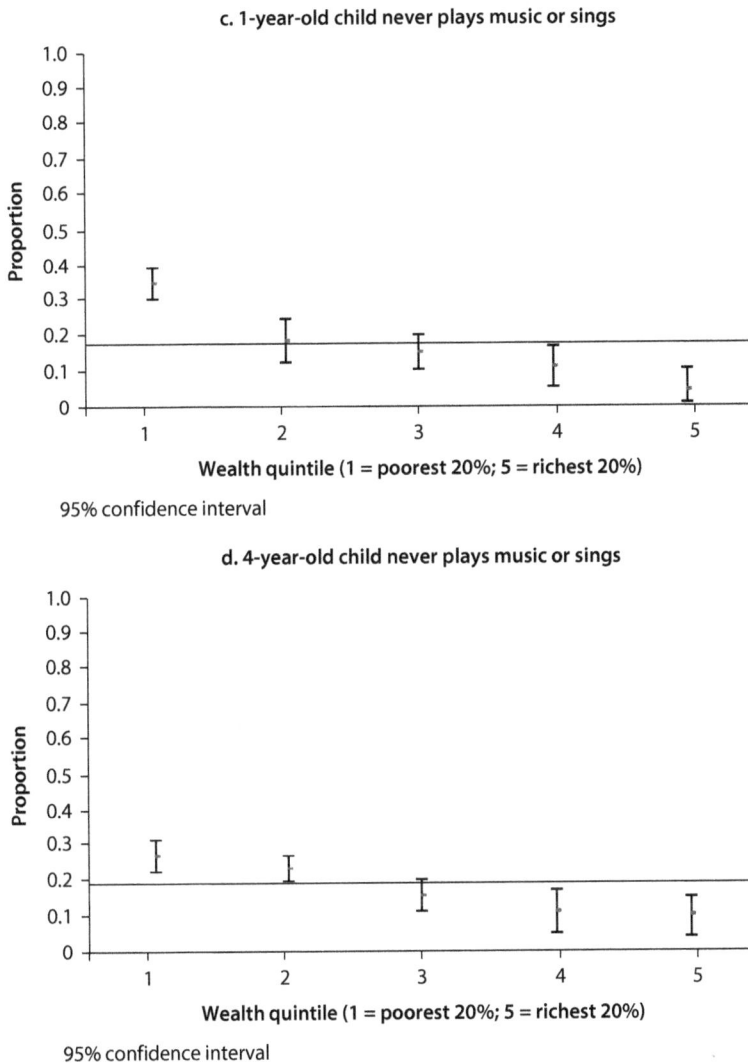

c. 1-year-old child never plays music or sings

Wealth quintile (1 = poorest 20%; 5 = richest 20%)

95% confidence interval

d. 4-year-old child never plays music or sings

Wealth quintile (1 = poorest 20%; 5 = richest 20%)

95% confidence interval

Source: Calculations using ECED survey data.
Note: Horizontal line shows sample average. For each wealth quintile, the mean and 95 percent confidence interval are shown.

recommended by nutritionists. In addition, we have already seen that this sample, and Indonesia as a whole, has high numbers of children who are stunted, wasting, or are underweight for their age. In some families, early feeding patterns may contribute to these problems. At a less-severe level, feeding patterns may also influence lower-than-optimal physical and intellectual development and longer-term health problems.

Virtually all mothers in this sample report breastfeeding their children (figure 2.4). But very few report exclusively breastfeeding their children for

6 months as is recommended. Two-thirds of mothers say they breastfed exclusively for 3 months, and only one-third of mothers say they breastfed exclusively for 6 months. It is striking that these patterns are the same irrespective of wealth.

Many children also appear to eat an unbalanced diet. In interviews, mothers report that 60 percent of their 1-year-olds and 70 percent of 4-year-olds have

Figure 2.4 Mothers' Feeding Practices and Knowledge May Be Making Children's Other Health Problems Worse

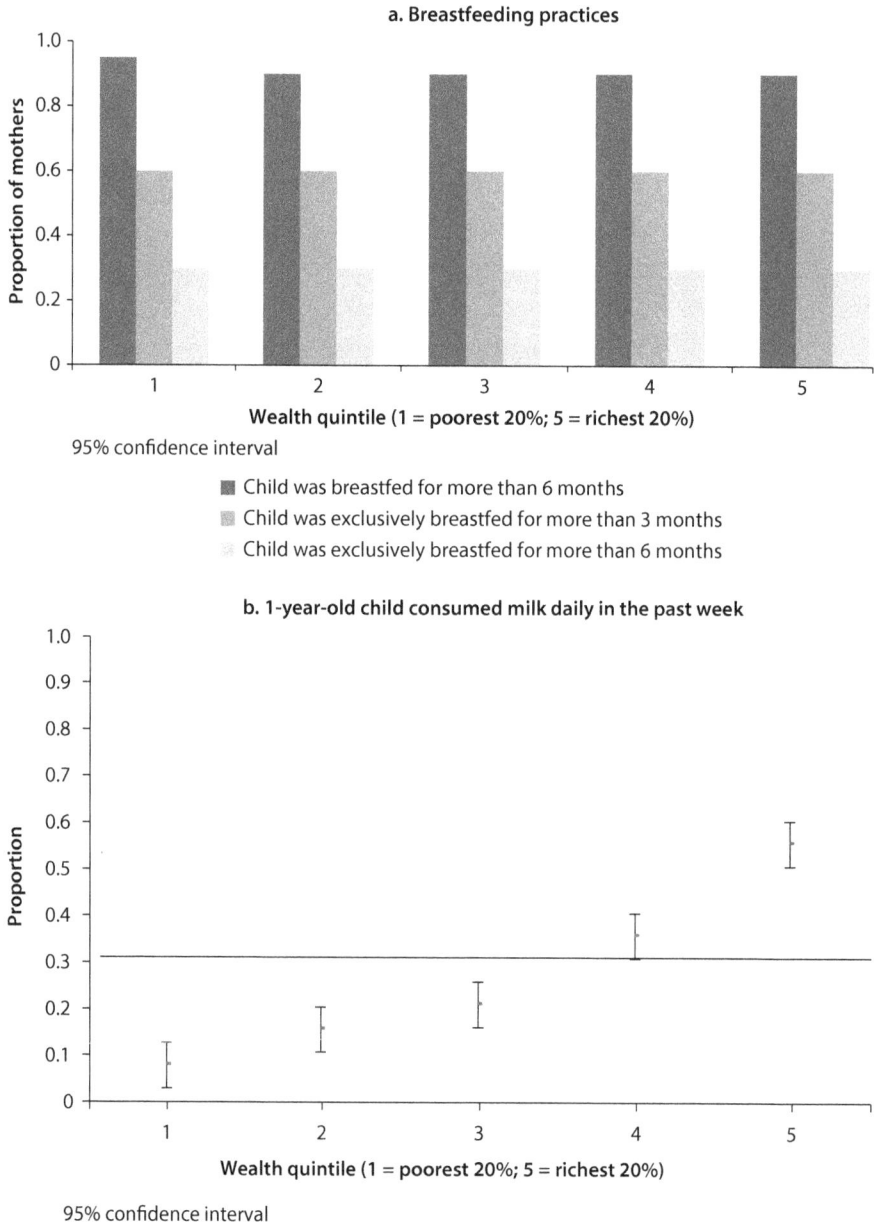

a. Breastfeeding practices

Wealth quintile (1 = poorest 20%; 5 = richest 20%)

95% confidence interval

■ Child was breastfed for more than 6 months
▨ Child was exclusively breastfed for more than 3 months
░ Child was exclusively breastfed for more than 6 months

b. 1-year-old child consumed milk daily in the past week

Wealth quintile (1 = poorest 20%; 5 = richest 20%)

95% confidence interval

figure continues next page

Figure 2.4 Mothers' Feeding Practices and Knowledge May Be Making Children's Other Health Problems Worse *(continued)*

c. 1-year-old child consumed snacks daily in the past week

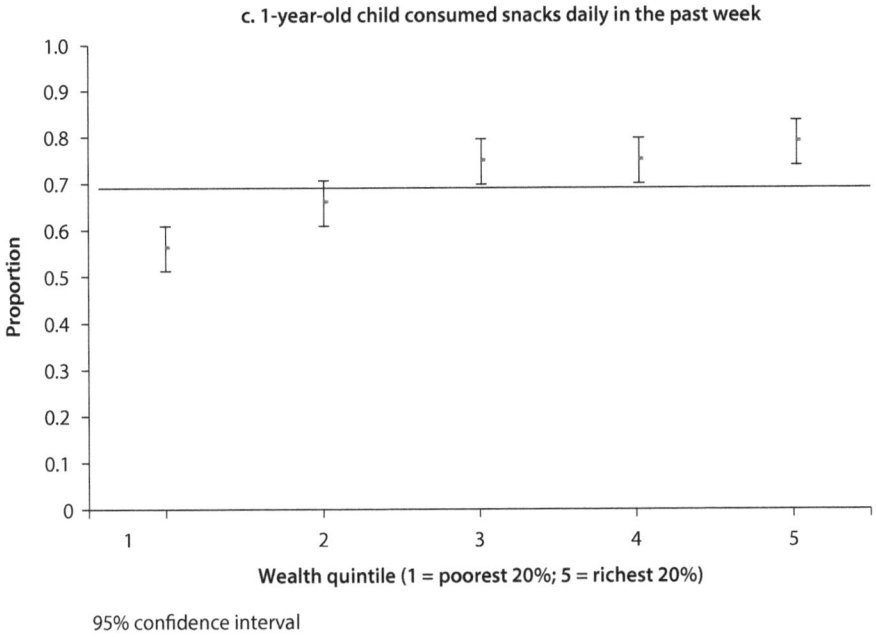

95% confidence interval

d. When 4-year-old child suffers from diarrhea,
more fluid than normal should be given

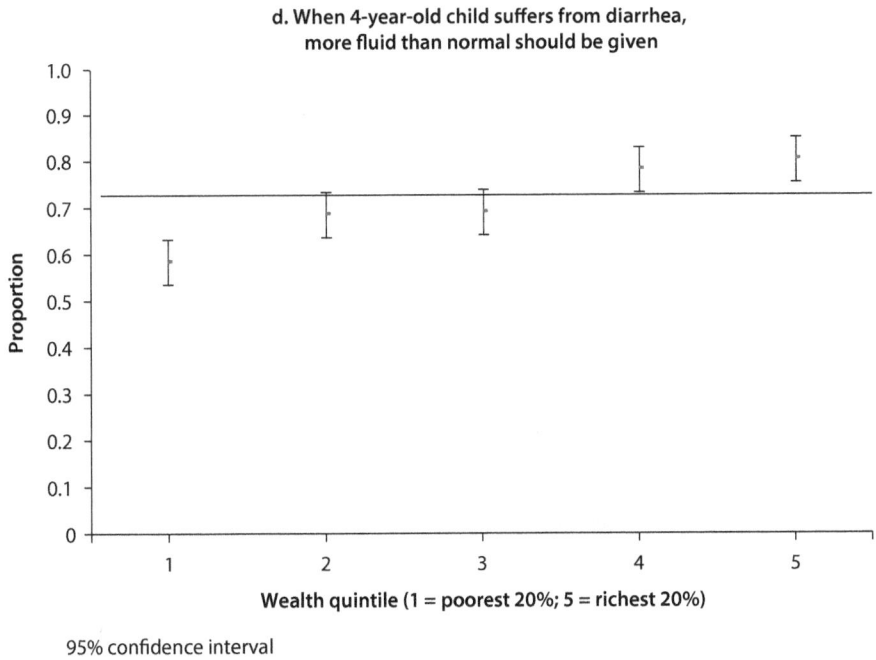

95% confidence interval

figure continues next page

Early Childhood Education and Development in Poor Villages of Indonesia •
http://dx.doi.org/10.1596/978-0-8213-9836-4

Figure 2.4 Mothers' Feeding Practices and Knowledge May Be Making Children's Other Health Problems Worse *(continued)*

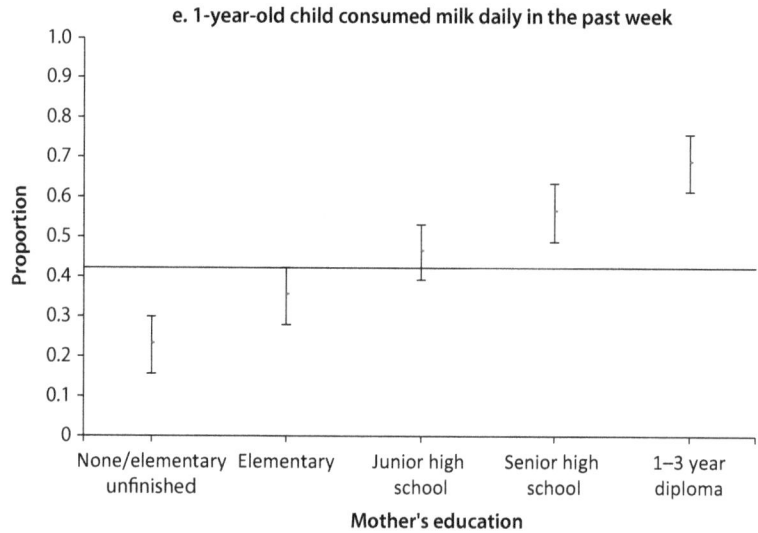

e. 1-year-old child consumed milk daily in the past week

95% confidence interval

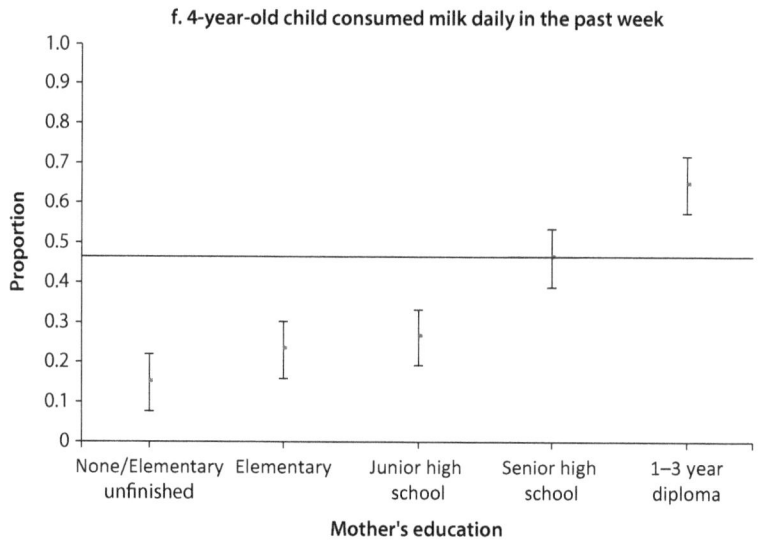

f. 4-year-old child consumed milk daily in the past week

95% confidence interval

Source: Calculations using ECED survey data.
Note: Horizontal line shows sample average. For each education level, the mean and 95 percent confidence interval are shown.

snacks daily—more than the percentage that eat vegetables every day (50 and 60 percent, respectively). More children eat snacks every day than drink milk every day—not only the 4-year-olds, but even the 1-year-olds. There is also evidence to suggest that children consume candy more frequently than fruit. Taken together, these findings suggest that parents could be provided with education and support about how to balance nutrition in everyday meals.

The evidence shows a strong association between parents' education and what they feed their children—but only for some food types (figure 2.4). Only 30 percent of mothers with less than an elementary education say that their 1-year-olds drink milk every day. For children who are 4 years old and whose mothers have a less than elementary school education, only 15 percent report consuming milk daily. In contrast, 70 percent of mothers with a diploma or higher education report that their children drink milk every day, at both age 1 and age 4. It seems, then, that less-educated parents may stop providing their children with milk—an essential nutrient—earlier than do more educated parents.

Mothers' feeding practices and beliefs may also be making children's other health problems worse. From the data just summarized, it seems that many young children, especially in the poorest families, are not getting enough milk. There is some indication that this problem may be related to parents' lack of knowledge about the importance of fluids (including milk) in children's diets. For example, when mothers were asked whether a child with diarrhea should be given more or less fluid than usual, 40 percent of mothers in the poorest quintile and 20 percent of mothers in the richest quintile were unable to offer the correct response, which is to provide more fluid than usual.

Mothers' Parenting Practices: Warmth, Consistency, Hostility

The preceding section described what activities the mothers in our sample typically do with their children, how the children spend their time at home, and what mothers usually feed their children. Chapter 1 emphasized that families also influence their children's development through their relationships with their children, such as the level of warmth or anger that mothers feel for their children and the kind of discipline that mothers tend to use when children misbehave. These practices are important because children living in an environment with higher-quality parenting are more likely to have higher pre-academic skills, better language skills, more social skills, and fewer behavior problems than children who received lower-quality parenting (NICHD Early Child Care Research Network 2002).

Therefore, mothers were asked to answer a series of questions about their parenting practices. These practices were measured using 24 items describing parent-child relationships adapted from the Longitudinal Study of Australian Children (LSAC) (Zubrick et al. 2008). The questions covered a range of possible practices that reflect different levels of warmth, consistency, and hostility. Mothers were asked how often they used each of a number of different parenting practices. Scores could then be created for each dimension separately, and a total positive parenting practices score could be created by adding together scores for each of the three parenting dimensions (with the negative items reversed).

Early Childhood Education and Development in Poor Villages of Indonesia •
http://dx.doi.org/10.1596/978-0-8213-9836-4

Table 2.12 Parenting Practices Do Not Change Much within a Year

Dimensions of parenting	2009 Mean (SD)	2010 Mean (SD)
Parental warmth (maximum score = 30)	23.06 (2.98)	22.85 (2.81)
Parental consistency (maximum score = 30)	18.77 (3.01)	19.30 (2.60)
Parental hostility (maximum score = 60)	39.87 (5.51)	38.47 (5.42)
Total (Maximum score = 120)	81.70 (7.29)	80.62 (7.10)
Number of observations	6,367–6,369	6,572–6,580

Source: Calculations using ECED survey data.
Note: SD = standard deviation.

The higher the score, the more likely it is that parents have high levels of warmth and consistency, and low levels of hostility toward their children.

Table 2.12 shows the mean scores and standard deviations for each parenting practices dimension and for the total positive parenting practices score. Mothers were asked these questions in 2009 and again in 2010. As table 2.12 shows, there was no real difference in their responses between the two data collection points.

It seems from these results that in our sample of mothers, parents are consistent in their style of parenting from year to year, but that there are also wide variations in the use of positive and negative parenting strategies.

What Kinds of ECED Services Are Available to Support Children's Development, and for Whom?

Just as families can support their children's development, ECED services in the communities in which children live can do the same. Chapter 1 defined ECED, described the goals of these services, and summarized research showing the short- and longer-term benefits of ECED services. We saw that the benefits are greatest when targeted to the poorest, most vulnerable children. The services that are most effective begin when children are young (often through parenting programs), are of sufficient length and intensity, and are holistic: they attend to all areas of children's development. This section examines how these kinds of services are provided in Indonesia.

ECED Service Provision in Indonesia

The Ministry of Education and Culture (MoEC), the Ministry of Religious Affairs (MoRA), the Ministry of Home Affairs (MoHA), and the National Family Planning Board (BKKBN) all provide some form of ECED services. At least eight different forms of service provision are available (table 2.13).

These different ECED services emphasize different aspects of children's development and have different ways of involving families. For example, Integrated Health Service Units (*Posyandu*) are available for families in the community to bring their young children to be weighed and measured, and for mothers to receive some information about health, nutrition, and child development. Usually

Table 2.13 Different Kinds of ECED Services Are Provided by Different Ministries

	Ministry of Education and Culture	Ministry of Religious Affairs	Ministry of Home Affairs with Ministry of Health Staff	National Family Planning Board
Formal	Kindergartens (*Taman Kanak-kanak*, TK)	Islamic kindergarten (*Raudhotul Atfal*, RA)	–	–
Nonformal	Playgroups (*Kelompok Bermain*, KB)	Islamic kindergarten (*Taman Pendidikan Quran*, TPQ)	Integrated health service unit (*Posyandu*)	Toddler family groups (*Bina Keluarga Balita*, BKB)
	ECED Posts (*Pos-PAUD*)	–	–	–
	Child care centers (*Taman Penitipan Anak*, TPA)	–	–	–
	Other early childhood units (*Satuan PAUD Sejenis*, SPS)	–	–	–

Note: ECED = early childhood education and development.

Posyandu are open once a month and staffed with volunteers from the community. In contrast, playgroups (KB) and kindergartens (TK) are more focused on education, with KB emphasizing learning through play and TK often having a more "academic" way of teaching, although not in every case. In terms of family involvement, in *Posyandu* the ECED services are delivered to the mother or other family caregiver; similarly, toddler family group (BKB) sessions, which may occur weekly or monthly, are parenting classes for mothers. Playgroups and kindergartens may have parent volunteers or perhaps occasional parent meetings, but the core of their services is directed at the children.

As seen in table 2.13, Indonesia has historically considered these services as falling into two categories: the formal and the nonformal systems, until recently administered under different directorates within the Ministry of Education and Culture. The majority of formal kindergartens are privately provided (figure 2.5).

Different forms of ECED services have been intended to cater to specific age-groups; in practice, however, these age-groupings are sometimes ignored (figure 2.6). For example, the government expects that children between the ages of 4 and 6 will attend kindergartens (TK or RA). But because of local conditions, service availability, and family preferences, some 4- to 5-year-old children may still be in playgroups (KB) and some 6-year-old children may have already started the first grade of primary school.

Not all ECED services are equally intensive. For example, child care centers *Taman Penitipan Anak* (TPA) are usually open from 8 a.m. to 4 p.m. to care for children of full-time working families. In contrast, kindergartens (TK), playgroups (KB), and ECED posts (Pos-PAUD) typically operate from 8 to 11 in the morning. Islamic kindergartens (TPQ) usually operate in the afternoons from 2 to 4 p.m., and many children are able to attend the TPQ after having attended another ECED center in the morning. Most of these services are available daily (5–6 times per week), although some playgroups meet only 3 days a week. Toddler family groups (BKB) meet less frequently; typically mothers attend one session a month.

Figure 2.5 The Vast Majority of Kindergarten Services Are Privately Provided

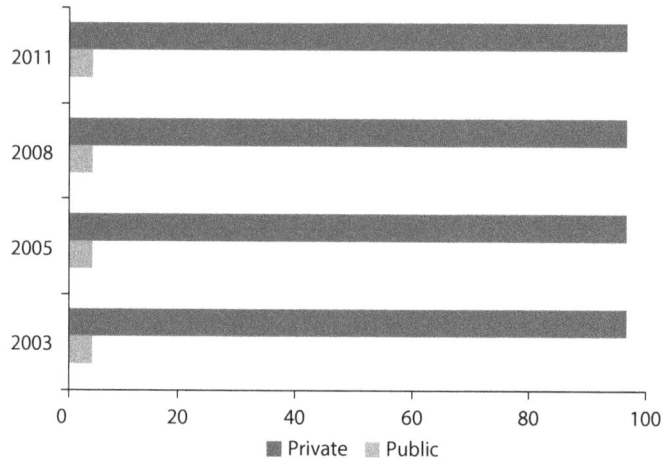

Source: Calculations using PODES data (various years).

**Figure 2.6 ECED Services Are Intended to Cater to Specific Ages,
but Intention Is Often Ignored**

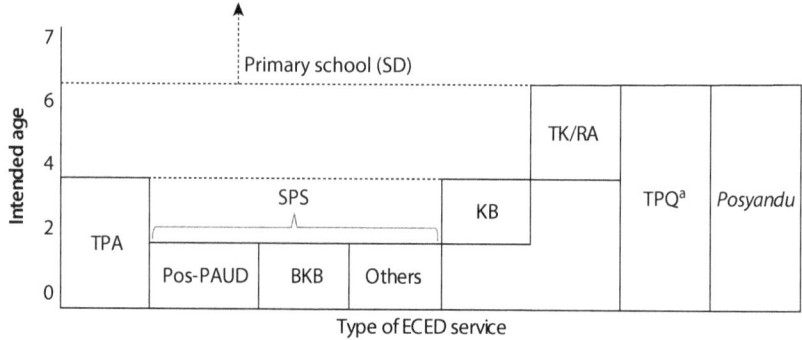

Note: BKB = *Bina Keluarga Balita* (toddler family groups); ECED = early childhood education and development; KB = *Kelompok Bermain* (playgroups); Pos-PAUD = ECED posts; *Posyandu* = Integrated health service unit; RA = *Raudhotul Atfal* (Islamic kindergarten); SPS = *Satuan PAUD Sejenis* (other early childhood units); TK = *Taman Kanak-kanak* (kindergartens); TPA = *Taman Penitipan Anak* (child care centers); TPQ = *Taman Pendidikan Quran* (Islamic kindergartens).
a. Also included in SPS.

Different types of services are subject to different standards. The government has established national standards on ECED, including a series of regulations on aspects such as class size. Regulations vary to some extent depending on whether the service is in the formal or nonformal category. Government regulations stipulate that formal kindergartens should have a teacher-to-child ratio of 1:20. In nonformal institutions such as playgroups, the teacher-child ratio varies depending on children's ages, ranging from 1:4 for children under

1 year of age up to 1:15 for 5- and 6-year-olds in a nonformal ECED center. In reality, ratios may vary locally depending on availability of teachers and demand for services.

Patterns of ECED Service Availability in a Sample of Villages

A number of reports have pointed out the lack of ECED services in poorer regions of Indonesia, compared to what is available in wealthier regions (figure 2.7) (World Bank 2006; UNESCO 2005). Because the sample we draw from is mostly poor villages in poor districts, we point out a few characteristics of ECED service availability in these settings.

By far the most commonly seen services in these villages are *Posyandu*. Kindergartens (TK) and playgroups (KB) are the next most common. Kindergartens serve only children age 4 and up and are almost entirely privately run. Therefore, this form of ECED service does not support the development of younger children (a critically important feature of effective ECED, as emphasized in chapter 1). Further, because kindergarten programs require fees from families, they are out of reach for the poorest families, whose children are most likely to need and benefit from ECED services.

A typical village in Indonesia has six subvillages or communities. Within the communities in our sample, we see that although virtually all subvillages have

Figure 2.7 Disparities in Enrollment Exist across Regions and Provinces

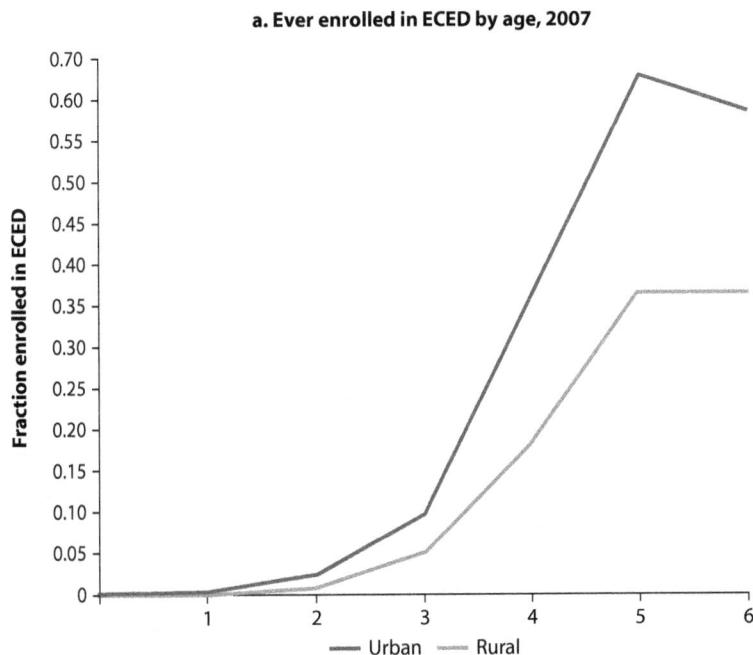

a. Ever enrolled in ECED by age, 2007

Source: Calculations using SUSENAS data.
Note: ECED = Early Childhood Education and Development.

figure continues next page

Figure 2.7 Disparities in Enrollment Exist across Regions and Provinces *(continued)*

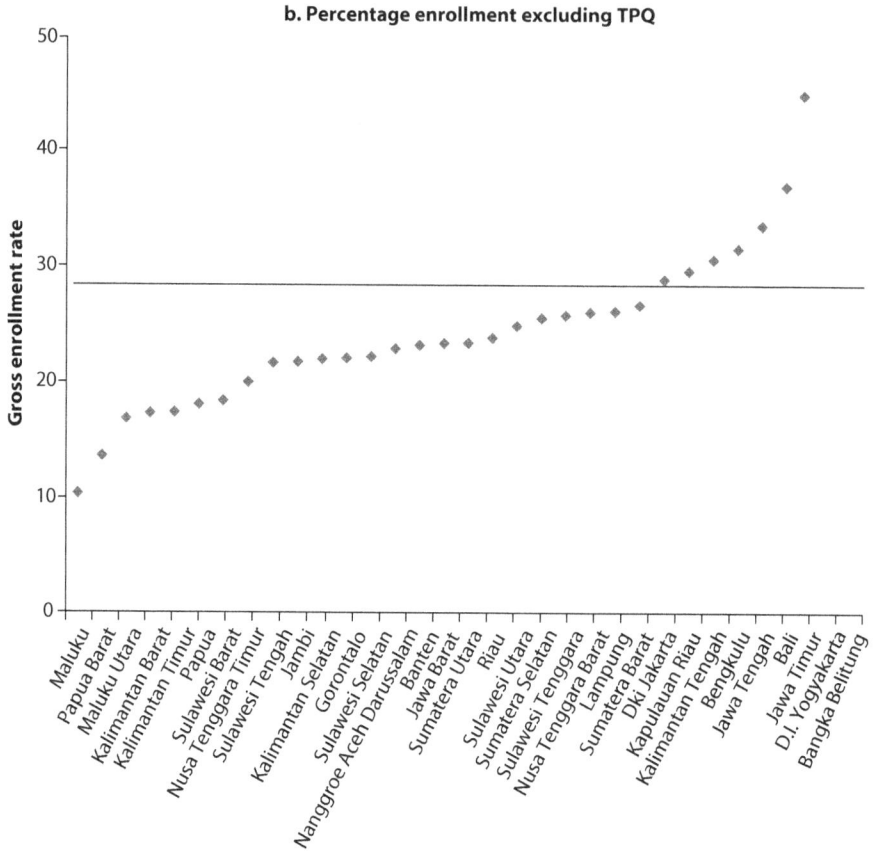

b. Percentage enrollment excluding TPQ

Source: Calculations using data from ECED grand design document.
Note: TPQ = Islamic kindergarten.

a *Posyandu* available, only one-third of all subvillages have a kindergarten or a playgroup available (figure 2.8).

What Can Make a Difference in Children's Development?

In chapter 1, we described the many circles of influence on young children's development (figure 1.5), noting that family characteristics are among the most influential. Among those characteristics are parents' level of formal education and their wealth—two factors that research has shown to have a large impact on children's development outcomes. Less-educated and poorer parents may be less able to provide adequate stimulation and material resources to their children. Perhaps as a result, research consistently shows that on most measures of development, the children of less-educated and poorer parents perform less well—another example of the effects of poverty on children's development.

Figure 2.8 Service Availability Varies Widely within a Sample of Villages, 2009

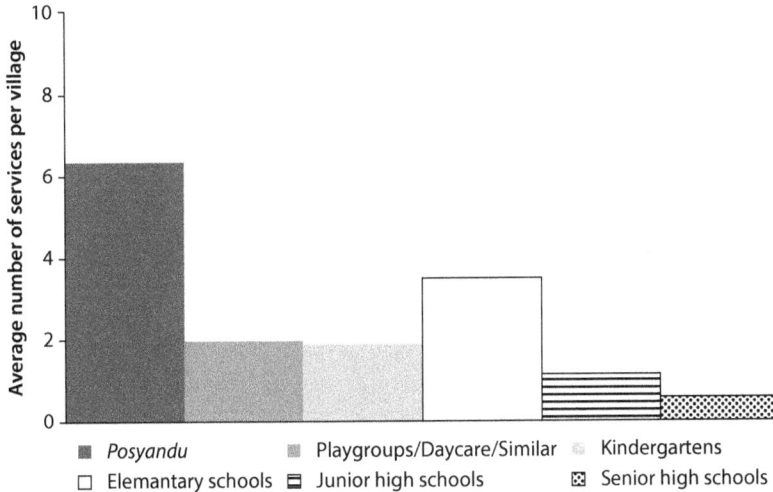

Source: Calculations using ECED survey.

In this study, districts and villages were selected because they were relatively poor, so it is unlikely that any families in the sample would be considered rich by Indonesian or other standards. Nevertheless, some mothers were better-educated than others, and some families had more assets or material resources than others. Figure 2.9 shows the distribution of education among parents.

Looking at the data in figures 2.10 through 2.13, we can see that low levels of mothers' education and family income are often associated with low levels of children's development as assessed with many of the measures used in this study. Even within a sample that is generally not highly educated or wealthy, the children with the least-educated mothers and the lowest level of material assets seem to be developing less well. This is the case on almost all of the child development measures used with the older cohort in this sample (children who were 4 and 5 years old when assessed). Results for the 1- and 2-year-olds, who were assessed with different measures, also show some associations between parents' education and wealth and levels of children's development, although the results are not as consistent. In part, the reason may be that very young children's development is more variable or uneven in general, and some of the measures used with the children at this age may not have been able to assess that development accurately.

Taken as a whole, these results show that even in low-income communities, the poorest children, and the children with the least-educated parents, tend to do less well in many aspects of their early development. This conclusion adds to concerns about the impact of poverty on inequality in child development and helps to make the case for ECED services targeting the poorest and most vulnerable children.

Figure 2.9 Fewer than Half the Parents in the Sample Have More than an Elementary School Education

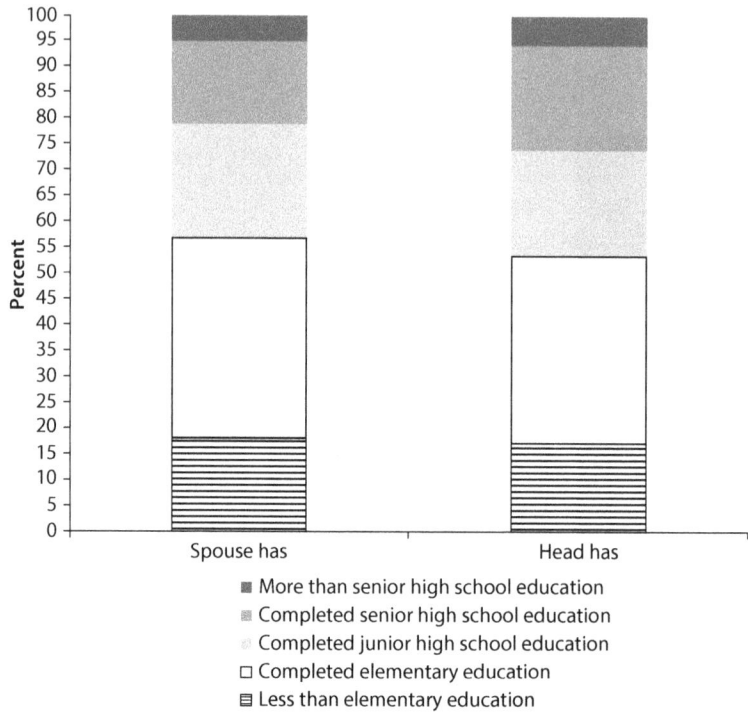

Legend:
- ■ More than senior high school education
- ▨ Completed senior high school education
- ▫ Completed junior high school education
- □ Completed elementary education
- ▤ Less than elementary education

Source: Calculations using ECED survey.
Note: Heads of household and their spouses were usually but not always the parents of the children.

Figure 2.10 Child Development Measures for 4-Year-Olds by Mothers' Education, 2009

a. Early Development Instrument (EDI)

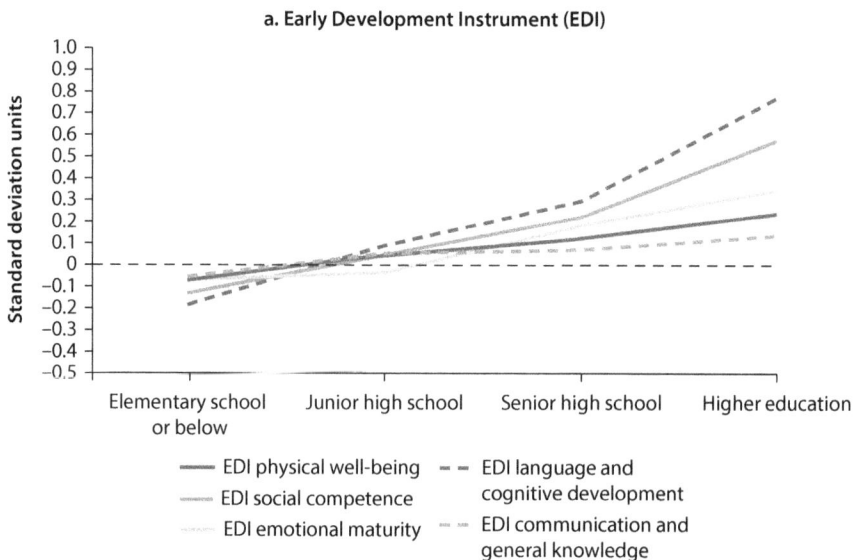

Legend:
- EDI physical well-being
- EDI social competence
- EDI emotional maturity
- EDI language and cognitive development
- EDI communication and general knowledge

figure continues next page

Figure 2.10 Child Development Measures for 4-Year-Olds by Mothers' Education, 2009 *(continued)*

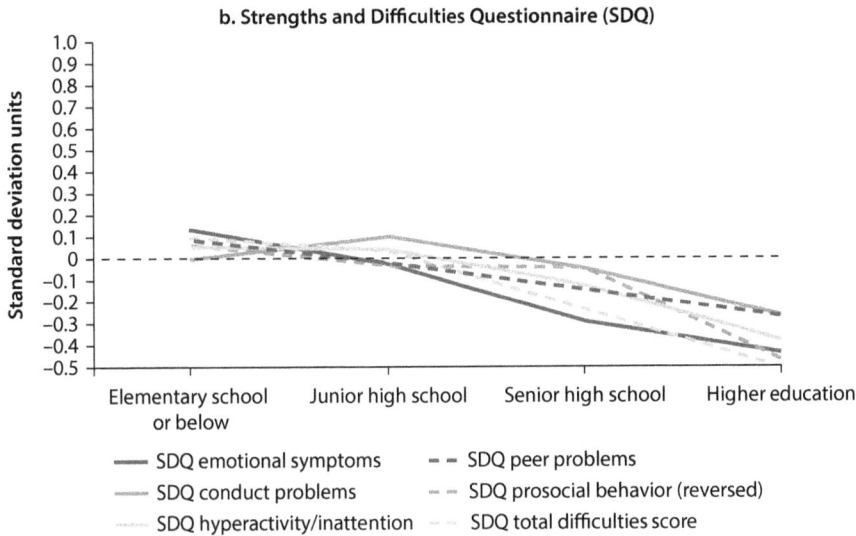

b. Strengths and Difficulties Questionnaire (SDQ)

Legend:
- SDQ emotional symptoms
- SDQ conduct problems
- SDQ hyperactivity/inattention
- SDQ peer problems
- SDQ prosocial behavior (reversed)
- SDQ total difficulties score

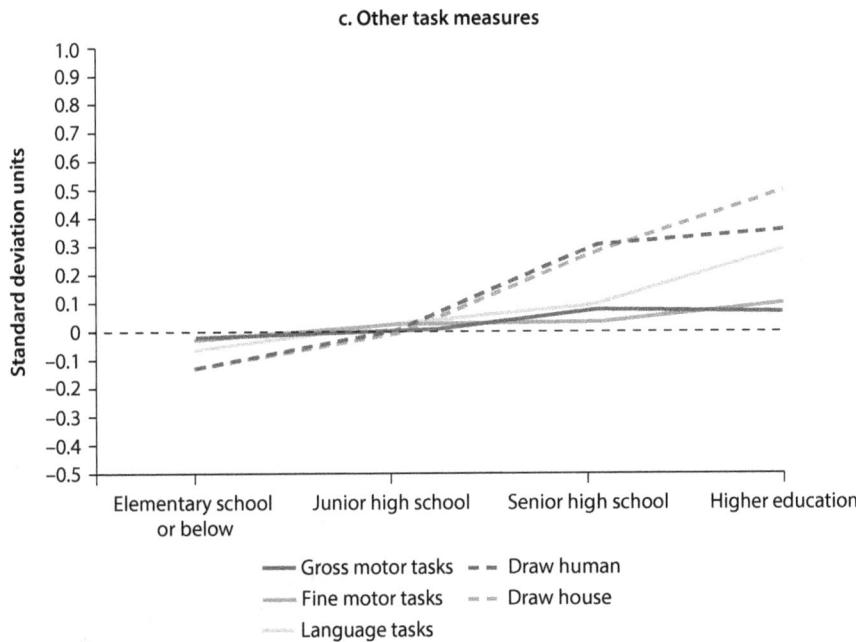

c. Other task measures

Legend:
- Gross motor tasks
- Fine motor tasks
- Language tasks
- Draw human
- Draw house

Source: Calculations using ECED survey.
Note: Standardized values of measures reported.

Early Childhood Education and Development in Poor Villages of Indonesia •
http://dx.doi.org/10.1596/978-0-8213-9836-4

Figure 2.11 Child Development Measures for the Same Children at Age 5 by Mothers' Education, 2010

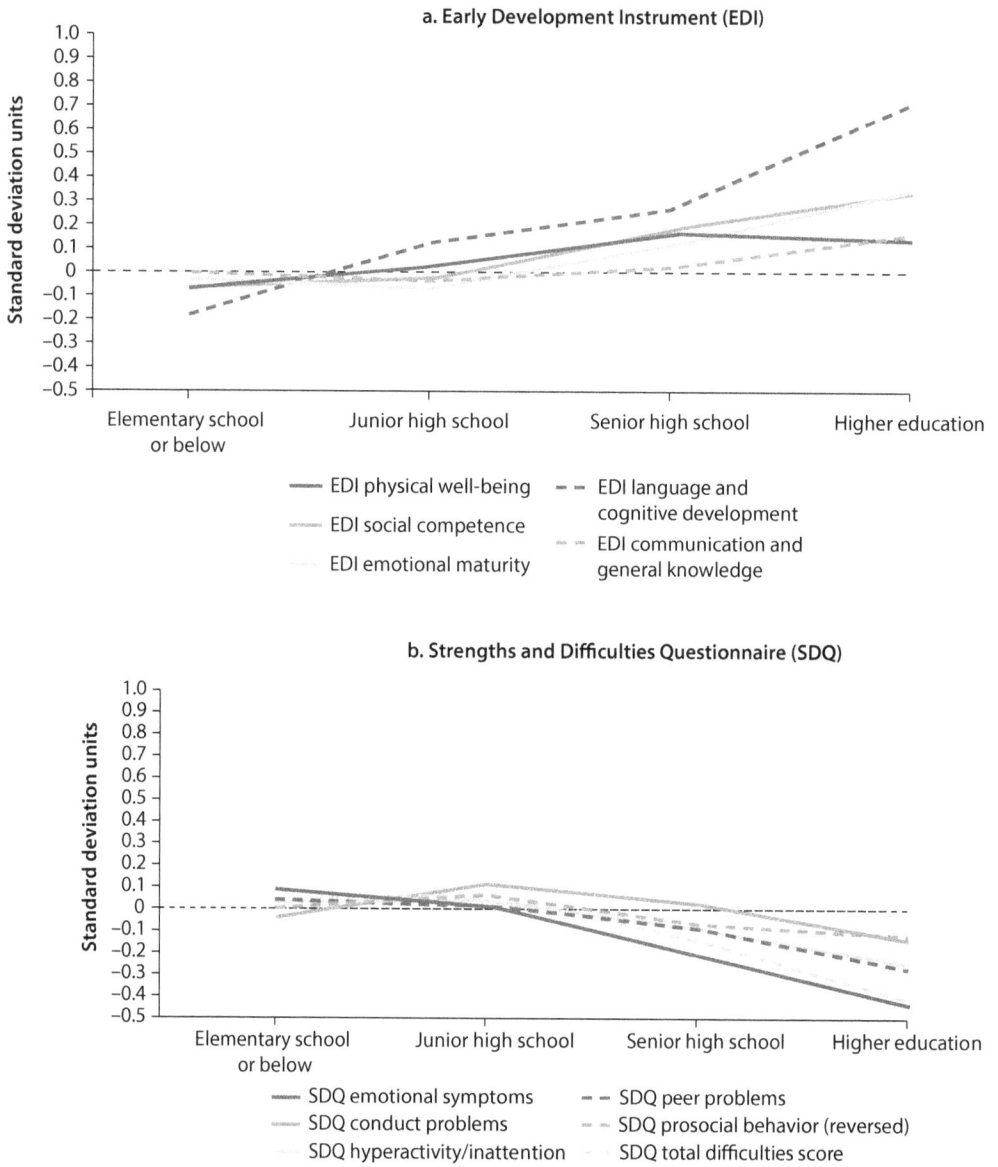

a. Early Development Instrument (EDI)

Legend:
- EDI physical well-being
- EDI social competence
- EDI emotional maturity
- EDI language and cognitive development
- EDI communication and general knowledge

b. Strengths and Difficulties Questionnaire (SDQ)

Legend:
- SDQ emotional symptoms
- SDQ conduct problems
- SDQ hyperactivity/inattention
- SDQ peer problems
- SDQ prosocial behavior (reversed)
- SDQ total difficulties score

figure continues next page

Figure 2.11 Child Development Measures for the Same Children at Age 5 by Mothers' Education, 2010

(continued)

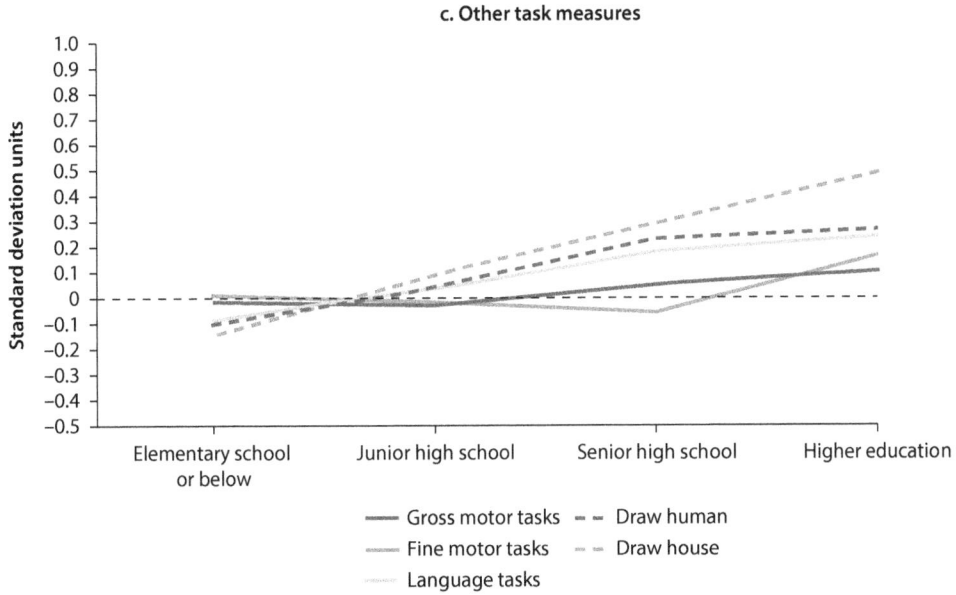

c. Other task measures

Source: Calculations using ECED survey.
Note: Standardized values of measures reported.

Figure 2.12 Child Development Measures for 1-Year-Olds by Mothers' Education, 2009

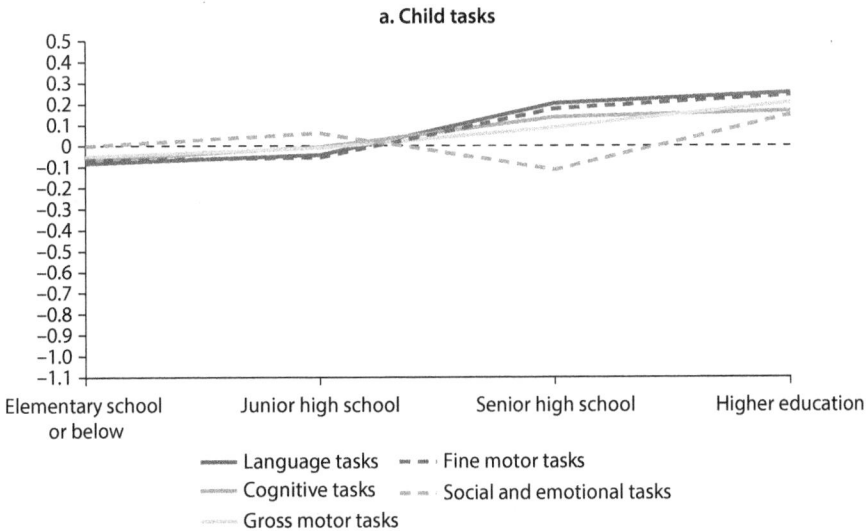

a. Child tasks

figure continues next page

Early Childhood Education and Development in Poor Villages of Indonesia •
http://dx.doi.org/10.1596/978-0-8213-9836-4

Figure 2.12 Child Development Measures for 1-Year-Olds by Mothers' Education, 2009 *(continued)*

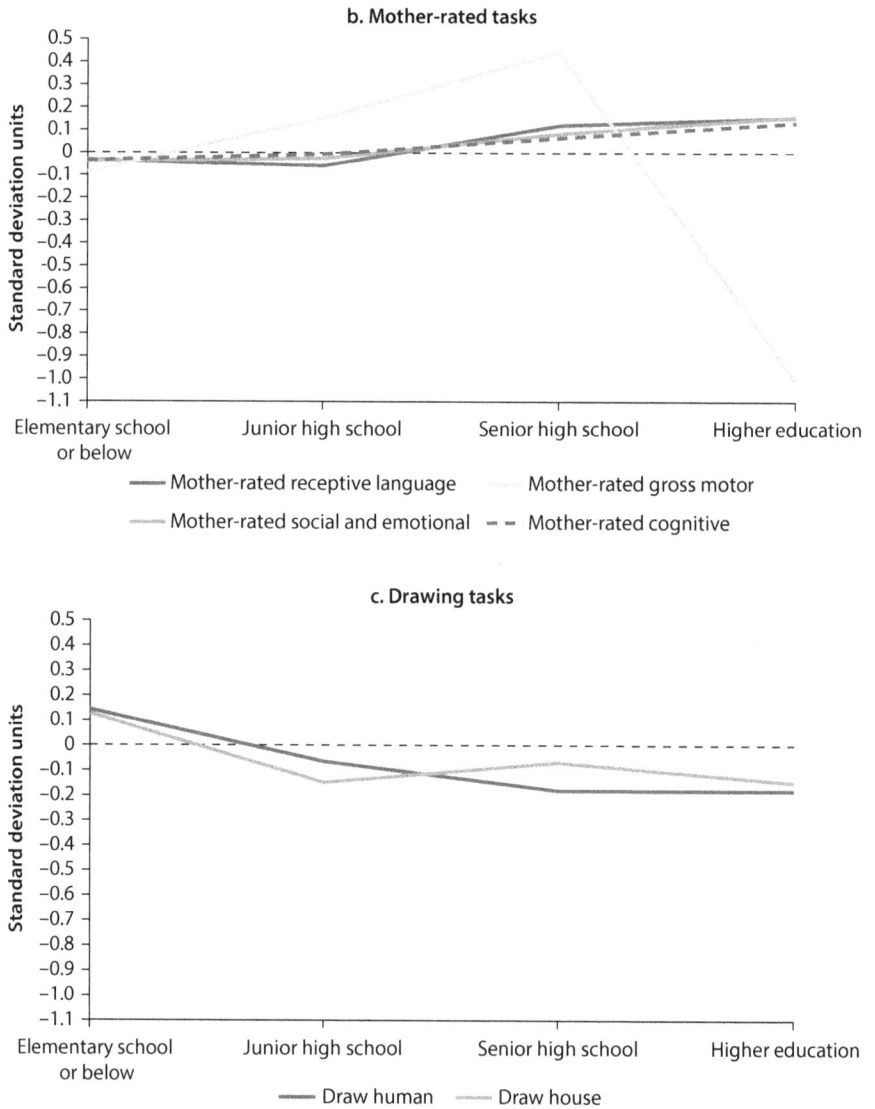

b. Mother-rated tasks

Mother-rated receptive language   Mother-rated gross motor

Mother-rated social and emotional   Mother-rated cognitive

c. Drawing tasks

Draw human   Draw house

Source: Calculations using ECED survey.
Note: Standardized values of measures reported.

Inequality in Child Development: What Do We Know?

Socioeconomic disparity in adulthood is related to disparity in child development (Irwin, Siddiqi, and Hertzman 2007). Children who are born into richer families with better-educated parents are more likely to develop well, while children born into poor families with poorly educated parents are less likely to develop as well and are at a greater risk of experiencing developmental delays. Naturally, exceptions occur, and children from all backgrounds may

Figure 2.13 Child Development Measures for the Same Children at Age 2 by Mothers' Education, 2010

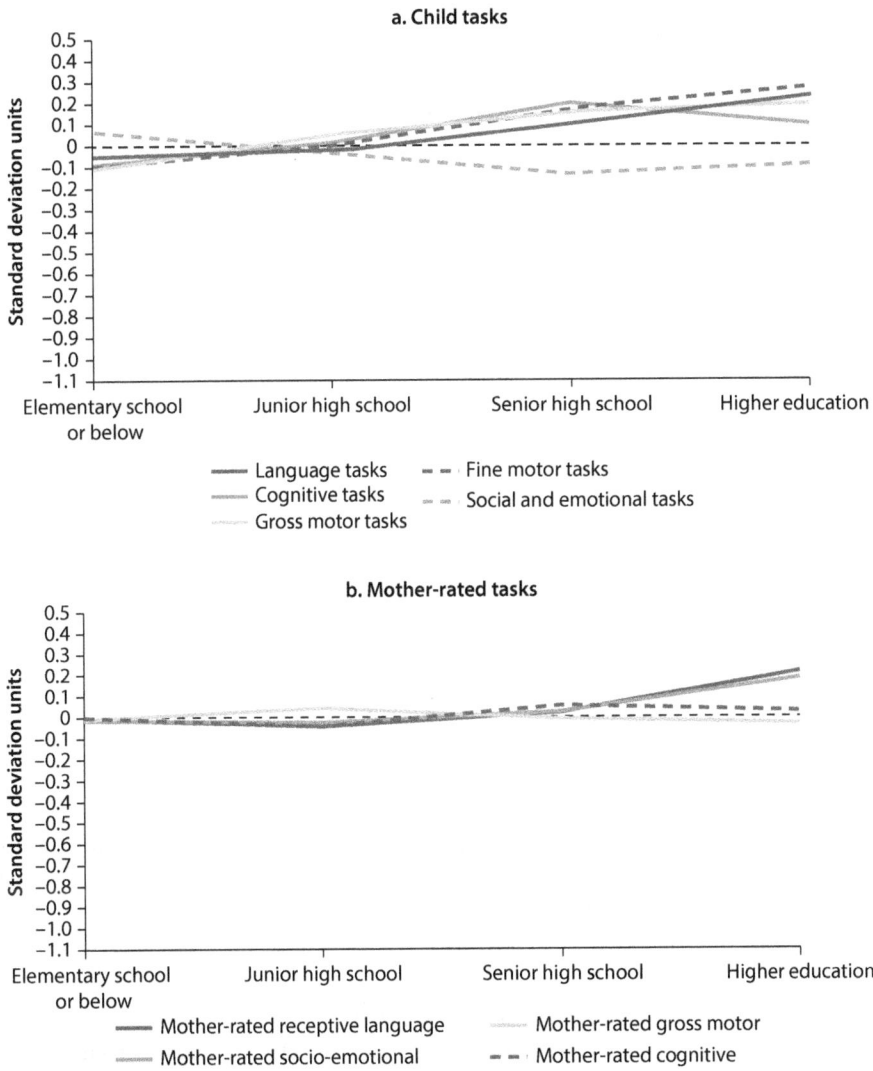

a. Child tasks

Legend:
- Language tasks
- Cognitive tasks
- Gross motor tasks
- Fine motor tasks
- Social and emotional tasks

b. Mother-rated tasks

Legend:
- Mother-rated receptive language
- Mother-rated socio-emotional
- Mother-rated gross motor
- Mother-rated cognitive

figure continues next page

Early Childhood Education and Development in Poor Villages of Indonesia •
http://dx.doi.org/10.1596/978-0-8213-9836-4

Figure 2.13 Child Development Measures for the Same Children at Age 2 by Mothers' Education, 2010 *(continued)*

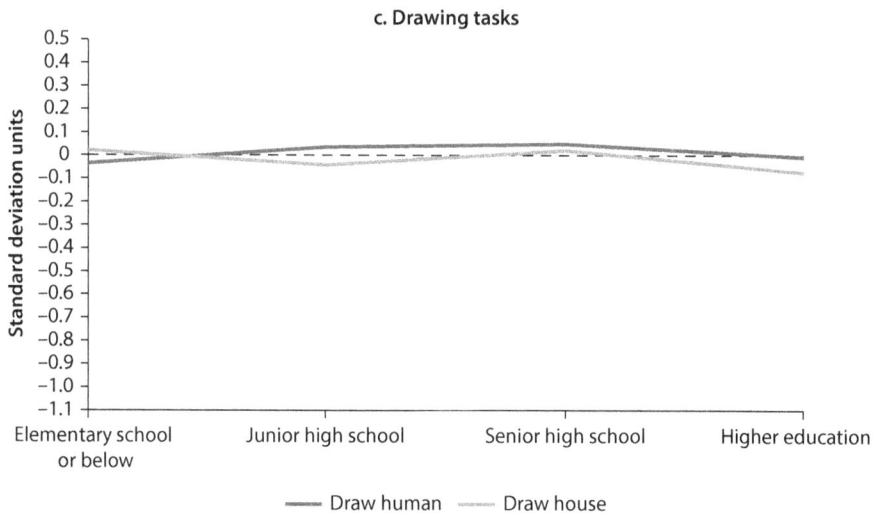

c. Drawing tasks

Source: Calculations using ECED survey.
Note: Standardized values of measures reported.

suffer from poor health and development. But it is still the case that the most disadvantaged are disproportionately more likely to suffer these negative outcomes.

Inequalities in child development on the basis of parents' education and wealth are present at every level—between countries of the world, within countries, as well as at the province, district, subdistrict, and village levels in Indonesia. Reducing inequality in child development prior to school should mean that all children would start school ready to learn with an equal chance of success throughout school and into adulthood.

This section investigates inequality in child development as a function of wealth within the sample of nine Indonesian districts (figures 2.14 and 2.15). Box 2.7 provides an example of a particular group of boys.

Such monitoring of child development over time enables communities and populations to determine if they are making any improvements. We can also compare how communities do in comparison to each other, which leads to questions such as:

1. Why are some communities doing better than others?
2. What are the strengths and weaknesses that help support families and children in some communities better than others?
3. What are the characteristics that explain why some high-risk communities are doing unexpectedly well in terms of their children's development?

Box 2.7 Measuring Inequality in Child Development: An Illustration Using Inequality on the Basis of Wealth for Boys in Lombok Tengah

Inequality of What?

To assess inequality, we use as our measure of child development whether a child is considered developmentally vulnerable on one or more domains of the Early Development Instrument (EDI).

Calculating differences in vulnerability within districts

Children in the sample were divided into two equal groups: those with above-average household wealth (high wealth) and those with below-average household wealth (low wealth).

In 2009, the EDI was completed for 390 boys in Lombok Tengah. Of these boys, 266 lived in a household with low wealth, and 124 lived in a household with high wealth.

Of the 266 boys with low wealth, 261 were developmentally vulnerable on one or more domains of the EDI; that is, 98.12 percent of low-wealth boys in Lombok Tengah were vulnerable. Of the 124 high-wealth boys in Lombok Tengah, 113 or 91.13 percent were also developmentally vulnerable.

The absolute developmental vulnerability gap for boys in Lombok Tengah was calculated by subtracting the percentage of high-wealth boys who were vulnerable (91.13 percent) from the percentage of low-wealth boys who were developmentally vulnerable (98.12 percent). For boys in Lombok Tengah in 2009, the absolute developmental vulnerability gap was 6.99 percent (98.12–91.13 = 6.99).

Calculating prevalence of vulnerability on one or more domains

We also want to look at the overall level of developmental vulnerability in each district. This finding is calculated irrespective of wealth. So, for Lombok Tengah, 374 (261 low wealth and 113 high wealth) of the 390 boys were considered developmentally vulnerable. That is, in 2009 the overall level of developmental vulnerability in Lombok Tengah was 95.90 percent. This calculation was repeated for each district and allows comparisons of inequality between districts.

Inequality in Indonesia at the District Level over Time

Figures 2.14 and 2.15 reveal patterns of child vulnerability that can mobilize policy makers and give service providers a better understanding of the determinants of child development in these districts.

Together, these figures show both the inequality within districts on the vertical axis and the overall prevalence of vulnerability in each district on the horizontal axis in 2009 and 2010, respectively. Each figure is split into two panels, one for boys and the other for girls, each drawn on the same scale for ease of comparison.

Using the example from box 2.7, we can see in panel A of figure 2.14 that the point representing Lombok Tengah is located at 95.90 percent on the horizontal axis, where the horizontal axis represents the prevalence of vulnerability on one

Figure 2.14 Prevalence of Vulnerability on One or More EDI Domains and Inequality Based on Household Wealth by District, 2009

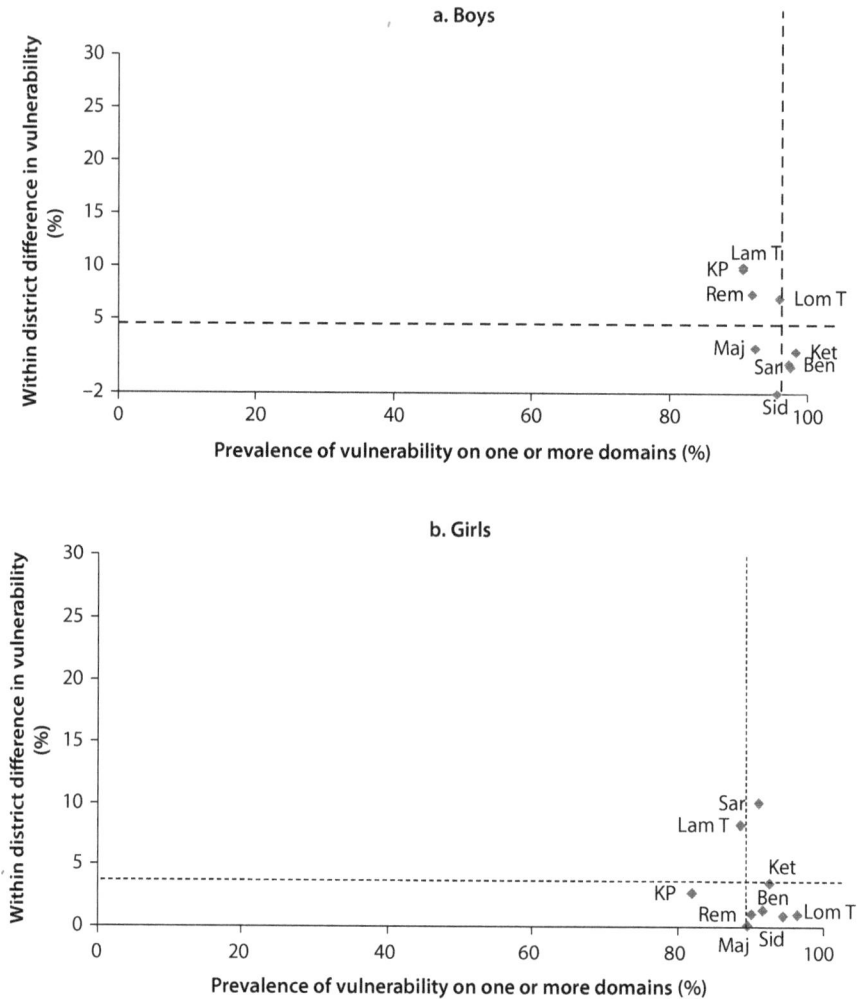

Source: Calculations using ECED survey.

Note: The point representing Sidrap for boys in panel a actually lies below the horizontal axis. The reason is that high socioeconomic status (SES) boys in Sidrap had higher levels of developmental vulnerability than boys with low SES. EDI = Early Development Instrument; Ben = Bengkulu; Ket = Ketapang; K P = Kulon Progo; Lam T = Lampung Timur; Lom T = Lombok Tengah; Maj = Majalengka; Rem = Rembang; Sar =Sarolangun; Sid = Sidrap.

or more domains. On the vertical axis, where we represent the difference in vulnerability within districts, Lombok Tengah is located at 6.99 percent.

To determine the change in the prevalence of developmental vulnerability at the district level and the change in inequality in developmental vulnerability within districts over time, we show data collection for 2 years, 2009 (figure 2.14) and 2010 (figure 2.15). We can see that, in 2009, the majority of villages are clustered in the bottom right-hand corners of the two graphs. This means that all

Figure 2.15 Prevalence of Vulnerability on One or More EDI Domains and Inequality Based on Household Wealth by District, 2010

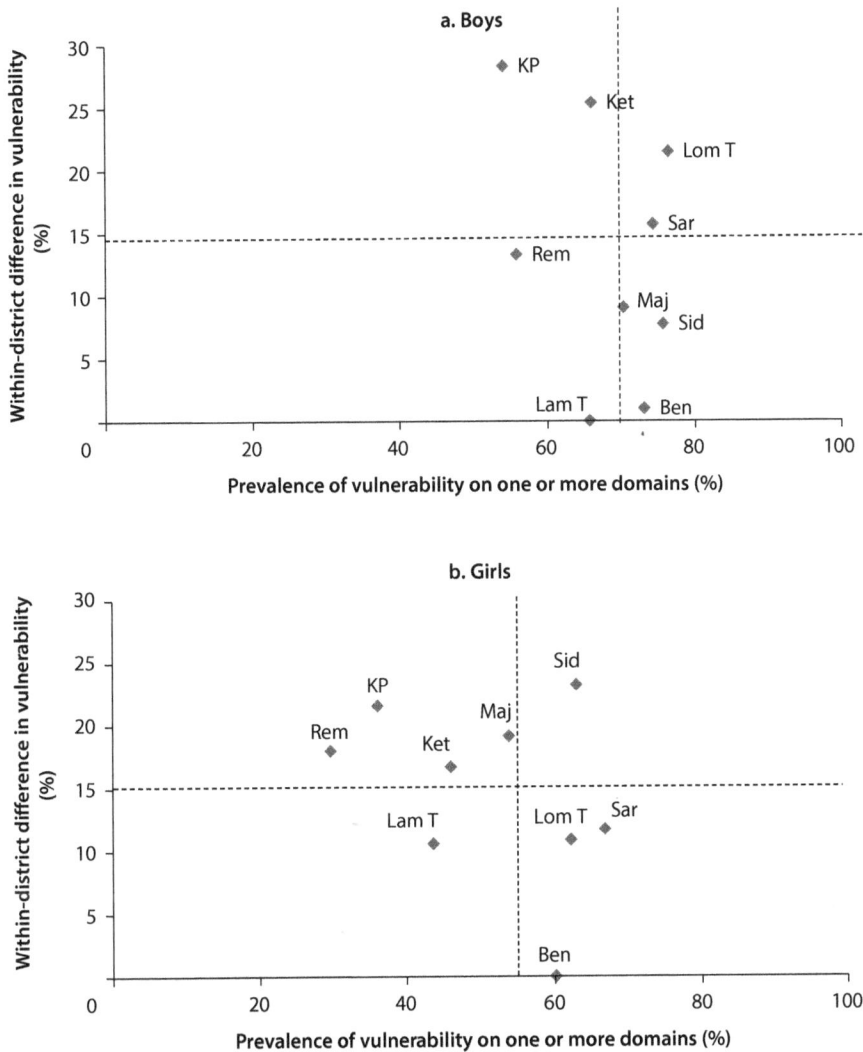

a. Boys

Y-axis: Within-district difference in vulnerability (%)
X-axis: Prevalence of vulnerability on one or more domains (%)

b. Girls

Y-axis: Within-district difference in vulnerability (%)
X-axis: Prevalence of vulnerability on one or more domains (%)

Source: Calculations using ECED survey.
Note: EDI = Early Development Instrument; Ben = Bengkulu; Ket = Ketapang; K P = Kulon Progo; Lam T = Lampung Timur; Lom T = Lombok Tengah; Maj = Majalengka; Rem = Rembang; Sar = Sarolangun; Sid = Sidrap.

districts have high levels of overall vulnerability and as a result quite low levels of inequality in vulnerability within districts.

The dotted lines on figures 2.14 and 2.15 represent the average absolute inequality in vulnerability within districts overall (horizontal line) and the median percentage of vulnerability overall (vertical line). The position of districts in relation to these lines is also important to consider. Districts to the right of the vertical line have a prevalence of vulnerability higher than the median across these nine districts, and those to the left of the line have lower than median developmental vulnerability. Districts positioned above the horizontal line have a level of within-district inequality that is greater than the average inequality across the nine districts, and those districts below the line have lower than average inequality.

A district located in the upper right-hand side of the graph has higher than median overall vulnerability and higher than average within-district inequality. A district in the upper left-hand side has high levels of inequality, but low overall vulnerability. A district in the bottom right-hand sector has a high overall level of vulnerability but experiences lower levels of inequality within district than others.

In 2010 (figure 2.15), the districts have changed locations within the graphs. In general, districts have moved left along the horizontal axis, indicating that the prevalence of vulnerability has gone down since 2009. However, the districts have also generally moved up the vertical axis, indicating that inequality within each district in 2010 was greater than it had been in 2009. These horizontal shifts are likely a result of the children becoming a year older between the two data collection points. Overall vulnerability levels begin to drop as children develop new skills across the developmental spectrum, but the vertical shifts suggest that some children have remained developmentally vulnerable while others have improved with age, experience, and support.

A district would be considered to be doing well in terms of child development if it fell in the bottom left-hand sector of the graphs. In this part of the graph, districts have both lower than median levels of vulnerability overall and lower than average differences in vulnerability between children. In 2009 for boys, Majalengka is the only district that lies in the bottom left-hand sector. For girls, the districts of Kulon Progo, Rembang, and Majalengka are all in the bottom left-hand sector. In 2010, Majalengka, Rembang, and Lampung Timur for boys and Lampung Timur for girls fall into this sector.

In 2009 and 2010, across all districts vulnerability was high overall on one or more of the EDI domains. The majority of children in this sample of Indonesian children (93.23 percent in 2009 and 60.95 percent in 2010) were vulnerable on the language and cognitive skills domain of the EDI. It is vulnerabilty on this domain that is primarily driving these overall high levels of developmental vulnerability in Indonesia.

Policy Implications: Addressing Inequality

Having identified that inequality in child development exists not only across districts, but also between socioeconomic groups within these districts, and that the level of inequality increases as the children get older, how can one attempt to level the playing field? Options include the implementation of universal, targeted, or proportionate universalism policy approaches.

A universal approach would ensure that all children living in these districts have access to some kind of intervention to reduce the overall proportion that is developmentally vulnerable. A targeted approach would concentrate on the districts with the most vulnerable children. For example, boys and girls living in

Lombok Tengah had a higher than average prevalence of developmental vulner-ability. A targeted approach to reducing inequality and vulnerability may be appropriate for a district like Lombok Tengah first.

Most governments and policy makers, however, realize it is important to have a mix of universal and targeted strategies to reduce the prevalence of poor outcomes and to mitigate the socioeconomic gradients of these poor outcomes. This approach is known as proportionate universalism. It would see all districts supported (as in the universal approach) but at a scale and intensity relative to the level of disadvantage (Human Early Learning Partnership 2011; Marmot 2010). Therefore, a district like Lombok Tengah would be the subject of a larger-scale intervention than a district like Majalengka, which had a lower than average prevalence of vulnerability and lower than average within-district inequality (with the exception of girls in the 2010 data collection). Using the proportionate universalism approach, we can take a step toward improving child outcomes for all Indonesian children while also reducing inequality in child development outcomes.

Promoting the Developmental Essentials: How Do Parenting Practices and Children's Involvement in ECED Services Contribute to Positive Development?

So far, this chapter has described the characteristics of children's development, of their families, and of existing ECED services in their communities. First, we described both the strengths and vulnerabilities of a sample of young Indonesian children in each area of their development—including their growth and weight for age, and in domains such as physical, socio-emotional, cognitive, language and communication. To do so, we relied on multiple measures of child development including mothers' reports and direct assessment of children's skills. We also described the characteristics of children's families in our sample, including their education and relative wealth and the specific parenting practices that mothers say they use with their children. Finally, we described the characteristics and availability of ECED services, especially in the communities where these children and families live.

From research summarized in chapter 1, we know that many factors can influ-ence the trajectory of that development. We began to examine some of these factors by looking at whether better-educated and relatively wealthier parents have children who typically score better on a comprehensive assessment of child development, and the answer was generally yes. We also were able to explore differences in children's development depending on the district where they live and the levels of poverty within those districts, keeping in mind that this sample is limited to relatively low-income districts and villages within those districts.

It is important to know what factors influence child development, so we can identify areas where interventions can improve children's outcomes. Naturally, some factors can be changed more easily than others: for example, it is difficult to make poor parents wealthy. Two potentially important factors that *are* more amenable to change through targeted interventions are the kinds of parenting practices used by families and children's participation in ECED services.

We know from research in developed and developing countries (Borkowski, Ramey, and Bristol-Power 2002; Lansford and Bornstein 2007) that parenting practices *and* children's participation in ECED services are both very influential. Both have the potential to increase young children's exposure to the developmental essentials described in chapter 1—opportunities for stimulating play, rich language experiences, practice in developing executive function skills, and more.

To learn more about the role of these two important influences, in this section we investigate whether parenting practices and ECED involvement are correlated with child development outcomes over and above the influence of other characteristics such as parents' education, characteristics of the child such as age and gender, characteristics of the child's household such as the number of people living there, household wealth, and education levels of other members of the household.

To do so, we test the correlation between parenting practices and ECED involvement on the one hand, and child development outcomes on the other, using a regression framework (box 2.8). A series of ordinary least squares (OLS) regressions was carried out to look at the influence of parenting practices and ECED involvement on child development outcomes. Parenting practices were measured using the total scores on the parenting practices measure, with higher scores reflecting warmer, more consistent, and less-hostile parenting. ECED involvement was measured by asking families if their child was engaged in ECED activities in the previous month. Specific questions were asked to find out what kind of ECED service the child was receiving.

Box 2.8 What Statistical Significance and Beta Values Tell Us

The statistical significance of parenting practices and early childhood education and development (ECED) involvement indicated by asterisks in figures 2.16 and 2.17 means that differences in parenting behavior and differences in ECED involvement continue to influence differences in development even when other child, household, and village characteristics are taken into account.

We report the results in terms of standardized coefficients—beta values, which allow the reader to compare the various estimates directly. The larger the beta value, the larger the influence of the parenting practices or ECED involvement on child development. If it is the case that parenting practices and ECED involvement do indeed influence children's development, then we would expect these two variables to have large beta values as well as statistical significance. Complete results are reported in appendix 2. For the physical health and well-being domain of the EDI, the value of 0.103 tells us that for every 1 standard deviation increase in the parenting practices score, there will be 0.103 standard deviation increase in a child's score on this domain. Simply put, if parents are warmer, more consistent, and less hostile toward their children, the children's physical health and well-being scores tend to be higher.

The first set of regressions included only parenting practices or ECED involvement in the previous month as the predictors. Figure 2.16 shows the impact of each of these variables on the child development outcomes for the 4-year-olds in our sample. The second set of regressions included a wide range of child, household, and village characteristics. These characteristics were the child's

Figure 2.16 Good Parenting Practices and ECED Involvement in the Previous Month Positively Influence Child Development Outcomes for the Older Cohort

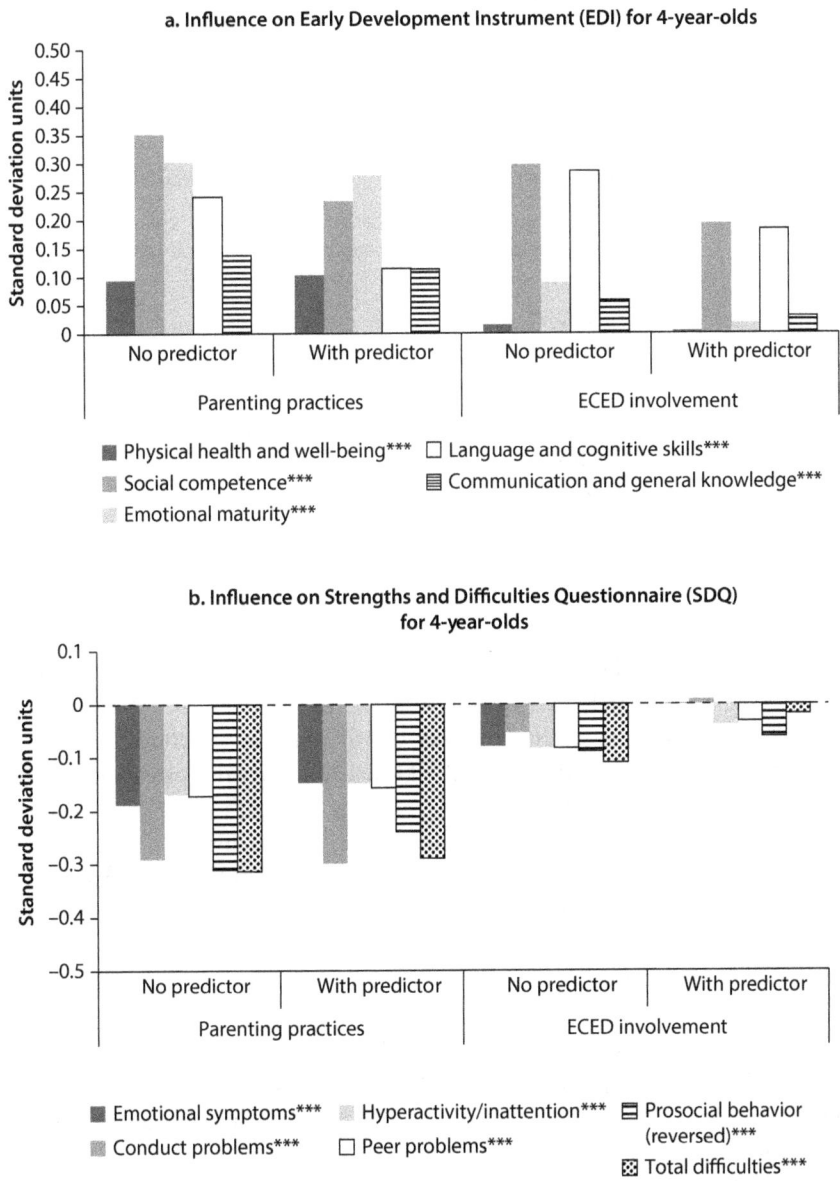

a. Influence on Early Development Instrument (EDI) for 4-year-olds

Physical health and well-being*** / Language and cognitive skills*** / Social competence*** / Communication and general knowledge*** / Emotional maturity***

b. Influence on Strengths and Difficulties Questionnaire (SDQ) for 4-year-olds

Emotional symptoms*** / Hyperactivity/inattention*** / Prosocial behavior (reversed)*** / Conduct problems*** / Peer problems*** / Total difficulties***

figure continues next page

Figure 2.16 Good Parenting Practices and ECED Involvement in the Previous Month Positively Influence Child Development Outcomes for the Older Cohort *(continued)*

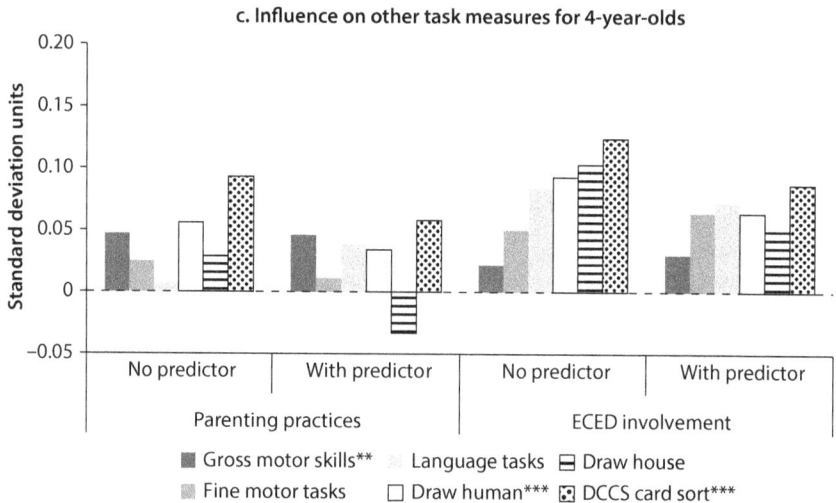

c. Influence on other task measures for 4-year-olds

Legend:
- Gross motor skills**
- Fine motor tasks
- Language tasks
- Draw human***
- Draw house
- DCCS card sort***

Source: Calculations using ECED survey.
Note: ECED = early childhood education and development. * = 10 percent, ** = 5 percent, *** = 1 percent.

sex, age, and weight and height information. Household characteristics included the composition of the household, including the number of adults, children of various ages, presence of other relatives, and the household size. Additional controls were also included for the head of the household and spouse. These characteristics included their highest education level and whether they had worked in the previous month. Mother's education and household wealth were also included.[4]

Figure 2.16 also shows the impact of parenting practices and whether the child was involved in ECED services during the last month on several child development outcomes when a number of other factors are controlled for.

Positive parenting practices and ECED involvement are both associated with better developmental scores for the 4-year-olds in this sample. When the child, household, and village characteristics were also taken into account, parenting practices significantly predicted higher scores on most of the child development measures for 4-year-olds including all EDI and SDQ domains, gross motor tasks, language skills, and the drawing and card sort tasks. ECED involvement in the previous month predicted better scores on the social competence, language and cognitive skills, and communication and general knowledge domains of the EDI over and above any contribution of child, household, and village characteristics. For the SDQ, ECED involvement predicted better scores on the hyperactivity/ inattention, peer problems, and prosocial behavior scales and was also a significant predictor of scores on all of the other child task measures.

For the 1-year-olds, better parenting practices had a statistically significant positive association with a child's language, cognitive, and fine motor skills, even when child, household, and village characteristics were taken into account (figure 2.17). More positive parenting practices were also significantly associated with higher levels of mother-rated child skills in the domains of receptive language, socio-emotional, and cognitive tasks. In this younger age group, reports of children's ECED involvement in the previous month predicted better scores on only a few tasks, namely language, gross motor and fine motor tasks, and mother-rated receptive language skills. This limited effect is likely because communities typically have fewer services appropriate for or targeted to children as young as 1, so these children are less likely to have been actively involved in ECED services. Of the children from this age group who did participate in ECED services in the previous month, almost all had attended either a *Posyandu* or toddler family group (BKB) service, which usually meet only once a month and are primarily focused either on health and nutrition monitoring (*Posyandu*) or parenting education (BKB).

Putting the Results in Context

These results suggest that parenting practices and ECED involvement are both associated with better child development outcomes even when differences in child, household, and village characteristics are controlled for. Figure 2.18

Figure 2.17 Good Parenting Practices and ECED Involvement in the Previous Month Positively Influence Child Development Outcomes for the Younger Cohort

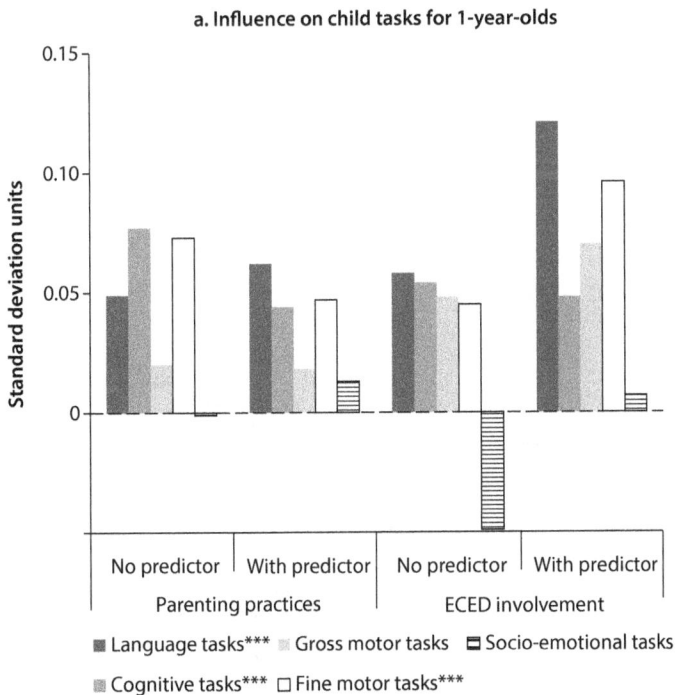

a. Influence on child tasks for 1-year-olds

■ Language tasks*** ▨ Gross motor tasks ▤ Socio-emotional tasks
▨ Cognitive tasks*** □ Fine motor tasks***

figure continues next page

Early Childhood Education and Development in Poor Villages of Indonesia •
http://dx.doi.org/10.1596/978-0-8213-9836-4

Figure 2.17 Good Parenting Practices and ECED Involvement in the Previous Month Positively Influence Child Development Outcomes for the Younger Cohort (continued)

b. Influence on mother-rated child skills for 1-year-olds

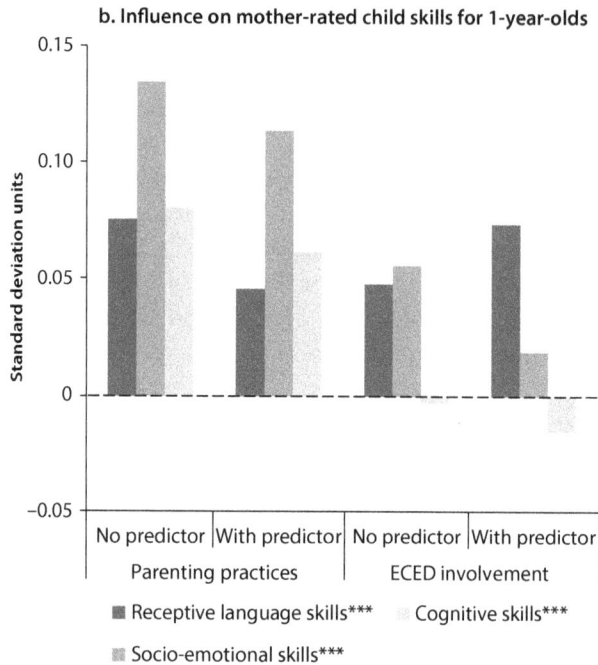

Receptive language skills***   Cognitive skills***

Socio-emotional skills***

Source: Calculations using ECED survey.
Note: ECED = early childhood education and development. * = 10 percent, ** = 5 percent, *** = 1 percent.

Figure 2.18 Good Parenting Practices and ECED Involvement Influence Child Development Outcomes Even When Controlling for Parental Wealth and Education

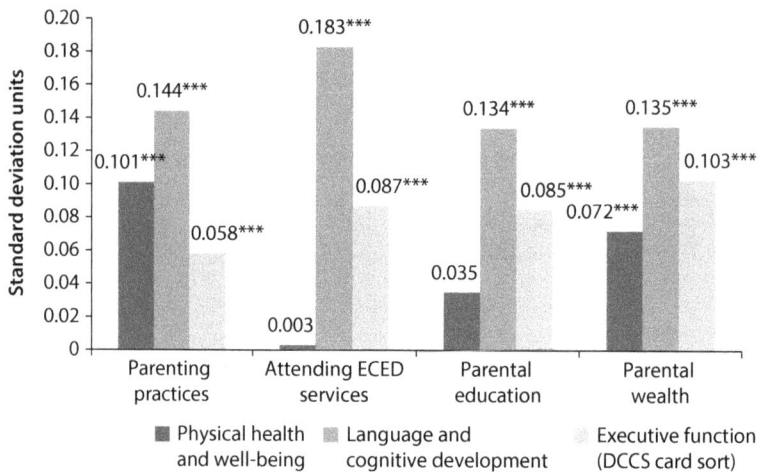

Physical health   Language and   Executive function
and well-being   cognitive development   (DCCS card sort)

Source: Calculations using ECED survey.
Note: ECED = early childhood education and development. * = 10 percent, ** = 5 percent, *** = 1 percent.

underscores that the strength of this association varies depending on the domain of child development being examined. For example, attending ECED services seems to have practically no association with better scores on the physical health and well-being domain of the EDI when parenting practices, education, and wealth are controlled for. In contrast, attending ECED services has the strongest association with higher scores on the language and cognitive development domain of the EDI even after controlling for parenting practices, parental wealth, and education. Likewise parenting practices have a much stronger association with better physical health and well-being than either parental education or wealth.

The message here is not that we should forget about how various child, household, and village characteristics affect children's early development. All are important and should be attended to in thinking of comprehensive or holistic approaches to promoting positive development. The message is that we should *also* be considering the role that parenting practices and ECED involvement play in these outcomes. Parenting practices and ECED involvement may be especially responsive to practical interventions that will help improve child development outcomes.

Notes

1. Usually the child's mother provided information; however, another primary caregiver such as a grandparent sometimes served as respondent if the mother was not available. In this book, *mother* is used throughout to represent mother or other family caregiver.

2. The dimension of child well-being, as opposed to developmental delay, allows for the measurement of both the positive and negative aspects of how a child is developing; it also allows for a holistic approach—social, emotional, cognitive, and physical well-being. Such measures have the potential to place a child on a developmental trajectory rather than a simple bimodal pass/fail outcome. In this study, we used a variety of child development instruments, such as asking the child's mother to rate her child's development and giving tasks for the child to do. Some of these instruments are milestone checks, and others try to place the children on a developmental trajectory.

3. These anthropometric measures were calculated in STATA using the user-written zanthro program. These calculations use the "1990 British Growth Charts: Version UK" as the reference population. Although other growth charts could have been used, the use of these specific growth charts allowed us to include very young children in our assessment of physical health. Results for older children in our sample were similar when using the World Health Organization (WHO) global growth standards, but the WHO standards would not have allowed us to include the youngest children. For further details on this program and the reference populations used, see the note to table 2.3 and the details provided in Vidmar et al. 2004.

4. Time-invariant village characteristics were included in the regression through a village fixed effects regression.

Bibliography

Borkowski, J. G., S. L. Ramey, and M. Bristol-Power. 2002. *Parenting and the Child's World: Influences on Academic, Intellectual, and Social-Emotional Development*. Mahwah, NJ: Lawrence Erlbaum.

Early Childhood Education and Development in Poor Villages of Indonesia •
http://dx.doi.org/10.1596/978-0-8213-9836-4

Brinkman, S. 2009. "The Impact and Reach of the EDI Around the World." Paper presented at the Early Development Imperative Conference, Winnipeg, Canada, November 6–18.

Brinkman, S., T. Gregory, J. Harris, B. Hart, S. Blackmore, and M. Janus. In press. "Associations between the Early Development Instrument at Age 5 and Reading and Numeracy Skills at Ages 8, 10 and 12: A Prospective Linked Data Study." *Child Indicators Research*.

Brinkman, S., S. Zubrick, and S. Silburn. In press. "Predictive Validity of a School Readiness Assessment on Later Cognitive and Behavioral Outcomes." *Child Indicators Research*.

Centre for Community Child Health and Telethon Institute for Child Health Research. 2009. *A Snapshot of Early Childhood Development in Australia*. Australian Early Development Index (AEDI) National Report 2009. Canberra: Australian Government.

Duncan, R. J. 2012. "Measures of Executive Function: Convergent Validity and Links to Academic Achievement in Preschool." Unpublished master's thesis. http://hdl.handle.net/1957/30264.

Duursma, E., M. Augustyn, and B. Zuckerman. 2008. "Reading Aloud to Children: The Evidence." *Archives of Diseases of Childhood* 93 (7): 554–57.

Forget-Dubois, N., J. P. Lemelin, M. Boivin, G. Dionne, J. R. Séguin, F. Vitaro, and R. E. Tremblay. 2007. "Predicting Early School Achievement with the EDI: A Longitudinal Population-based Study." *Early Education and Development* 18 (3): 405–26. doi:10.1080/10409280701610796.

Frye, D., P. D. Zelazo, and T. Palfai, 1995. "Theory of Mind and Rule-Based Reasoning." *Cognitive Development* 10: 483–527.

Goodenough, F. L. 1954. *Measurement of Intelligence by Drawings*. New York: Harcourt, Brace, and World.

Goodman, R. 1997. "The Strengths and Difficulties Questionnaire: A Research Note." *Journal of Child Psychology and Psychiatry* 38 (5): 581–86. doi:10.1111/j.1469-7610.1997.tb01545.x.

Hart, B., and T. R. Risley. 1995. *Meaningful Differences in the Everyday Experience of Young American Children*. Baltimore, MD: Paul H. Brookes.

Harris, D. B. 1963. *Children's Drawings as Measures of Intellectual Maturity: A Revision and Extension of the Goodenough Draw-a-Man Test*. New York, NY: Harcourt, Brace & World.

Hawes, D. J., and M. R. Dadds. 2004. "Australian Data and Psychometric Properties of the Strengths and Difficulties Questionnaire." *Australian and New Zealand Journal of Psychiatry* 38 (8): 644–51.

Human Early Learning Partnership. 2011. *Proportionate Universality*. Policy Brief, University of British Columbia, Vancouver.

Irwin, L. G., A. Siddiqi., and C. Hertzman. 2007. *Early Child Development: A Powerful Equalizer*. Final Report for the World Health Organization's Commission of the Social Determinants of Health, Human Early Learning Partnership, Vancouver, Canada.

Janus, M., S. Brinkman, E. Duku, C. Hertzman, R. Santos, and M. Sayers. 2007. *The Early Development Instrument: A Population-based Measure for Communities. A Handbook on Development, Properties and Use*. Offord Centre for Child Studies, McMaster University, Hamilton, Ontario.

Janus, M. and E. K. Duku. 2005. *Development of the Short Early Development Instrument (S-EDI)*. Offord Centre for Child Studies, McMaster University, Hamilton, Ontario.

Janus, M., and D. Offord. 2007. "Development and Psychometric Properties of the Early Development Instrument (EDI): A Measure of Children's School Readiness." *Canadian Journal of Behavioural Science* 39: 1–22.

Laak, J. T., M. de Goede, A. Aleva, and P. van Rijswijk. 2005. "The Draw-a-Person Test: An Indicator of Children's Cognitive and Socio-emotional Adaptation?" *Journal of Genetic Psychology* 166 (1): 77–93.

Lansford, J. E., and M. H. Bornstein. 2007. *Review of Parenting Programs in Developing Countries*. New York: United Nations Children's Fund.

Marmot, M. 2010. "Fair Society, Healthy Lives: The Marmot Review." http://www.marmotreview.org/AssetLibrary/pdfs/Reports/FairSocietyHealthyLives.pdf.

Muris, P., C. Meesters, and F. van den Berg. 2003. "The Strengths and Difficulties Questionnaire (SDQ): Further Evidence for its Reliability and Validity in a Community Sample of Dutch Children and Adolescents." *European Child and Adolescent Psychiatry* 12: 1–8.

NICHD ([Eunice Kennedy Shriver] National Institute of Child Health and Human Development) Early Child Care Research Network. 2002. "Early Child Care and Children's Development Prior to School Entry: Results from the NICHD Study of Early Child Care." *American Educational Research Journal* 39 (1): 133–64.

Office of Population Studies. 2005. *A Study of the Effects of Early Childhood Interventions on Children's Physiological, Cognitive and Social Development*. Cebu City, Philippines: Office of Population Studies, University of San Carlos.

Perren, S., S. Stadelmann. A. von Wyl, and K. von Klitzing. 2007. "Pathways of Behavioural and Emotional Symptoms in Kindergarten Children: What is the Role of Pro-social Behaviour?" *European Child and Adolescent Psychiatry* 16 (4): 209–14. doi:10.1007/s00787-006-0588-6.

Raikes, H., G. Luze, and J. Brooks-Gunn. 2006. "Mother-child Bookreading in Low-Income Families: Correlates and Outcomes during the First Three Years of Life." *Child Development* 77 (4): 924–53.

Raver, C. C. 2002. "Emotions Matter: Making the Case for the Role of Young Children's Emotional Development for Early School Readiness." *Social Policy Report* 16 (3): 3–19.

Stone, L. L., R. Otten, R. C. M. E. Engels, A. A.Vermulst, and J. M. A. M. Janssens. 2010. "Psychometric Properties of the Parent and Teacher Versions of the Strengths and Difficulties Questionnaire for 4- to 12-Year-Olds: A Review." *Clinical Child and Family Psychology Review* 13 (3): 254–74. doi:10.1007/s10567-010-0071-2.

Tamis-LeMonda, C. S., and E. T. Rodriguez. 2009. "Parents' Role in Fostering Young Children's Learning and Language Development." In *Encyclopedia on Early Childhood Development*. http://www.child-encyclopedia.com/pages/pdf/tamis-lemonda-rodriguezangxp_rev-language.pdf.

Turner, K. A., M. W. Lipsey, D. C. Farran, N. Dong, S. J. Wilson, M. W. Fuhs, and D. Meador. 2012. "Academically Relevant Measures of Executive Function: Development and Validation of Assessments for Preschool Children." Paper presented at the Spring 2012 Annual Conference of the Society for Research on Educational Effectiveness (SREE), 8–11 March 2012, Washington, DC.

UNESCO (United Nations Educational, Scientific, and Cultural Organization). 2005. *Policy Review Report: Early Childhood Care and Education in Indonesia*. Paris: UNESCO.

Vidmar, S., J. Carlin, K. Hesketh, and T. Cole. 2004. "Standardizing Anthropometric Measures in Children and Adolescents with New Functions for Egen." *Stata Journal* 4 (1): 50–55.

World Bank. 2006. *Early Childhood Education and Development in Indonesia: An Investment for a Better Life*. Jakarta, Indonesia: World Bank.

Zelazo, P. D. 2006. "The Dimensional Change Card Sort (DCCS): A Method of Assessing Executive Function in Children." *Nature Protocols* 1 (1): 297–301. doi:10.1038/nprot.2006.46.

Zelazo, P. D., U. Müller, D. Frye, S. Marcovitch, G. Argitis, J. Boseovski, J. K. Chiang, D. Hogwanishkul, B. V. Schuster, A. Sutherland, and S. M. Carlson. 2003. "The Development of Executive Function in Early Childhood." *Monographs of the Society for Research in Child Development* 68 (3): 1–151. doi:10.2307/1166202.

Zubrick, S., G. J. Smith, J. M. Nicholson, A. V. Sanson, and T. A. Jackiewicz. 2008. *Parenting and Families in Australia*. Canberra: FaHCSIA (Department of Families, Housing, Community Services and Indigenous Affairs).

CHAPTER 3

Providing and Evaluating Services for Low-Income Young Children

This chapter describes the planning, implementation, and midline evaluation of a community-driven Early Childhood Education and Development (ECED) project in 50 districts. Conditions and concerns about Indonesia's young children similar to those reported in chapter 2 prompted the government of Indonesia to develop plans to expand access to ECED services in 3,000 villages across 50 low-income districts.

The chapter is divided into two sections. The first section describes planning the project and its implementation. Using a community-driven process, local facilitators helped village members prepare proposals for small grants, primarily used to establish new playgroups in renovated facilities and primarily serving children ages 3–5. Staffed by teachers selected from the community and trained through the ECED project, these centers to date have served more than 500,000 children. The second section describes short-term effects of the project on ECED enrollment and children's development from an ongoing randomized impact evaluation. This evaluation uses both experimental and nonexperimental approaches and takes advantage of the fact that not only were villages phased into the project in randomly assigned batches, but also that information was collected on a set of villages that never received project services. For this reason, communities that had project services for 20 months can be compared with communities that had services for 9 months, and communities with the ECED project can be compared with communities that did not. The results suggest some impacts appearing in the short term, but also identify areas in which few or no effects can yet be seen. The chapter ends by describing the goals of the final round of data collection, to occur early in 2013.

An Overview of the ECED Project

Chapter 1 summarized research on the individual and societal benefits of participation in ECED services, especially for poor children and families. As noted in chapter 2, however, enrollment in ECED services has been historically low in Indonesia, with services either unavailable or unaffordable to low-income families. And many children in Indonesia's villages have been and continue to be vulnerable in the domains of physical (e.g., stunting) and cognitive development, potentially limiting their ability to benefit from subsequent schooling and restricting their later success in life. Chapter 2 also provided encouraging evidence from a sample of rural children: the evidence showed that their development may be enhanced by positive parenting practices and by involvement in ECED services.

With this background, chapter 3 focuses on a community-driven project implemented by the government of Indonesia in nearly 3,000 villages since 2007. Project activities have included the government's ECED capacity-building efforts at the central and local level, sensitization about the importance of ECED within villages, and training for community members to serve as ECED center teachers. The World Bank is supporting the monitoring and evaluation of project activities and has been involved in a variety of related ECED initiatives such as policy development at the central level. A brief timeline of the trajectory of ECED initiatives is provided in figure 3.1.

The ECED project discussed in this chapter harnesses World Bank experience working on ECED issues. Among other lessons learned from these experiences, including a pilot project, was that to ensure ownership and sustainability, local participation by both the community and local government was critical.

The government initiated the community-driven ECED project in 50 districts. Within each district, priority villages were identified according to fixed criteria. Given the wide disparities that exist within districts, 60 villages with the highest number of children ages 0–6 and the highest poverty rates were identified and targeted as priorities within each district.

The overall development objective for the ECED project was to improve poor children's access to ECED services and enhance children's school readiness. The project was launched through a series of sequentially delivered components:

1. Community facilitation: Sensitization of communities to the importance and benefits of ECED and training on how to submit a proposal to obtain and use project funds (provided as block grants).
2. Block grants: Block grants to each selected village (US$18,000 over 3 years) with which to set up and operate ECED services. Villages usually chose to divide the funds and establish center-based/group ECED programs for preschool-age children in two communities within the village.
3. Teacher training: 200 hours of training to 2 ECED program staff per center.

To ensure that project objectives are being met and to build the evidence base for future ECED policy decisions, an impact evaluation study has been ongoing since 2009. So far, the government has collected two rounds of data with World Bank support, and a final round is planned for early 2013. These data follow two cohorts of children born in 2005 and 2008. When data were collected in 2009, these cohorts of children were 4 years old and 1 year old, respectively.

Figure 3.1 ECED Project Milestones in Indonesia

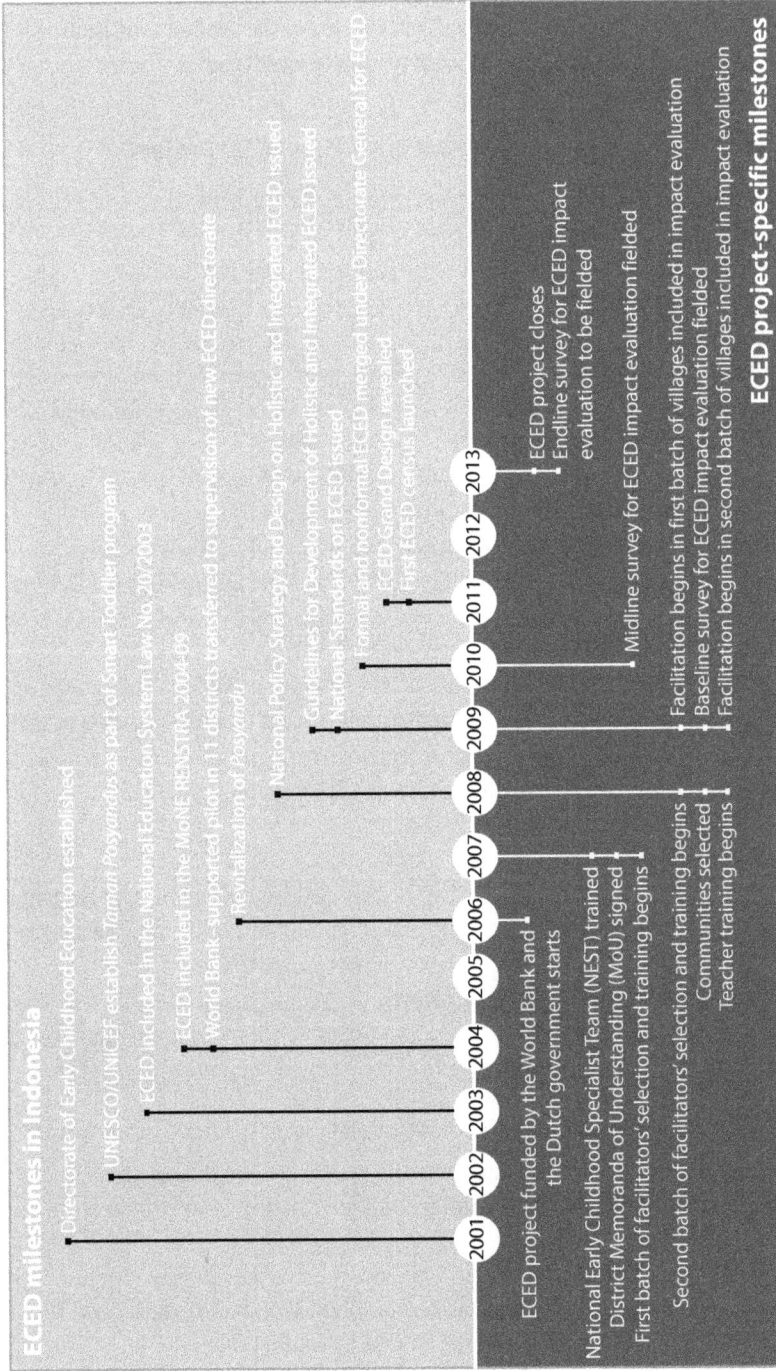

ECED milestones in Indonesia

2001	Directorate of Early Childhood Education established
2002	UNESCO/UNICEF establish *Taman Posyandu* as part of Smart Toddler program
2003	ECED included in the National Education System Law No. 20/2003
2004	ECED included in the MoNE RENSTRA 2004-09
	World Bank–supported pilot in 11 districts transferred to supervision of new ECED directorate
	Revitalization of Posyandu
2008	National Policy, Strategy and Design on Holistic and Integrated ECED issued
2009	Guidelines for Development of Holistic and Integrated ECED issued
	National Standards on ECED issued
2011	Formal and nonformal ECED merged under Directorate General for ECED
	ECED Grand Design revealed
	First ECED census launched

ECED project-specific milestones

2006	ECED project funded by the World Bank and the Dutch government starts
2007	National Early Childhood Specialist Team (NEST) trained
	District Memoranda of Understanding (MoU) signed
	First batch of facilitators' selection and training begins
2008	Second batch of facilitators' selection and training begins
	Communities selected
	Teacher training begins
2009	Facilitation begins in first batch of villages included in impact evaluation
	Baseline survey for ECED impact evaluation fielded
	Facilitation begins in second batch of villages included in impact evaluation
2010	Midline survey for ECED impact evaluation fielded
2013	ECED project closes
	Endline survey for ECED impact evaluation to be fielded

Timeline years shown: 2001, 2002, 2003, 2004, 2005, 2006, 2007, 2008, 2009, 2010, 2011, 2012, 2013

Note: ECED = early childhood education and development; MoNE = Ministry of National Education; UNESCO/UNICEF = United Nations Educational, Scientific, and Cultural Organization/United Nations Children's Fund.

The first section of the chapter describes the rationale, planning, and implementation of the key components of the ECED project, primarily emphasizing the service delivery component. The second section presents findings from the ongoing impact evaluation, summarizing how the project influenced ECED enrollment and children's development in the short run.

Section 1—Planning and Implementing an ECED Project

Rationale, Development Objective, and Key Components of the ECED Project

The plans for the ECED project were influenced by the following:

- International evidence on the benefits of ECED services, especially for poor children and families. As outlined in chapter 1, research has identified many benefits of well-designed and well-implemented early childhood interventions. Benefits include improved child development and school success, more positive development in adulthood, and enhanced earning power. Cost-benefit analyses make a convincing case for investments in the early years.
- Evidence from Indonesian sources of poor children's inadequate school readiness and academic difficulties, as well as continuing high levels of stunting and related problems. This evidence is confirmed by more recent assessments of child development as reported in chapter 2.
- Positive experiences on the part of the World Bank and the government of Indonesia with community-driven development (CDD), a poverty reduction strategy that aims to increase local control over planning decisions and provides resources for locally identified projects (Brinkman et al. 2007).

Development Objective

The ECED project aims to improve poor children's overall development and readiness for further education within a sustainable quality ECED system.

Key Components of the ECED Project

To accomplish this objective, three key components were identified. The ECED project would do the following:

- Increase integrated ECED service delivery through community-driven mechanisms in targeted poor communities. Included in this component would be staff development, community-level facilitation, and provision of community block grants.
- Develop a sustainable system to ensure ECED quality. Included in this component would be standards and quality assurance systems and the institutionalization of ECED at the district and provincial levels.
- Establish effective program management, monitoring, and evaluation. Included here would be overall project management and a system for

Figure 3.2 Key Components of the ECED Project in Indonesia

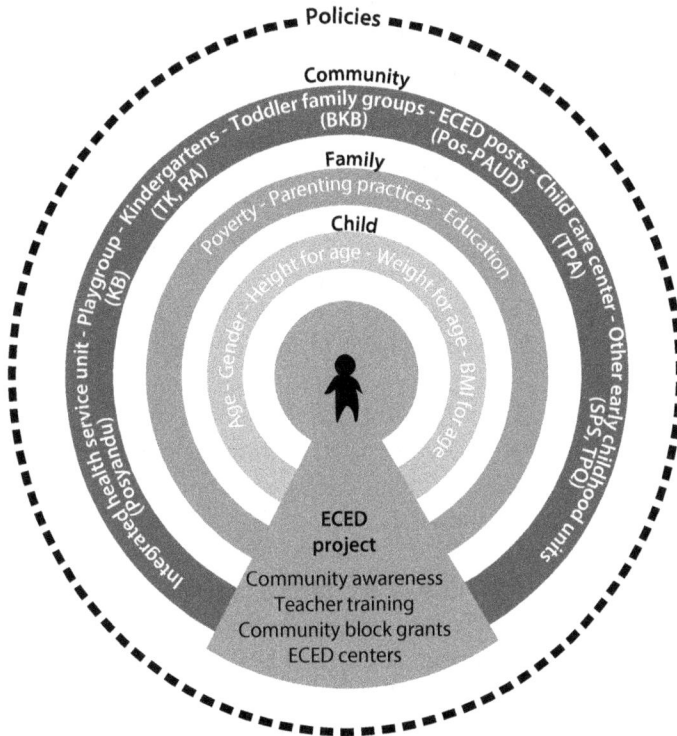

Note: Posyandu = Pos pelayanan terpadu; ECED = early childhood education and development; KB = Kelompok Bermain; TK = Taman Kanak Kanak; RA = Raudotul Atfal; TPQ = Taman Pendidikan Quran; BKB = Bina Keluarga Balita; Pos-PAUD = Pos Pendidikan Anak Usia Dini; TPA = Taman Penitipan Anak; SPS = Satuan PAUD Sejenis.

monitoring, supervising, and evaluating ECED programs at the village and district levels.

The primary focus of this chapter is on the first component, although we discuss the others as they relate to the establishment and implementation of ECED services. Paralleling the Circles of Influence figure introduced in chapter 1, figure 3.2 summarizes how the components of the ECED project were intended to influence children's positive development and school readiness.

Moving toward Targeted ECED Services for Low-Income Communities: The Steps

Based on these identified needs, the development objective, and project components, the ECED project used a step-by-step process to identify target communities and help those communities prepare proposals to obtain funds with which to provide ECED services for their children. Important considerations were the need to ensure broad engagement of community members and for full

Early Childhood Education and Development in Poor Villages of Indonesia •
http://dx.doi.org/10.1596/978-0-8213-9836-4

transparency throughout the process. The use of local, trained facilitators was important in helping community members gain a practical understanding of what ECED is and why ECED services are valuable for young children, families, and the community as a whole.

Step 1: Selecting Poor Districts and the Communities within Them

Criteria were established for selecting districts and communities, with the aim of targeting those that seemed most likely to benefit from ECED services and those whose district governments showed commitment and therefore the potential for sustainability beyond the life of the project.

With these aims in mind, districts in Indonesia were scored using the criteria below and then the 50 districts most likely to benefit from the project were selected:

- low participation rate of children from birth to age 6 in ECED services;
- low Human Development Index (HDI), a composite statistic of education, life expectancy, and income indices;
- high poverty rates;
- classification as a poor district by the Decree on Disadvantaged Districts (*Kepmen Pembangunan Daerah Tertinggal*) 2005;
- commitment to developing a district-level ECED agenda, measured by indicators such as having an ECED budget allocation, an ECED unit in district government, and an early childhood forum of key stakeholders. Appendix 3 describes the results from this scoring and the measures of district commitment used.

Within each of the 50 participating districts, 60 villages (120 communities) were selected for inclusion in the project. A community is typically a subvillage or *dusun*. Indonesian villages usually consist of about five *dusuns*, each with approximately 60 children ages 0–6. The goal was to select communities with high poverty and evidence of need for services. Like the process used at the district level, and again to ensure objectivity and transparency, the community selection process also used scoring criteria, in this case applied by districts. The criteria included overall community population, high numbers of children ages 0–6, and high poverty rates (see appendix 4 for details). The project had resources to provide villages an average of two centers per village for service delivery. These resources were provided to villages in batches. The impact evaluation design, discussed in further detail in the second section of the chapter, relied on villages being phased into the project in batches over time.

A series of activities led to final selection of these villages: preliminary selection through information dissemination, expression of community interest, field verification, and final approval by the district heads (*Bupati*). Table 3.1 describes each activity in this sequence. Again, an objective process was designed to ensure trust, transparency, and community engagement.

Table 3.1 Activities Involved in the Community Selection Process

Activity	Description
Preliminary identification and scoring of villages	Districts identified and scored all eligible villages, using the agreed indicators.
Long-listing	Using the scores, districts ranked and grouped villages into a long list; if a district had fewer than 60 villages, then all villages were entitled to participate in the program. If there were more than 60 villages, a cut-off score was used.
Short-listing	Having assessed all the letters received within a predetermined period of time (usually 30 days), districts decided upon a short list of villages (maximum of 60 villages), each of which would receive a block grant (actually, 1 grant to each of 2 subvillages/*dusun*).
Information dissemination at the district level	Districts invited subdistrict (*kecamatan*) and village representatives to meet, in order to inform them about the ECED project and the eligibility of the villages to participate.
Expression of community interest	After meetings with districts, communities responded by organizing village meetings to develop letters of interest, in which they stated whether they believed they were capable of meeting all requirements (including full commitment to the participatory planning process and provision of community contributions).
Field verification	Districts conducted field visits to verify that the selected villages met all requirements.
District head (*Bupati*) decree	Districts submitted the short list to the district head (*Bupati*), who issued a decree identifying all 60 participating villages in that district.

Box 3.1 What Is Community-Driven Development?

Community-driven development (CDD) is an initiative that provides control of the development process, resources, and decision-making authority directly to community groups. The CDD process assumes that people within a community are in the best position to judge what they need to improve their lives. If they are given information and resources, they are capable of using these to meet their own needs.

Step 2: Helping Communities Identify ECED Service Needs and Prepare Their Proposals

The next step in the process also promoted community engagement in decision making and aimed to increase the likelihood that ECED services would respond to community preferences and needs and not be imposed from the top down. The approach was adapted from the general CDD process, with adaptations to make it suitable to the domain of ECED, which in many ways is different from community planning for a new bridge or road (box 3.1).

After villages were selected, districts nominated candidates to serve as facilitators to help the villagers identify their ECED service needs and prepare proposals. The final selection and facilitator training was done at the national level.

Early Childhood Education and Development in Poor Villages of Indonesia •
http://dx.doi.org/10.1596/978-0-8213-9836-4

Facilitators were mostly well-educated local residents with some experience in community development. Their familiarity with local languages, customs, and community patterns helped them in this role (see appendix 5 for details). Similar to the typical CDD facilitation cycle, the facilitators prepared the community for participation in the ECED project by:

1. raising awareness in the community about the importance of early childhood development and ECED services;
2. helping the community to identify target groups and to select the type, specific delivery systems, and location of the ECED services;
3. establishing an activities management or implementing team, known as *Tim Pengelola Kegiatan* (TPK), to oversee the project; and
4. assisting community members in developing a proposal for project funding.

The detailed process by which community facilitation was carried out is illustrated in figure 3.3.

As mapped out in figure 3.3, the core phases in which communities were empowered to participate in a democratic and participatory decision-making process were threefold.

The First Phase: Community Preconditioning

In the CDD process, time spent in a preconditioning phase creates the conditions that will allow future planning to take place in an informed way. In the ECED project, facilitators first got to know people in the village informally, building trust and meeting with key leaders in conjunction with district officials. Then a series of meetings were held at venues such as mosques, churches, community events, and village health posts (*Posyandu*). Meetings had diverse participation from the entire village, including mothers, expectant mothers, couples of child-bearing age, health post volunteers, midwives, members of the village women's association (PKK), teachers, village leaders, and the elderly.

Through this process, district officials and facilitators ensured that members of eligible villages were:

- aware of the importance of the early years and early interventions for young children;
- informed about the opportunity to get a grant to establish/improve ECED services in their community; and
- aware of the collective responsibility they would need to assume to receive a grant.

The Second Phase: Community Participatory Planning

After the initial preconditioning, the facilitators helped the entire village membership engage in a planning process. With facilitators' help, villagers mapped the existence and location of ECED services already in their communities, identified unmet needs or existing but weak services, and identified spaces that

Figure 3.3 The Community Facilitation Process

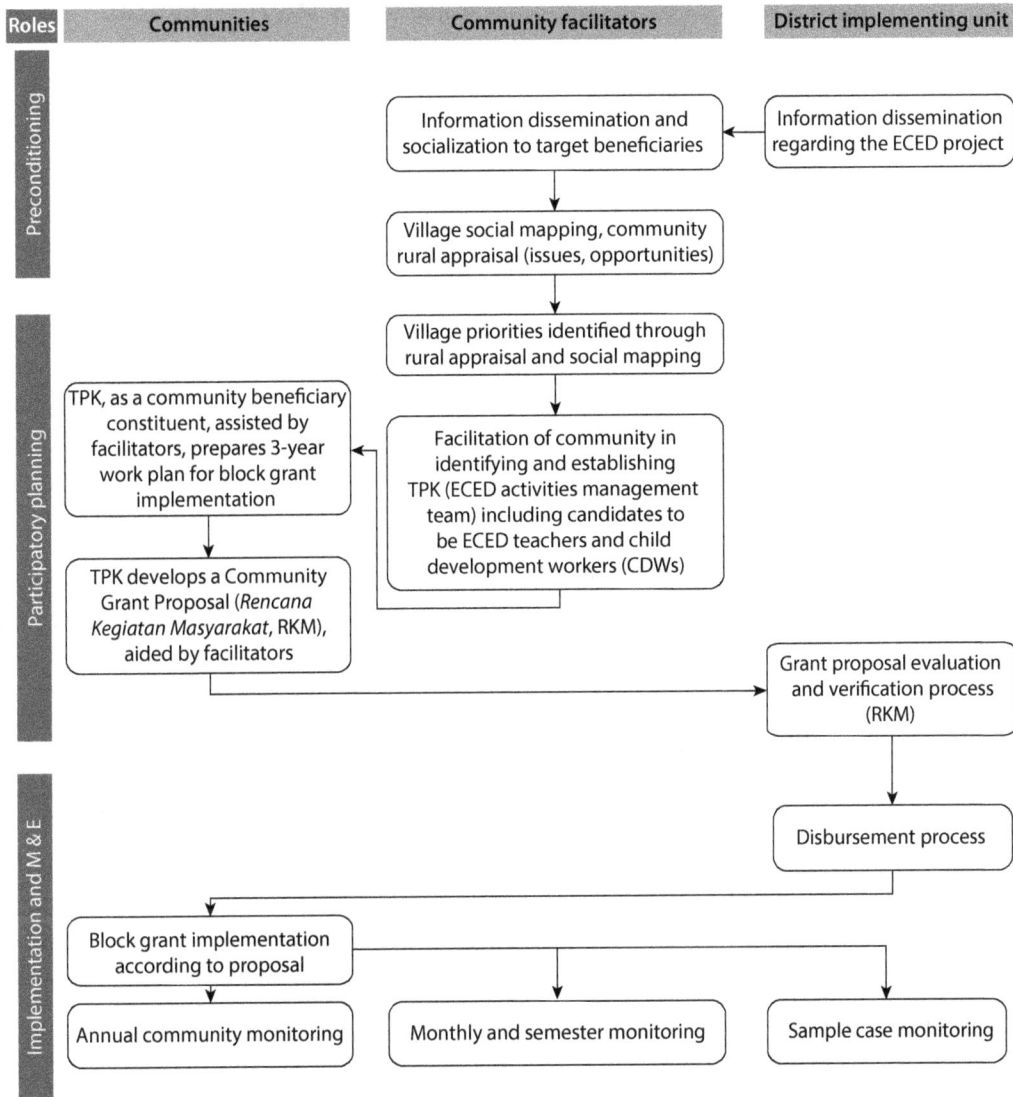

Roles	Communities	Community facilitators	District implementing unit

Preconditioning

Information dissemination regarding the ECED project → Information dissemination and socialization to target beneficiaries

Village social mapping, community rural appraisal (issues, opportunities)

Village priorities identified through rural appraisal and social mapping

Participatory planning

Facilitation of community in identifying and establishing TPK (ECED activities management team) including candidates to be ECED teachers and child development workers (CDWs)

TPK, as a community beneficiary constituent, assisted by facilitators, prepares 3-year work plan for block grant implementation

TPK develops a Community Grant Proposal (*Rencana Kegiatan Masyarakat*, RKM), aided by facilitators

Grant proposal evaluation and verification process (RKM)

Disbursement process

Implementation and M & E

Block grant implementation according to proposal

Annual community monitoring | Monthly and semester monitoring | Sample case monitoring

Note: ECED = early childhood education and development.

might be used to house some ECED services. The villagers also identified who would be their representatives on the activities management team (TPK). With these tasks completed, facilitators helped the community write simple grant proposals using a format provided in a manual from the project (box 3.2). Finally, in this phase the villagers established a village forum to organize meetings about all of these activities, emphasizing broad civic involvement (youth, women, the poorest in the community) to avoid domination of decision making by local elites. See appendix 6 for details.

Box 3.2 What Is a Community Grant Proposal? How May Funds Be Used?

Each community has different needs and priorities for its young children and the services they may need, so in a sense each community grant proposal might be unique. Nevertheless, to assist and manage the process, the early childhood education and development (ECED) project provided a manual to help villagers construct their proposals and to avoid proposing that funds be spent for inappropriate activities. Examples of legitimate uses of funds included the following:

Education and Learning Program: Educational toys (outdoor and indoor), salaries of ECED personnel, furniture, books, teaching materials, teacher transport to conduct outreach services.

Health and Nutrition Program: Scheduled supplementary feedings, vitamin and mineral supplements, first aid box, deworming, measuring tape, scale, trash cans, toothpaste, hand washing sink.

Renovation Program: Costs incurred because of small renovation activities, including labor costs. The use of funds for major renovations or new construction were not encouraged, so villages' proposed allocation for renovation could not exceed 20 percent of the total budget.

Management and Operation of Activities Management Team (TPK): TPK transport to conduct banking and to attend district meetings, TPK training, electricity and water bills, photocopies.

Village activities were financed mainly by the ECED project block grants. However, the management units also received contributions from the parents, community, and local government (in cash or in-kind).

The Third Phase: Proposal Submission and Final Selection
Once village members finished their proposals and received the village head's approval, proposals were submitted to the district office for further review. Following previously established criteria, the district team was to see that each proposal:

- showed commitment to reaching the poorest children and families, with specific plans for how the village would do it;
- targeted both age groups (0–3 and 3–6), with a specific emphasis on children aged 2–4;
- enhanced, rather than replaced, what already existed, such as *Posyandu*, playgroups, Islamic schools, or Sunday schools; and
- had a plan to sustain ECED services after the end of project-specific support.

Following district approval, grants were disbursed directly to village management unit bank accounts (not individual accounts) after the issuance of a disbursement contract between the village and district. The grant disbursements were made in three payments or tranches: 40 percent (US$3,600), 30 percent (US$2,700), and a final 30 percent (US$2,700).

Early Childhood Education and Development in Poor Villages of Indonesia •
http://dx.doi.org/10.1596/978-0-8213-9836-4

ECED Services as Selected by and Implemented in Villages

Villages were able to select various options for services and service delivery, within established guidelines. Figure 3.4 shows patterns in the types and key features of the services supported by ECED project funds.

Services Implemented in Villages: Playgroups Dominate

Villages that were part of the ECED project were expected to address the developmental and learning needs of children from birth to age 6. In theory, the potential range of ECED services that could contribute to this goal was wide. As described in chapter 2, Indonesia has services under many auspices, services that

Figure 3.4 Characteristics of Services Available under the Project

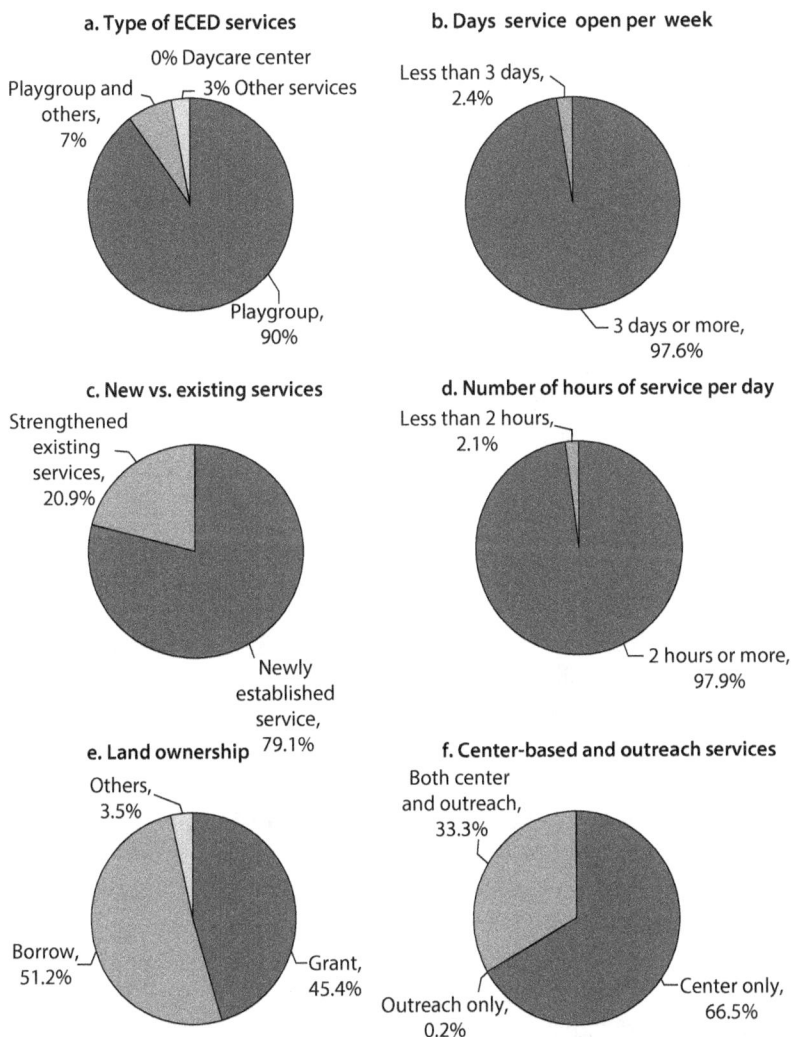

a. Type of ECED services
- 0% Daycare center
- Playgroup and others, 7%
- 3% Other services
- Playgroup, 90%

b. Days service open per week
- Less than 3 days, 2.4%
- 3 days or more, 97.6%

c. New vs. existing services
- Strengthened existing services, 20.9%
- Newly established service, 79.1%

d. Number of hours of service per day
- Less than 2 hours, 2.1%
- 2 hours or more, 97.9%

e. Land ownership
- Others, 3.5%
- Borrow, 51.2%
- Grant, 45.4%

f. Center-based and outreach services
- Both center and outreach, 33.3%
- Outreach only, 0.2%
- Center only, 66.5%

Source: Calculations using project monitoring data.
Note: ECED = early childhood education and development. Percentage totals may exceed 100 because of rounding.

Early Childhood Education and Development in Poor Villages of Indonesia •
http://dx.doi.org/10.1596/978-0-8213-9836-4

focus on different developmental domains and cater to different age groups—for example, playgroups (KB), daycare centers (TPA), *Posyandu*, community health posts integrated with ECED services (Pos-PAUD), kindergartens (TK), and a number of other kinds of services. Villages could have initiated or enhanced any of these, although the manual used in the planning process focused on playgroups and related outreach services. Those services could potentially take many forms; for example, teachers from a centrally located ECED playgroup might travel once or twice a week to provide similar experiences for children living farther away from the playgroup location. Home visiting or informal mother-child play-and-learn meetings facilitated by ECED project staff were other potential outreach options, especially for the youngest children. For children from 0 to 3, ECED services would typically be provided through parenting education and support.

The project monitoring and evaluation data displayed in figure 3.4 reveal that 90 percent of services offered were center-based playgroups (KB). Most children enrolled in these centers were between the ages of 3 and 6. From the government's point of view, playgroups—traditionally part of Indonesia's nonformal education system and until recently under a separate directorate that oversaw the ECED project—serve children ages 2–4, while kindergartens (TK), part of the formal system, serve 4- to 6-year-olds. In the real world of rural villages, however, these distinctions were less clear-cut. Whatever the age range served, project-supported village teachers described their services as playgroups, seeing kindergartens as formal schooling that used different, less play-oriented methods.

Establishing New ECED Services vs. Strengthening Existing Ones: New Services Predominate

In submitting their proposals, villages were able to propose either (1) establishing new ECED services (though they could not build a whole new facility to house the service) or (2) using funds to enhance the quality of existing services; for example, providing current teachers with additional training or purchasing much-needed materials. Figure 3.4 shows that almost 80 percent opted to establish new services. The reasons for this pattern were not clear, but certainly establishing new centers was more likely to increase overall enrollment within the community, especially in areas where no existing ECED services were close by or where the available services (often kindergartens) were not affordable for very poor families.

Communities Donated or Loaned Space for ECED Centers

The ECED centers established under the ECED project were intended to be community-based services requiring community support. This expectation was stated in proposals submitted for funding. One type of community contribution was the provision of land where the center was to be located. Most often, project-supported ECED centers used existing community space belonging to government, communities, or individuals. Examples of locations for the centers, usually playgroups, were rooms in school buildings, village halls, mosques, churches, or sites for the *Posyandu*. About half of the centers were established on donated land from the community (45 percent). A little over half (51 percent) of the centers were provided with land or a building borrowed rent-free from members of the communities. No rent was to be charged to the project's management for borrowed land or buildings.

Most Project-Supported ECED Centers Operated 3 or More Days a Week for 2 or More Hours a Day

Government regulations expect playgroups (90 percent of the ECED project-supported services) to operate at least 3 days per week especially for 3- to 6-year-olds. Figure 3.4 shows that the majority of these services operate 3 or more days per week, fulfilling the government requirement of service days.[1]

The government also sets regulations about the length of the day in nonformal ECED programs, recommending 3 hours per day, if the program primarily serves 3- to 6-year-olds. Figure 3.4 suggests that almost all ECED project-supported centers meet for at least 2 hours a day.

Curriculum in Project-Supported ECED Centers

Box 3.3 describes the rationale for and emphasis of the curriculum typically implemented in ECED project centers. With this information as a basis, box 3.4 outlines an example of activities that might occur in a typical 2-hour session at one of these centers.

Box 3.3 Curriculum in Project-Supported ECED Centers

Although the classrooms for 3- to 6-year-olds in the early childhood education and development project do not use a specific mandated curriculum, most use the government's Generic Menu, which follows the general principles of the Beyond Centers and Circle Time (BCCT) curriculum.

This play-based methodology, using learning centers to promote holistic development, is introduced to teachers during their training. The essential principles are: (1) children learn through play and social relationships; (2) toys and other learning materials should be concrete (hands-on) and, when possible, locally made; (3) teachers "scaffold" children's learning by being involved in their activities but do not teach in a didactic way; and (4) the day should include a balance of quiet and active and child-initiated and teacher-guided activities that support all areas of child development.

Typically, the day begins with welcoming the children and with songs or movement activities. Next, the teacher may introduce and discuss with the class a topic or theme based on recommendations in the Generic Menu. The topic would be something familiar and interesting to the children and would be reflected in other activities during the day and week. A substantial part of the day is devoted to center time, during which small groups of children choose to play in different areas such as blocks, dramatic (make believe) play, creative arts, puzzles, or other fine motor activities. With the teacher's planning and guidance, during this time children may learn concepts and skills that are important for their holistic development and school readiness. Outdoor play, both teacher-planned games and free play, is also part of a typical day.

Box 3.4 A Sample Schedule for a 2-Hour Day in a Project-Supported ECED Center

Prior to 8 a.m., teachers prepare materials and toys and then welcome children as they arrive.

1. 08:00 Opening activities (20 minutes). Usually takes place outdoors. The teacher gathers the children in a circle. The activity may include music, movement, and games.
2. 08:20 Transition (15 minutes). Children conclude the opening activities by singing, praying, or doing a gym activity. They are requested to drink and go to the wash room before entering class.
3. 08:35 Main program (60 minutes). The teacher checks attendance, explains the day's learning theme, and then helps children explore the theme and other concepts through learning centers and other activities: reading, storytelling, games, and pretend play. Teacher goes around to learning centers, facilitating each group's activities. At the end of the main program, children are asked to tidy up; then all children will sit in a circle to recall and discuss what they have done.
4. 09:35 Lunch/snack (15 minutes). Children have lunch or snack together (parents bring the food, teacher demonstrates table manners), then wash their hands.
5. 09:50 Closing (10 minutes). In a circle, children end the class by singing or reciting a poem. The teacher explains the next day's theme. One child in turn will lead the prayer. Children then line up to kiss the teacher's hand before leaving for the day at around 10 a.m.

The curriculum and typical schedule are consistent with good early childhood education practices and follow the government's recommendations. Children are encouraged to learn through first-hand activities and by using locally produced materials that connect them with their culture and community. As we will see in chapter 4, however, there are questions about whether the training and supervision provided to teachers (who have no prior experience) are sufficient to support consistently good curriculum implementation. Additionally, the 2-hour schedule followed by the majority of project-supported centers actually includes no more than an hour for the main program.

Beyond Center-Based Services: The Role of Outreach Options in ECED Service Delivery

Although we have seen that center-based ECED services (mostly playgroups) were the choice of almost all communities, figure 3.4 also shows that many communities used funds both to establish those services and to implement what were called outreach services.

A number of kinds of services might be implemented in the outreach services category. For example, they might include:

• Home visiting to mothers of children, especially children up to age 3. Such services often involve the visitor and the mother (or other family caregiver) observing the child's development, demonstrating the child's abilities to use toys and everyday materials, and encouraging mothers to do more of the good things they are already doing to promote child development.

- Informal, small group play-and-learn sessions with mothers and their children (often under age 3), also to observe the children and encourage the mothers. These might take place at a *Posyandu*, at the ECED center, or other venue.
- Satellite ECED programs: The satellites could be considered subcenters, connected with and staffed by the main ECED center, but operating in different locations. This form of service delivery, though not originally planned, evolved because in many communities there were remotely located or marginalized families with children who could benefit from services. In these cases, teachers often managed to schedule regular visits to implement curriculum similar to that used in the ECED center. In many communities, volunteer teachers were recruited to support this work, although training was not provided to them.

Connecting with Young Children's Families

As emphasized in chapters 1 and 2, families are among the most important circles of influence on young children's development. Early childhood research indicates that involving mothers and other family members, and helping them strengthen home practices, can multiply the positive effects of ECED services (Weiss, Caspe, and Lopez 2006).

In the ECED project, parenting services were part of the menu of ECED options available for support through the project. Although involvement of families is important for children at all ages, it was considered especially important in planning ECED services for children from birth through age 3. Unless parents are working full-time and there is no one else available to care for the child, in Indonesia and many other countries, enhancing the development of infants and toddlers occurs through the engagement of parents. Although it was expected that villages would prioritize outreach to parents and other family members to strengthen the impact of other ECED services, data show that this was done in only one-third of centers.

More recently, because of increased government attention to parenting services, centers' focus on this area has increased. According to the third round of ECED monitoring results as shown in table 3.2, parent-class engagement (volunteering in the classroom) is the most frequent parenting program implemented by ECED centers, followed by home visits and parent meetings. Most home visits seem to occur in connection with the satellite or subcenter services and target younger childen who do not attend center-based programs.

Table 3.2 Half of the Centers Have Some Parent-Class Engagement, 2010

Type of parenting services	No. of service centers	Percentage
Parent-class engagement (volunteering)	2,717	49.50
Home visits	2,315	43.40
Parent meetings	1,622	30.20
Individual consultation day (teacher and parent discussing a child)	1,156	21.80

Source: Calculations using third round of ECED service monitoring results, 2010.

Early Childhood Education and Development in Poor Villages of Indonesia •
http://dx.doi.org/10.1596/978-0-8213-9836-4

Research on ECED services repeatedly emphasizes that even the best planning and the best curriculum will not be effective unless those who work with children and families are well-prepared and motivated to implement high-quality services (Engle *et al.* 2007; Fukkink and Lont 2007).

In this community-based implementation of ECED services, it was important to identify people from the communities to be the service providers. Considering that these were poor communities with relatively low levels of education, this task was challenging. Yet if the strategy were successful, it could empower villages to continue providing locally grown services for their own children—a key to sustainability.

Following is a summary of how the ECED project's personnel were identified, provided with professional development, and supervised. Chapter 4 discusses lessons learned from this process in light of the long-range plans for future ECED teachers' training and continuing professional development.

ECED Project Teachers: Selected by Villages to Support ECED Services for Children 0–6

Because villages agreed to provide services for children from birth through age 6, the project asked them to identify community members who were able to perform two roles: (1) teacher, who would be prepared to lead a playgroup or other center-based program for children 3–6, and (2) child development worker (CDW), who would be prepared to implement parenting meetings, home visiting, or other informal parent-child programs for children 0–3 with their mothers.

Villages used objective criteria to identify potential teachers and CDWs. As with the selection of districts and villages, the project provided villages with criteria to use in identifying two individuals from each site. Although everyone agreed that greater amounts of formal education were desirable, in response to the realities of typical education levels in project villages, a minimum requirement of secondary school completion (SMA) was set. Additional criteria were interest in young children and commitment to ECED. Because of a lack of local opportunities, few candidates had any prior experience in ECED services, although some were *Posyandu* volunteers and some had children of their own.

Training Design, Content, and Methods

The training design and modules were developed by members of a national ECED team in collaboration with a consultant who prepared the team to deliver training. The project identified a national early childhood specialist team (NEST) of 32 individuals with backgrounds in government, higher education, ECED program leadership, training and professional development, and other specializations relevant to the project. The NEST received 400 hours of in-residence professional development, as well as observations and study tours of exemplary ECED programs within and beyond Indonesia. The goals were to build NEST members' capacity in each of the key areas in which they would be responsible for training others and to create a critical mass of ECED leaders whose commitment and influence would extend beyond this project. The NEST members adapted the materials used in their own training to create a comprehensive set of training modules, with topics including the concept and importance of ECED, child development, health and nutrition, curriculum and materials, lesson planning, inclusion of children with disabilities, the arts, and creativity.

Using a cascade approach, the NEST conducted 500 hours of training of trainers for almost 200 district-level personnel. These master trainers in turn were responsible for training village teachers and CDWs.

Training occurred in two blocks of 100 hours each, combining background on child development and ECED with practical information on setting up and teaching in an ECED center, but not including an explicit curriculum manual. Decisions about the amount and timing of training again balanced a desire for extensive training with a realistic appraisal of trainees' and trainers' other responsibilities and practical constraints. During the training, groups of trainees from the same region were in residence, usually at one of the government-sponsored regional centers for nonformal adult education.

Consistent with what the NEST members had been provided in their own training, the total hours were divided into a set of modules delivered by different members of the training team, with similar content as mentioned. In this training, the primary emphasis was on preschool-age children and programs that serve that age group. Relatively little training was provided on parenting programs, home visiting or other outreach techniques, or other service options intended for children 0–3.

Participants received extensive printed resources based on all of the modules that were presented during the training. Because of the interest in promoting teachers' flexibility and autonomy, teachers were not given step-by-step manuals.

Training methods emphasized interactive learning, demonstrations, and role play. Although some trainers initially leaned toward didactic methods, with the benefit of feedback and further training, the methods evolved to emphasize hands-on learning, interaction among participants, demonstrations, and simulations. The trainees had no opportunity to work directly with children, but a limited number of ECED program visits, combined with role play, helped them begin to envision what it might be like to lead a group of young children.

Section 2—Evaluating the Impact of New ECED Services

An Overview of the Evaluation

In section 1, Planning and Implementing an ECED Project, we described the rationale, objective, key components, and implementation process for the ECED project, which helped poor rural communities initiate or enhance ECED services. With that background, this section presents estimates of the short-run impact of having such services in these communities. The estimates use data from an

Early Childhood Education and Development in Poor Villages of Indonesia •
http://dx.doi.org/10.1596/978-0-8213-9836-4

ongoing randomized impact evaluation on four possible clusters of outcomes within these communities:

1. Children's enrollment in ECED services
2. Children's development
3. Parenting practices
4. Children's nutritional status.

How Old Are the Children?

The ECED project's impact evaluation uses data from two cohorts of children that were studied first in 2009 (baseline) and then again in 2010 (midline). Endline data will be collected early in 2013.

Children in the younger cohort were 1 year old when they were first studied in 2009 and 2 years old when they were studied a second time the following year. Children in the older cohort were 4 years old in 2009 and 5 years old in 2010.

Where Do They Live?

These children live in 310 villages, which were organized into three batches. Two of these batches (217 villages in all) participated in the project through a randomized lottery and received funds to begin ECED services at different points in time. Another batch (93 villages) was not part of the project; rather, these villages served as comparison locations and were not part of the randomization process. The impact evaluation takes advantage of the fact that the two batches of villages that initiated project-supported ECED services were randomly assigned to do so and that information is available on villages not part of the project.

The evaluation took advantage of the phased roll-out by randomly assigning villages to Batch 1 or Batch 3. The evaluation did not use data from villages in Batch 2, as they were to be incorporated into the project too soon after Batch 1 to be useful for comparison purposes. The result is that the set of project villages (217 in all) are of two types—those that had project-supported services for a longer duration and those that had services for a shorter duration.

1. Batch 1 villages had project services for a longer duration: 105 villages had been receiving project-supported services for 20 months when data were collected in 2010.
2. Batch 3 villages were exposed to the project for a shorter duration: 112 villages had been receiving project-supported ECED services for 9 months when data were collected in 2010.
3. The 93 nonproject villages never received ECED services supported by this project. Like the project villages, they may already have had services such as kindergartens, playgroups, and Poysandu. Data were collected on a sample of children and families in these villages for comparison purposes. These villages were not picked by random assignment.

What Impact Are We Studying?

We estimate short-run impacts of exposure to the project. It is important to keep in mind that whether or not the villages were exposed to the project for a short or long duration in no cases were project services in villages for more than 20 months. For this reason, all the impacts we estimate are short-run impacts.

Not All Children Who Were Studied Were Enrolled in Project-Supported Services

Many other ECED services such as kindergartens and playgroups were located in both project villages and villages that never received the project. Some of the children in our sample would have attended these services instead of project-supported services.

Why Include 1- and 2-Year-Olds?

We included the younger age group because, as explained in chapter 2, the ECED project was designed to address the needs of children from birth through age 6 through various kinds of services to children and their families. Although the reality was that most villages focused on establishing playgroup-type centers for children primarily between ages 3 and 5, an assessment of impact on younger children was important in light of project objectives.

What Exactly Is Being Evaluated? The Scope of the Evaluation

When analyzing the impact of the project, we are analyzing the impact of the availability of new or enhanced ECED services in the selected ECED project villages for a sample of children living in those villages regardless of whether those children actually attended the ECED project-supported centers.

Why Not Just Study the Children Who Were Actually Enrolled in ECED Project-Supported Services?

The question of impacts on children who were enrolled in project centers is important and interesting. For two reasons, however, the question cannot be answered in this report:

1. Using data on enrolled children to measure impacts would have been technically difficult. Because we do not know in advance the characteristics of the children who will enroll in the project-supported ECED centers, it is impossible to know whether their child development outcomes measured later are a result of their attending project-supported centers or of some other factors, such as parenting practices.

2. Even children not enrolled in ECED project services might benefit *indirectly*. In designing this evaluation, we believed that all children living in the targeted villages might potentially benefit, not just those who participated in the project-supported centers. Other children could benefit through other types of outreach services or through spill-over effects—what they might learn informally from children or parents that do participate.

The Evaluation Design: Taking Advantage of Phased Implementation of the Project

To determine impacts we compared enrollment, child development, and family outcomes in villages with different amounts of exposure to project-supported services. As mentioned in the first section of this chapter, project funds were provided in phases, with different batches of villages receiving funds and therefore able to begin offering services at different points in time. Villages included in Batch 1 began their ECED project services first, and villages in Batch 3 began around 11 months later.[2] Villages in the comparison group were not part of the ECED project. One would expect—assuming that the project services have positive effects on villages' children and families—better outcomes in Batch 1 compared to Batch 3 villages because the people in Batch 1 villages had longer opportunities to benefit, directly or indirectly, from the project-financed services. For the same reason, one would expect better outcomes in Batch 3 villages compared to the group of villages that were not part of the project.

But Were All These Villages the Same to Start with?

To be confident that differences are related to the ECED project and not to something else that was different about Batch 1, Batch 3, and the comparison villages, we needed to check that the villages were similar on average before the project started. For Batch 1 and Batch 3 villages, this was ensured by conducting public lotteries in the selected villages to decide which villages would be part of Batch 1 and which would be part of Batch 3. Because a lottery is random, we can assume that on average the villages in Batch 1 and 3 are the same. Unfortunately, it was not possible to use the same method to determine whether the comparison villages were equally similar. Comparison villages were suggested by local officials who typically used their knowledge of the surrounding villages to suggest those with similar characteristics. An analysis of the data suggests that they made these selections quite well: for example, the child outcomes measured at baseline in Batch 3 and comparison villages were very similar. Appendix 7 reports tests of the evaluation design using village characteristics reported in the Survey of Village Potential (PODES).[3]

Challenges of Using a Phased-in Evaluation Design: Expectations versus Reality

Unfortunately, the planned timing of the data collection and the implementation of the ECED project in villages were not well synchronized. The expectation was that we would collect baseline data in communities before any of the project villages established their ECED services. We also planned that the midline data collection would occur just before Batch 3 villages, the last to receive ECED project funds, started their ECED services.

In reality, Batch 1 villages had already been providing project-supported ECED services for 6 months by the time the baseline data were collected. And by the time of the midline data collection, Batch 3 villages were already 9 months into providing services, instead of just beginning, as was expected. Faced with this reality, we adjusted our analyses accordingly.

Different Batches Make Different Comparisons Possible—An Overview

A randomized impact evaluation usually involves comparing outcomes in two groups: a randomly assigned treatment group, which receives some kind of intervention, and a randomly assigned control group, which does not receive an intervention but is otherwise similar to the treatment group. Despite the problems with the timing of data collection, we benefited from having more than the usual number of groups to make different comparisons (see box 3.5). Therefore, we had an opportunity to learn about the relative effects of the ECED project on villages that had different amounts of project exposure.

The comparisons that form the basis for the impact estimates of the ECED project are presented in figure 3.5. The lines in the graph show the number of months the different groups of villages had ECED project-supported services. On the horizontal axis is the age of the child, separately for the younger or 1-year-old cohort (which was around 18 months old when the baseline data were collected), and older for the 4-year-old cohort (which was around 54 months old when the baseline data were collected). There are three possible comparisons:

Figure 3.5 Comparisons Used for Impact Evaluation

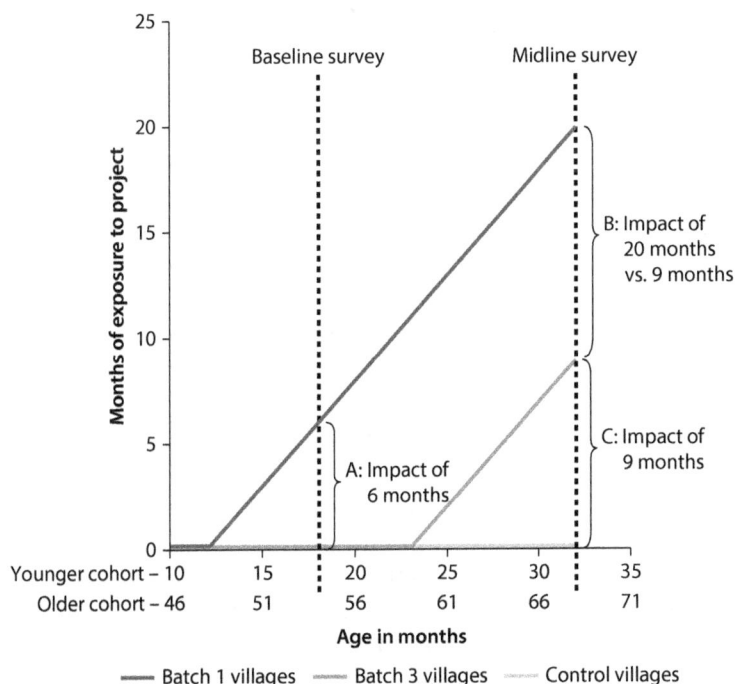

1. Comparison A compares the outcomes in Batch 1 and Batch 3 in 2009, the time of initial data collection (baseline). By that time, because of the timing problems, the Batch 1 villages had project-supported services for 6 months, and Batch 3 villages had not yet started their project-supported services. In this comparison, the age cohorts of children we examine are on average 18 and 54 months old, with some living in Batch 1 villages and some in Batch 3 (although the children in the sample might or might not have been enrolled in the project's ECED services or, indeed, in any ECED services.)

2. Comparison B compares these same children in 2010 (midline). Now they are 14 months older. By that time their average age was around 32 months for the younger cohort and 68 months for the older cohort. Also at this time Batch 3 villages had begun implementation of services. Batch 1 villages had now been providing ECED project-supported services for 20 months, and Batch 3 villages had provided their services for 9 months.[4]

3. Comparison C relies on two rounds of data, takes a difference-in-differences approach, and compares how children's outcomes in villages with project-supported services for 9 months changed over time when compared with changes in children's outcomes in villages that did not participate in the project.

Being able to analyze our child, family, and enrollment data using three different types of comparisons is potentially valuable. Each comparison measures different levels of exposure to ECED project services at different times. For this research, timing (at what ages the children were assessed) is particularly important, as children change and grow substantially over the course of a year.

Comparisons A and C are the usual type of comparisons in this kind of evaluation, comparing villages with ECED project services in place to villages not having such services. The villages differ in the length of exposure to these activities. For comparison A it is 6 months, and for comparison C it is 9 months. But more important, the time at which the data are collected differs by 14 months. For comparison C, most of the children in the younger age cohort are 2 years old and 5 in the older cohort. Comparison C has an additional advantage: Baseline data are available for the comparison, which makes it possible to analyze the impact of the ECED project services among a range of subgroups (such as girls, children from poor households, and those who were never enrolled). Having different points in time for these villages also increases statistical power, the ability to reliably detect differences between different groups.

Comparison B answers the question of whether 11 months difference in exposure to the project still makes a difference 9 months after the latter group started. One would not expect this to make a difference for short-term effects, such as increasing enrollment. But for child development indicators, the effects of early exposure may persist over time.

Box 3.5 A Methodological Guide to the Comparisons

Some readers may be interested to know what parameters are being reported in our discussions of comparisons A, B, and C. This box specifies the methodology we follow.

Comparison A compares a group of villages randomly assigned to treatment status (Batch 1) with a group of villages randomly assigned to control status (Batch 3) in the first round. Treatment villages have received program services for 6 months and control villages have not yet received the project. We estimate comparison A using ordinary least squares regressions as follows:

$$y_{ij}^A = \beta_0^A + D_j\delta^A + x_{ij}\beta^A + u_{ij}^A \tag{1}$$

Where y_{ij}^A is enrollment (1 if ever-enrolled and 0 if never-enrolled) or child development outcomes at baseline for a child i in village j. D_j is the dummy variable indicating 1 for treatment village and 0 for control village. Thus, δ^A is the program impact coefficient after 6 months. x_{ij} is a vector of explanatory variables that include caregiver, household, and child characteristics.[5]

Comparison B compares these same groups of villages at midline. Treatment villages have received program services for 20 months and control group villages have received program services for 9 months. Again, we estimate comparison B using ordinary least squares regressions as follows:

$$y_{ij}^B = \beta_0^B + D_j\delta^B + x_{ij}\beta^B + u_{ij}^B \tag{2}$$

Where y_{ij}^B is enrollment (1 if ever-enrolled and 0 if never-enrolled) or child development outcomes at midline for a child i in village j. D_j is the dummy variable indicating 1 for treatment village and 0 for control village. Thus, δ^B is the program impact coefficient after 11 months of differential treatment. x_{ij} is a vector of explanatory variables that include caregiver, household, and child characteristics.

Comparison C estimates the impact of the early childhood education and development (ECED) project using a difference-in-differences approach. The basic logic of this method is to follow two groups of villages that are similar at baseline and to estimate the difference in the outcomes of children in these villages at midline after the project has started in one group of villages and no project exists in the other group. We take advantage of the fact that at baseline the project had not yet started in Batch 3 villages (randomly assigned to control status), but at midline these villages had been part of the project for 9 months. In addition we have data on a group of villages that had no intervention at either baseline or midline (the comparison group).

The regression model is as follows:

$$y_{ijt}^C = \beta_0^C + D_j\delta_1^C + T_t\delta_2^C + D_jT_t\delta_3^C + x_{ij}\beta^C + u_{ijt}^C \tag{3}$$

y_{ijt}^C is enrollment (1 if ever-enrolled and 0 if never-enrolled) or child development outcomes at baseline ($t = 1$) and midline ($t = 2$) for a child i in village j. D_j is a dummy variable which is 1 for Batch 3 and 0 for the villages with no project, and T_t is a dummy variable indicating 1 for baseline and 0 for midline. Thus, δ_1^C captures the difference between Batch 3 and comparison villages at baseline. If the two groups being compared are similar in terms of child development

box continues next page

Early Childhood Education and Development in Poor Villages of Indonesia •
http://dx.doi.org/10.1596/978-0-8213-9836-4

Box 3.5 A Methodological Guide to the Comparisons *(continued)*

outcomes and enrollment, our estimates should be close to 0. δ_2^C captures the change in children's outcomes and ECED enrollment as they get older. $D_j T_t$ is an interaction between the treatment group dummy and the time dummy. Thus, δ_3^C indicates the difference between Batch 3 and comparison villages as a result of the project after 9 months. If there had been no ECED project, we would expect that the midline differences in outcomes between Batch 3 and comparison villages should be the same as those at baseline, implying that $\delta_3^C = 0$. x_{ij} is a vector of explanatory variables that includes caregiver, household, and child characteristics at baseline. Robust standard errors clustered at the village level are used. We also run a fixed effects model on regression model (3), which controls for all observed and unobserved time-invariant characteristics. These results are not reported here but are available upon request.

Reading the Graphs: A Preview of How the Impact Evaluation Results Are Presented

In the following pages, the short-run impacts of the project are presented for each comparison—A, B, and C—and for each age cohort, as represented in the case of enrollment in figure 3.6. (The corresponding data used to construct these graphs are reported in appendixes 8–10.) For each possible outcome, the bars show the estimated expected outcome without the ECED project and the estimated impact of the project. The bar labeled "without ECED project" indicates the expected outcome in the absence of project-supported services. The bar labeled "impact of ECED project" indicates how much change in this outcome is a result of having project services in the community. Again, remember that the children whose development is being assessed might or might not have been enrolled in ECED project services or in other ECED services available in the community.[6]

Showing Positive and Negative Impacts and the Degree of Confidence in the Results

When the impact is positive, the two bars are stacked on top of each other so that the combined bar indicates the estimated outcome for children from project villages. With a negative impact, the "impact" is stacked on the left side of the bar, indicating that this amount should be subtracted to obtain the expected outcome for children from project villages. This result is possible for those outcomes where lower scores are better and in those few instances when outcomes appear to have gotten worse in the short run.

Asterisks next to the comparisons indicate whether the impact is statistically significant. The more asterisks, the more certain we are that the difference between villages would not simply occur by chance.

Increases in Child Development Outcomes: Sometimes Just because Children Improve as They Get Older

Note that the bars for the various outcomes are generally higher when we look at the results from comparisons B and C than the results from comparison A.

Figure 3.6 The Project Resulted in Increases in Enrollment Rates among Younger and Older Cohorts

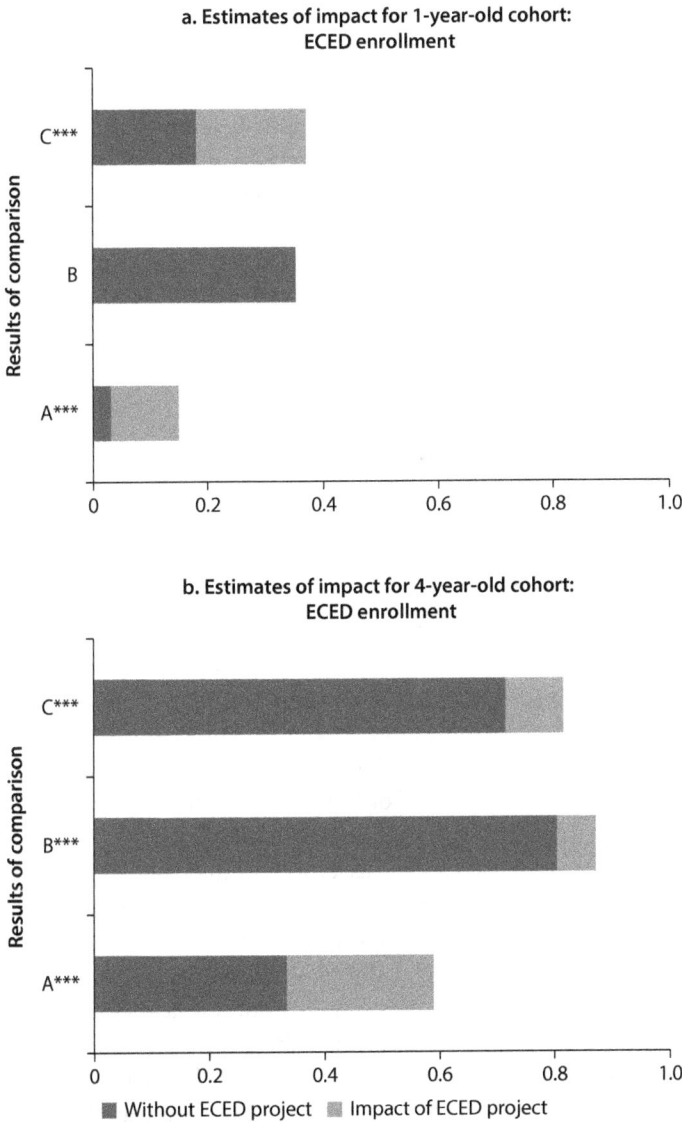

a. Estimates of impact for 1-year-old cohort:
ECED enrollment

b. Estimates of impact for 4-year-old cohort:
ECED enrollment

■ Without ECED project   ■ Impact of ECED project

Source: Calculations using ECED survey data.
Note: ECED = early childhood education and development.
*** = 1%, ** = 5%, * = 10 % significance.

This reflects the expected improvements in most areas as the children grow older. On many indicators of child development, such as physical or social skills, children will typically get better with age just as a result of growth, maturation, and increased experience. Poor children's development, however, is often both slower/behind that of children from better-off families and more likely to improve with the added value of ECED services.

Early Childhood Education and Development in Poor Villages of Indonesia •
http://dx.doi.org/10.1596/978-0-8213-9836-4

The Impact Evaluation Results: Enrollment, Child Development, Parenting Practices, Nutritional Status

To discuss the impact evaluation results according to type of outcome variable, we start with an analysis of how project-supported services impacted ECED enrollment in general. Next, we present the impacts on children's development in various domains, using results from the measures introduced in chapter 2—the Early Development Instrument (EDI), Strengths and Difficulties Questionnaire (SDQ), and other child tasks. We unpack these average results by looking at particular subgroups of interest. Finally, we present impacts on parenting practices and nutrition outcomes. In each case, we discuss the findings from all comparisons. For reasons that we have highlighted, we believe estimates based on comparison C (Batch 3 villages compared with villages not part of the ECED project) provide the most informative results.

Impacts on Enrollment in ECED Services

The project has a positive impact on children's enrollment in ECED services. Recall that in chapter 2 we described the many kinds of ECED services in Indonesia—such as playgroups and kindergartens. We also saw in this chapter that most villages, whether part of the ECED project or not, had some kind of services for young children and families.

Our analyses show that the ECED project had a clear positive impact on enrollment in ECED services (including but not limited to project-supported services). Figure 3.6 shows the estimated impacts by age of the child. It shows the average rates of enrollment in villages without the project and the impact we estimate is caused by the project. For both cohorts, the impact is clear and statistically significant.

Looking at figure 3.6, we can see, as expected, that the percentage of children who have ever been enrolled in an ECED service increases with the age of the child. This pattern in the data matches the national patterns of ECED enrollment described in chapter 2. Looking at the two panels together, specifically at comparisons A and C for the two cohorts, we also find that the impact of providing new or enhanced ECED services through this project increases as children get older, up to about age 4. After that point, the impact begins to decrease. (Recall that children are older in comparison B than they are in A.)

These findings are in line with what we expected from the kinds of in-the-field observations noted in the first part of this chapter. There is much evidence that the ECED centers set up in this project were generally targeted to children ages 3–5. Looking again at figure 3.6, we see that the impact of villages' having these ECED project services is lower for 4-year-olds. This relatively low project impact may be explained because in many villages the children who are 4 or older may already be enrolled in some kind of service such as kindergartens.

This point is confirmed by data showing that in contrast to the results for the 4-year-olds, enrollment rates for 1- and 2-year-olds are lower even when new or enhanced ECED services are provided.

Finally, we asked whether having new ECED services in project villages might increase enrollment in ECED programs (either ECED project-supported or other), especially for girls—who in many countries have limited access to education—and children from very poor families. Data presented in appendices 8–10 show that there was limited evidence of an increase for girls' ECED enrollment and for enrollment by children from the poorest families.

If Services Are Available when Children Are Younger (but Not Too Young!), Families Are More Likely to Enroll Them

Opening new centers can increase enrollment, but how old children are when centers are opened matters for the enrollment effect. If they are too old when the centers open, many may already be enrolled in some other service, and the impact of the new project-supported services is lower. The enrollment effect on the 4-year-old cohort is higher than for the 5-year-old cohort.

It is interesting to investigate whether the baseline differences in enrollment observed in Batch 1 and Batch 3 villages persisted through the midline data collection. By the midline, both groups of villages had established ECED project-supported centers, but some (Batch 1) had received the services for 20 months, and some (Batch 3) for only 9 months. And again, most villages had some preexisting ECED services available in the community.

An important question is, does it matter for children's outcomes whether the ECED centers had been available in the village for a relatively longer time (Batch 1) or a shorter time (Batch 3)—though in neither case had the centers been there very long? It appears that how long the ECED project's services had been in the villages had some impact on overall ECED enrollment for the older children, who by the time midline data were collected were 5 years old. The number of months that ECED project-supported centers had been in the villages does not matter for the younger cohort, who were 2 years old when midline enrollment data were collected—probably because it turned out that very few centers were intended to serve children under age 3. Five-year-olds from Batch 1 villages have a 7 percentage point higher chance of being enrolled in an ECED center, compared to 5-year-olds in Batch 3 villages, where the centers were relatively new. So for the 5-year-old children it is important that they enroll in the centers when they are 4 or maybe even younger, but we cannot tell because of limitations of the data. The data suggest that if the centers are not established until children are older (age 5), it may be more difficult to enroll them.

Impacts on Children's Development

The most important question one can ask in the impact evaluation is whether ECED services make a positive difference in young children's development (figures 3.7 and 3.8). Given the timing challenges, an analysis of this project that looked only at randomized treatment and control villages or that looked only at the average child in these villages would find disappointing results. When we look at villages with and without project services, and when we look at especially

Figure 3.7 The Short-Run Effects of the Project on the Younger Cohort of Children Were Small on Average

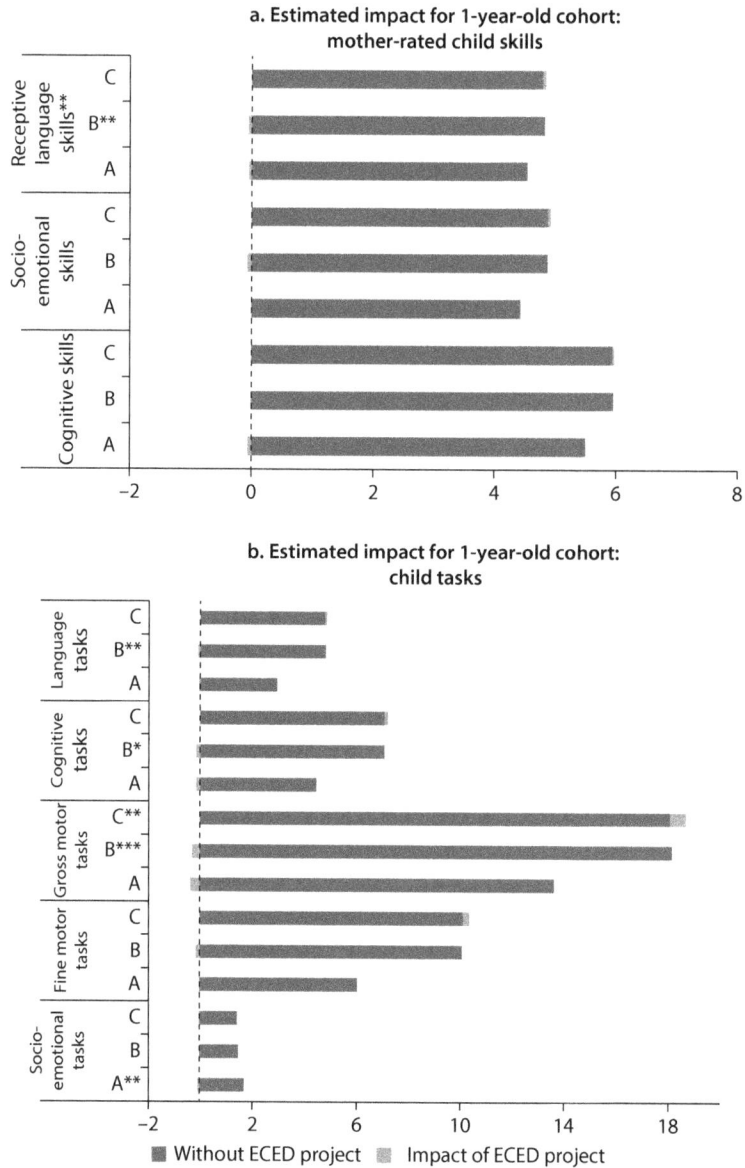

a. Estimated impact for 1-year-old cohort:
mother-rated child skills

b. Estimated impact for 1-year-old cohort:
child tasks

■ Without ECED project ▨ Impact of ECED project

Note: ECED = early childhood education and development.
*** = 1%, ** = 5%, * = 10 % significance.

disadvantaged groups, we can discern a more nuanced picture of the short-run impacts of the project.

When assessed after ECED project-supported services had been in place for a year or less, the average children living in ECED project villages showed only limited improvements in their development, but the most disadvantaged children showed more substantial benefits.[7] When looking at the average child, we see that most of the estimates of the impact of having ECED project services on children's development are in the positive direction as expected, but most are not statistically significant. Disaggregating results further reveals some positive and significant impacts of the project for very poor children, girls, and those who had never been enrolled in ECED services before the project.

These results are likely to be a conservative estimate of impact for two reasons:

1. The new ECED services had been in place within project villages for less than a year. Comparisons A and C measure the impact after services had been in villages for either 6 or 9 months (compared to villages without the project), while comparison B measures the impact when the difference in villages' exposure to project services is 11 months. It would be surprising for an ECED intervention to show large effects on child development outcomes within such a short time period.

2. The children whose development was assessed were not necessarily enrolled in the project's ECED centers or other ECED services. Recall that the design of this impact evaluation did not allow us to compare children who were enrolled in project-supported services with children who were not enrolled. Instead, children living in ECED project villages, which had services available for varying but short periods of time, were compared with those who lived in non-ECED project villages. Most other ECED impact evaluations compare the development of enrolled vs. not-enrolled children who were randomly assigned to these categories. As noted, this kind of comparison was not possible in the evaluation reported here.

The Younger Cohort of Children

When comparing children in villages with project services for 6 months to children in villages without those services (comparison A), we find a negative impact on socio-emotional skills (assessed by child tasks) for the younger cohort of children—those who are 1 year old when we first observe them. There are reasons to be cautious in interpreting this finding because the measure of socio-emotional tasks relied on only two questions. Also, as noted, the development of 1-year-olds is difficult to assess in field settings. Finally, these results are not confirmed by mothers' ratings of their children's socio-emotional skills, which were assessed using six questions (figure 3.7).

In addition, in this comparison we find evidence of negative effects on gross motor skills among girls. These results are reported in appendixes 8–10.

We also find some negative effects for the younger cohort when we compare villages that had project services for 20 months with those that had them for 9 months (comparison B). At this point, children in the younger cohort were 2 years old. Two-year-old children living in villages where project playgroup services were established earlier had lower scores on receptive language skills (mother-rated) and gross motor skills (child tasks) when compared to children living in villages

Figure 3.8 The Short-Run Effects of Project Services on the Older Cohort of Children Were Small on Average

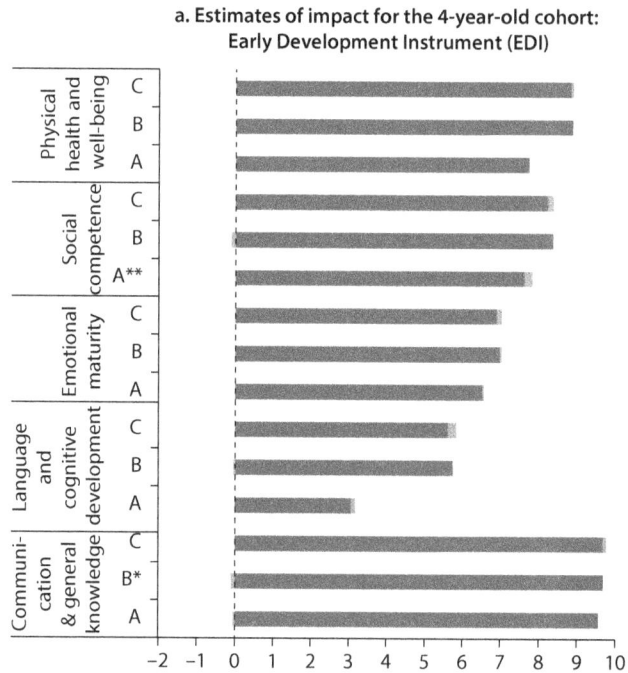

a. Estimates of impact for the 4-year-old cohort:
Early Development Instrument (EDI)

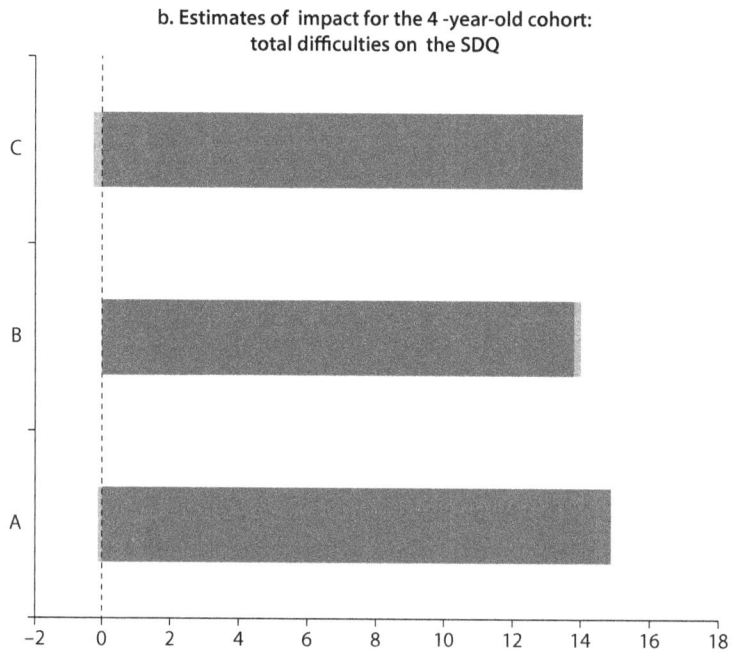

b. Estimates of impact for the 4 -year-old cohort:
total difficulties on the SDQ

figure continues next page

Figure 3.8 The Short-Run Effects of Project Services on the Older Cohort of Children Were Small on Average *(continued)*

c. Estimates of impact for the 4-year-old cohort:
Strengths and Difficulties Questionnaire (SDQ)

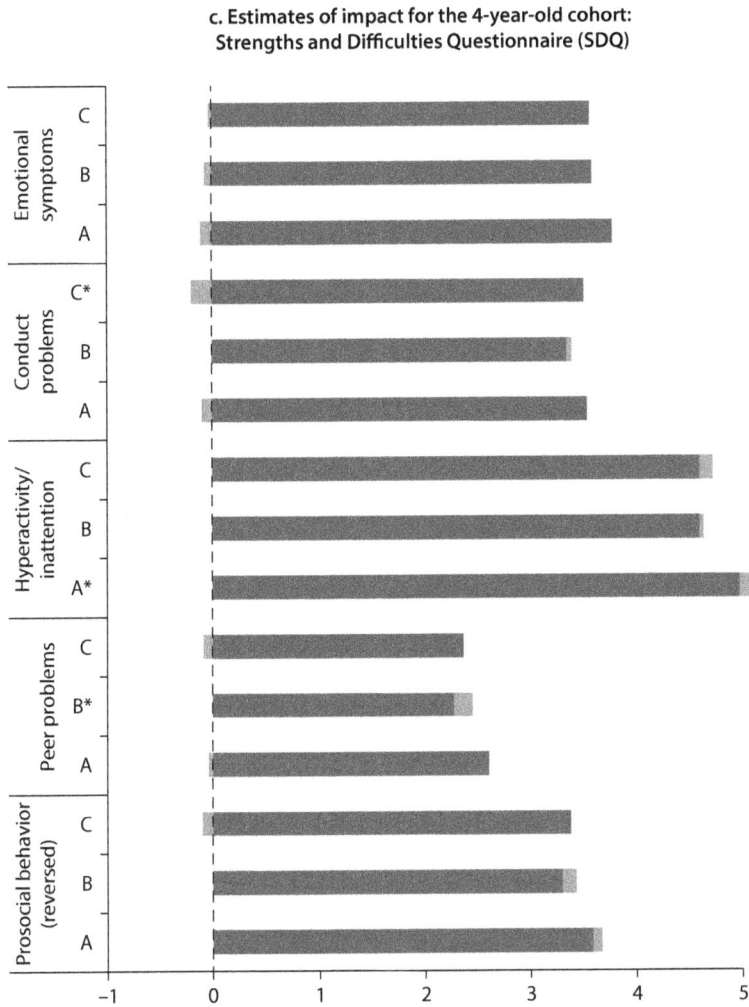

figure continues next page

Early Childhood Education and Development in Poor Villages of Indonesia •
http://dx.doi.org/10.1596/978-0-8213-9836-4

Figure 3.8 The Short-Run Effects of Project Services on the Older Cohort of Children Were Small on Average *(continued)*

d. Estimates of impact for the 4-year-old cohort: Other task measures

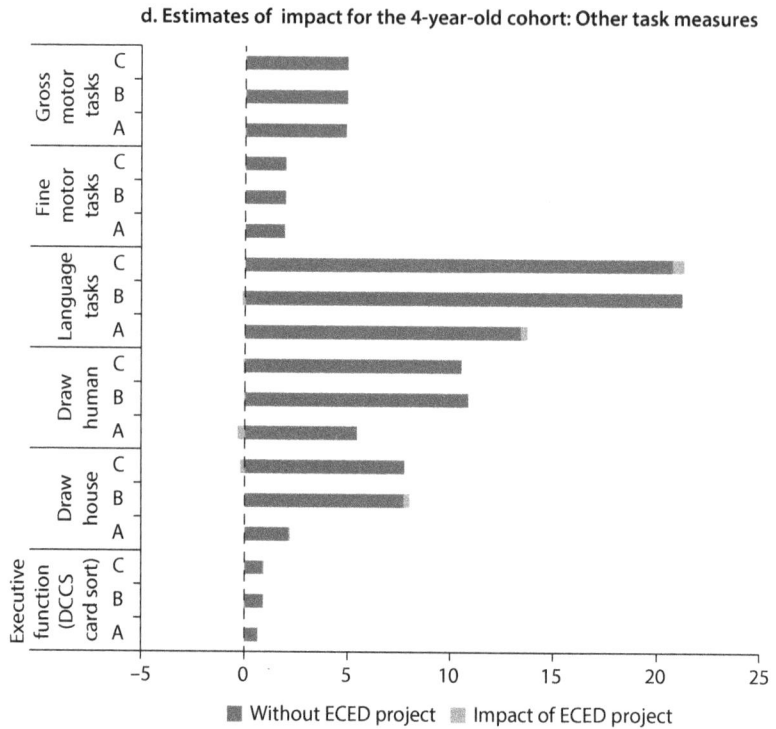

Source: Calculations using ECED survey data.

Note: ECED = early childhood education and development; SDQ = Strengths and Difficulties Questionnaire.

* = 10 percent, ** = 5 percent, *** = 1 percent.

where ECED centers were established 11 months later. The negative effects on gross motor skills among girls are also apparent in this comparison.

In contrast to the results above, impact estimates comparing villages that had project services for 9 months to villages without such services at two points in time (using comparison C) are all in the positive direction, although most are not statistically significant. Given what we have noted about the short duration of exposure, these results are understandable. We find none of the negative effects. On the contrary, we find a positive effect on gross motor skills. Children from poor families benefit more than the average in this domain.

The Older Cohort of Children on Average

On most measures of development, the average impacts for 4-year-olds are in the expected positive direction, yet most are not statistically significant.

We find a positive effect of living in a project village for 4-year-olds on the EDI's social competence score (comparison A: 4-year-olds in villages where project services have been in place for 6 months versus 4-year-olds in nonproject villages). Although the differences seem small, they are significant both statistically and practically.

Recall the research discussed in chapter 2 on differences in children's development as predicted by differences in their mothers' education. The differences associated with living in a non-ECED project village and a village with ECED project services are quite similar in magnitude to those we find for children whose mothers have either lower (junior secondary) or higher (senior secondary) education.

There is no difference one year later, when both Batch 1 and Batch 3 villages have implemented project services. By that time there is no statistical difference between children in these two groups in their social competence scores. Note that at this age most children are likely to be enrolled in some sort of ECED service, and the distinctive impact of the services that are strictly ECED project-supported is limited.

Beyond the Average: Subgroups Provide a More Nuanced Picture of Impacts on Child Development

Unpacking the average results reveals some positive and significant impacts of the project for subgroups of disadvantaged children: children from the poorest families, girls, and those who had never been enrolled in ECED services before the project services were implemented in their village.

We find generally stronger positive impacts for the 4-year-old age group for girls, children who are from families in the lower half of the asset index, and children who were not enrolled in any services before the start of the project's services. This last subgroup analysis is only possible for comparison C, as neither of the groups being compared had project services in their villages at baseline (figure 3.9).

We find clear positive effects of villages' project participation on the EDI language and cognitive development domain for children from poorer families and for children who were not enrolled in any ECED services at baseline. This result comes from comparison C, which compares how outcomes change over time in villages that have had project services for 9 months with those that have never had project services. This result is important because it was in the language and cognitive domain that the children in the sample were most behind at baseline. The effects are substantial (14 percent for poor children and 10 percent for girls and for those not enrolled at baseline).

The positive effects for poorer children and for girls are further confirmed by results from the Dimensional Change Card Sort task described in chapter 2. This measure is a widely used assessment of children's cognitive development, especially their executive function skills, which are the foundation of many aspects of later academic and social outcomes. On this same task, using comparison C, we find a positive, significant effect of living in an ECED project village on 4-year-olds' performance on this measure. For the group not enrolled in any ECED services at baseline, we see an effect on the card sort task (with a fixed effects specification not shown here).

We also explore whether children whose parents have below-average parenting practices have bigger impacts from exposure to the project. Figure 3.10

Figure 3.9 The Project Services Had Larger Effects on Children from Poorer Families Compared to the Average

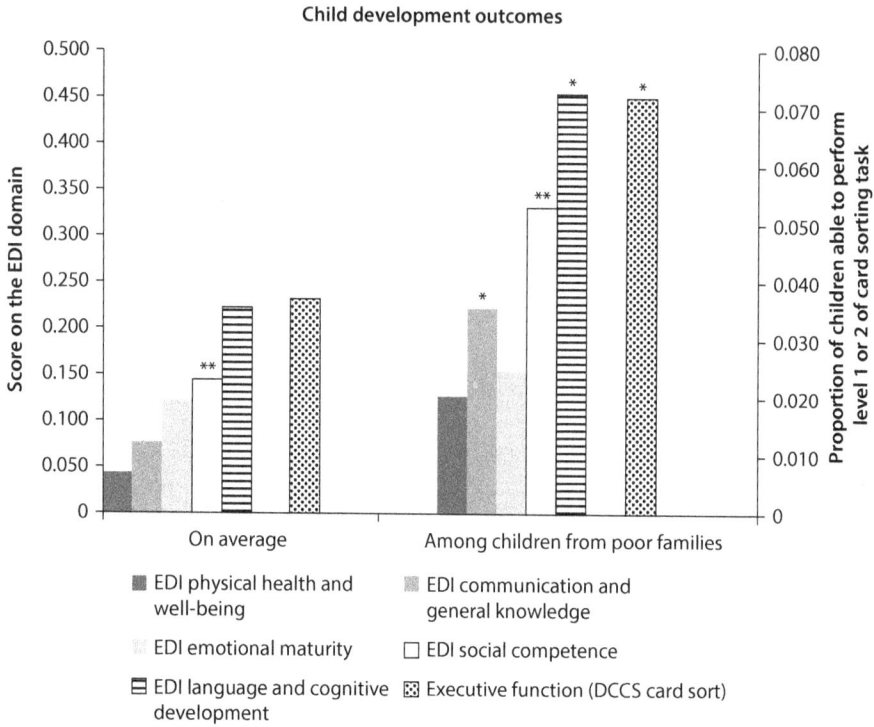

Source: Calculations using ECED survey data.
Note: EDI = Early Development Instrument.
* = 10 percent, ** = 5 percent, *** = 1 percent.

shows that such children have larger improvements in their development outcomes than the average child residing in these villages. This is particularly so on domains where children lag behind international norms, such as the EDI's language and cognitive development domain.

The effects for girls and children from poorer households are not evident for the 4-year-olds in comparison A. Recall that comparison A measures impact by comparing villages that have had 6 months of ECED project services with villages that have not yet received any ECED services. The estimates generally point in the same direction, perhaps because the comparison measures only 6 months of having project services instead of 9, and that comparison A has lower power (statistical ability to detect differences) than comparison C.

Parenting and Nutrition Outcomes

The analysis did not identify impacts of the project on parenting practices or children's nutritional outcomes. We find no impact of having the ECED project services in villages on parents' use of more positive parenting practices or on children's nutritional indicators. This finding is true both for the younger and

Figure 3.10 Children Whose Parents Have Below-Average Parenting Practices Benefit More than Average Children

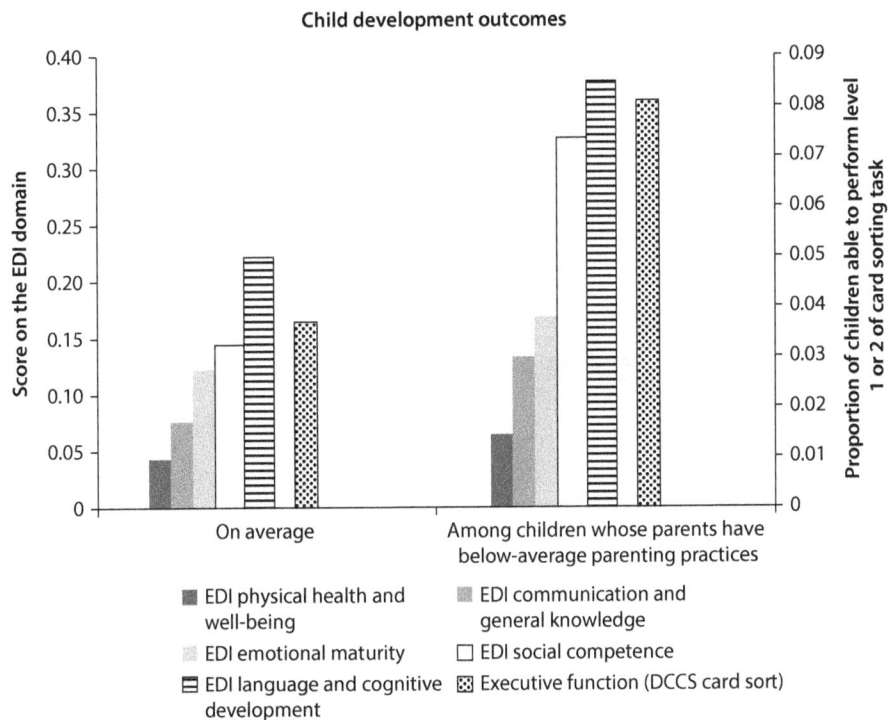

Child development outcomes

Note: EDI = Early Development Instrument.

older cohorts in the sample (figure 3.11). Recall that parenting practices were assessed by interviewing mothers about practices that reflected different levels of warmth, consistency, or hostility toward their children, resulting in a positive parenting score. Children's nutrition was assessed using their height and weight and calculating whether the child was considered to be stunted or wasting.

As noted in section 1 of this chapter, few project centers tried to address parenting practices, and few formed close relationships with *Posyandu*. In addition, the training provided to teachers did not emphasize this aspect of ECED programming. Together, these factors may, in part, explain why no impact of the project on parenting practices or children's nutritional status was identified.

It should be reiterated that this analysis shows only the absence of an impact in the short term. Because behavior can be slow to change and because nutritional outcomes take a long time to manifest, it may take some time to establish whether there is a long-term impact of the project on parenting practices and children's nutritional outcomes. In chapter 2, we saw that many parents were not taking advantage of everyday opportunities to stimulate and nurture their children and that many children are stunted or underweight and are not being provided with nutritious food. Additional follow-up in 2013 will allow for a longer-term assessment of these potential impacts.

Early Childhood Education and Development in Poor Villages of Indonesia •
http://dx.doi.org/10.1596/978-0-8213-9836-4

Figure 3.11 In the Short Run, the Effects of the Project Services Did Not Extend to Parenting Practices or Nutritional Outcomes

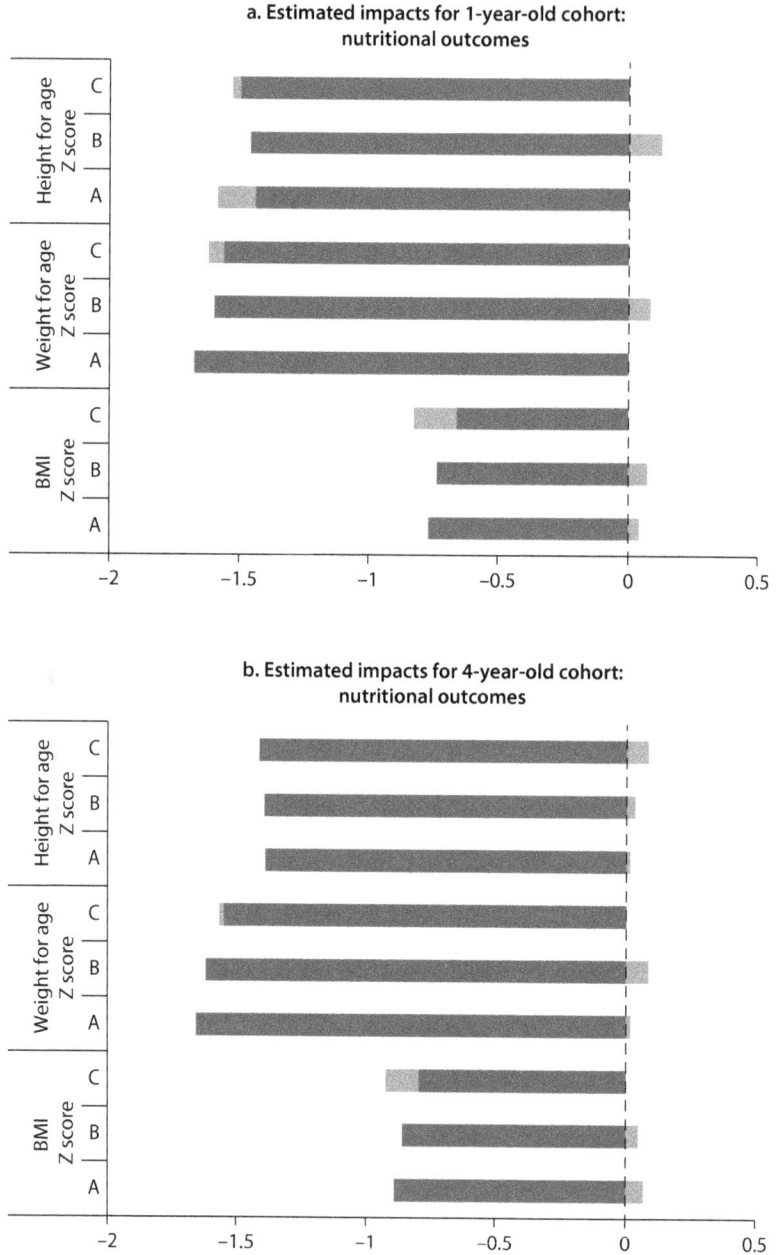

a. Estimated impacts for 1-year-old cohort: nutritional outcomes

b. Estimated impacts for 4-year-old cohort: nutritional outcomes

figure continues next page

Early Childhood Education and Development in Poor Villages of Indonesia ·
http://dx.doi.org/10.1596/978-0-8213-9836-4

Figure 3.11 In the Short Run, the Effects of the Project Services Did Not Extend to Parenting Practices or Nutritional Outcomes (continued)

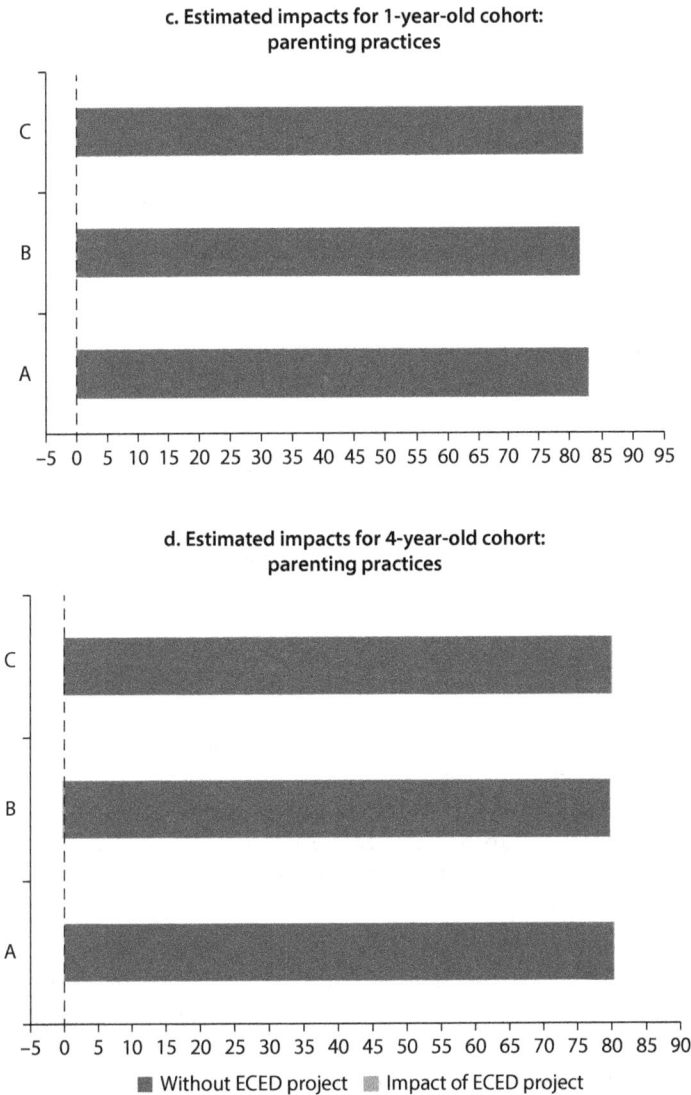

c. Estimated impacts for 1-year-old cohort:
parenting practices

d. Estimated impacts for 4-year-old cohort:
parenting practices

■ Without ECED project ■ Impact of ECED project

Source: Calculations using ECED survey data.
Note: BMI = body mass index; ECED = early childhood education and development.

Looking Ahead: Final Data Collection in 2013

The results presented in this chapter show some signs of positive impacts of expanding the provision of center-based ECED services, especially for children aged 2–4, who are neither too young for the services that most villages provided nor old enough to have access to existing services in their villages.

As we have seen, there are relatively few impacts on most areas of child development for the average child in ECED project villages, as compared to those

Early Childhood Education and Development in Poor Villages of Indonesia •
http://dx.doi.org/10.1596/978-0-8213-9836-4

living in villages not part of this effort. Looking beyond averages, however, there is some indication that the availability of project services had larger effects on children from poorer families, on children who had never enrolled in ECED services before the project services were implemented, and on girls (comparison C).

The next round of data collection, to occur in 2013, will provide additional valuable information, allowing a longer-term assessment of the impact of ECED services on child development, parenting practices, and nutritional status in these poor rural communities. By that time, the youngest group of children will be about 4–5 years old. They are likely to be the group that ultimately shows the greatest benefits from having the project's ECED services in their villages because—as we know now from our midline data—the enrollment tends to increase each year up until age 4. By this age, it will be easier to assess their cognitive development than was the case when they were babies and toddlers. Also, at the time of endline data collection, the older children in our sample will be about 7–8 years old. This is an age at which we can assess how they are doing in school through direct assessments and through their first-grade teachers' use of the EDI as an assessment of school readiness. This kind of information will allow us to see how successful the ECED project has been in meeting its core development objective: to increase school readiness of Indonesian children.

Notes

1. The ECED center operates every week within the academic calendar year. The Ministry of Education and Culture decree (Permendiknas No.58/2009) sets these requirements. If the center has a small space, it can organize two class sessions.

2. There was a group of Batch 2 villages, but they are not part of this evaluation. We used Batch 1 and Batch 3 to try to create the greatest possible contrast between longer and shorter exposure to project-supported services.

3. Appendixes 6 and 7 present tests of internal and external validity also using the Survey of Village Potential (PODES).

4. Comparisons A and B are estimated using a linear regression, correcting for child background characteristics and district fixed effects, and with errors clustered at the village level.

5. We control for caregiver, household, and child characteristics as follows: sex, age, education, health, literacy, and number of children of a caregiver; sex, age, education, literacy, and health of a household head and wealth, neighborhood, marital status, religion, and social integration of a household; sex, health, and age in months of a child. Robust standard errors are clustered at the village level.

6. Where possible, we display the values for both the mean and the impact. When this is not possible, in the interests of clarity we report only the estimated impact. Statistical significance is noted using *s next to each comparison, A, B or C.

7. There are two areas where we observe a statistically significant result for the analysis, which looks at all children living in the village. The first is a negative impact of ECED enrollment at age 1 on various dimensions of child development. The second is a positive effect of ECED enrollment at age 4 on the social competence domain of the EDI.

Bibliography

Brinkman, S., S. Silburn, D. Lawrence, S. Goldfeld, M. Sayers, and F. Oberklaid. 2007. "Investigating the Validity of the Australian Early Development Index." *Early Education and Development* 18 (3): 427–51. doi:10.1080/10409280701610812.

Engle, P. L., M. M. Black, J. R. Behrman, M. Cabral de Mello, P. J. Gertler, L. Kapiriri, R. Martorell, and M. E. Young. 2007. "Strategies to Avoid the Loss of Developmental Potential in More Than 200 Million Children in the Developing World." *The Lancet* 369 (9557): 229–42.

Fukkink, R. G., and A. Lont. 2007. "Does Training Matter? A Meta-Analysis and Review of Caregiver Training Studies." *Early Childhood Research Quarterly* 22 (3): 294–311.

Weiss, H. B., M. Caspe, and E. L. Lopez. 2006. *Family Involvement in Early Childhood Education*. Cambridge, MA: Harvard Family Research Project.

CHAPTER 4

Insights from Indonesia: Implications for Policy and Practice

This chapter identifies insights from new data on Indonesian children's development and from the Early Childhood Education and Development (ECED) project's planning, implementation, and evaluation. It suggests how these insights may inform future ECED initiatives within each of the circles of influence that have framed this book (figure 4.1). We begin by considering how comprehensive background data about young children's development may be used to guide future policies and services. Moving to the influence of families, we consider the data obtained about children's home environments and parenting practices and about the extent to which ECED services may support positive parenting. Next, we look at community supports for children's development, in particular this project's implementation of ECED services through a participatory planning process, again considering the extent to which these services may promote improved development. And, finally, we turn to the broad context of policies, systems, and resources at the national, provincial, and district levels and consider how they may be deployed in the service of young children's development.

Looking Back and Looking Forward

Chapter 4 integrates all of the circles of influence on children's development that have been the focus of the book so far. In this chapter, we look back at the portrait of Indonesian children in poor rural villages, their families, and the ECED services they may or may not have received, highlighting impacts on their development and identifying areas that still need more effective intervention. Looking forward, we examine broader influences—emerging ECED priorities and policies in Indonesia and elsewhere—in light of what has been learned from the data presented in this book (figure 4.2).

The first three chapters have laid out a rationale for early childhood services to promote positive outcomes for children, especially those living in poverty. Data from two cohorts of low-income children between birth and age 6 provided

Figure 4.1 Looking toward the Future of ECED in Indonesia and Beyond

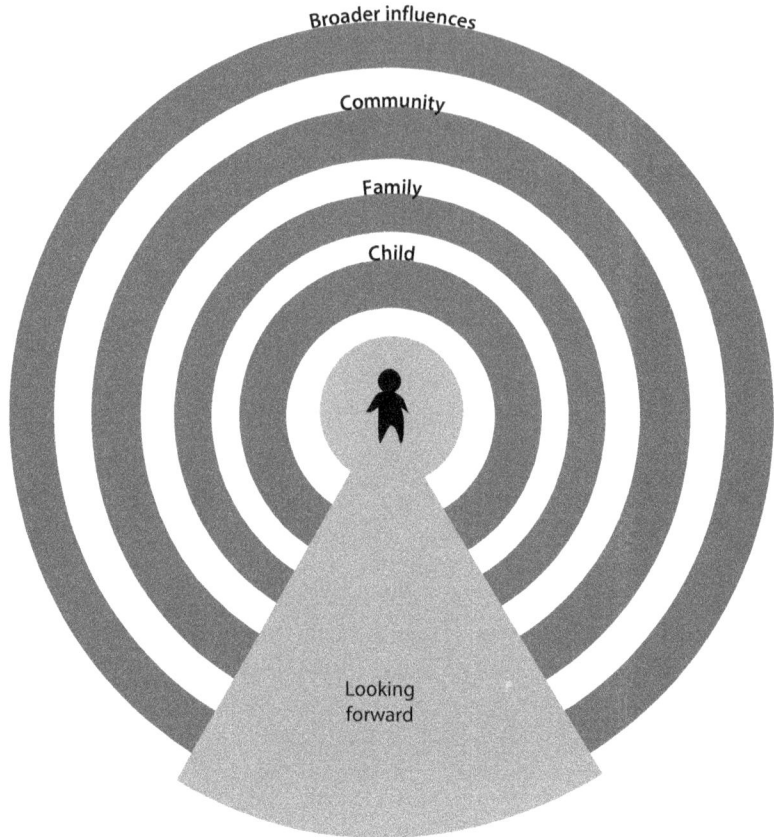

Source: Adapted from Bronfenbrenner 1979.
Note: ECED= early childhood education and development.

a comprehensive picture of development on a range of internationally validated measures. This picture was given further detail with descriptions of the characteristics and parenting practices of the children's families and the extent to which ECED services may be available in their communities.

Against this background, the government of Indonesia and the World Bank designed a project aiming to increase access to ECED services through a community-based approach in 50 districts across 21 provinces, while building ECED capacity at the district and provincial government levels and supporting the development of standards and other features of a sustainable, quality ECED system.

Focusing primarily on the village ECED services, this report described the approach that was adopted and the processes through which these services were implemented in poor rural communities. Midterm results from the impact evaluation of the project showed some gains on some domains of development for some groups of children and revealed lingering challenges on other domains.

Figure 4.2 Milestones for the Future

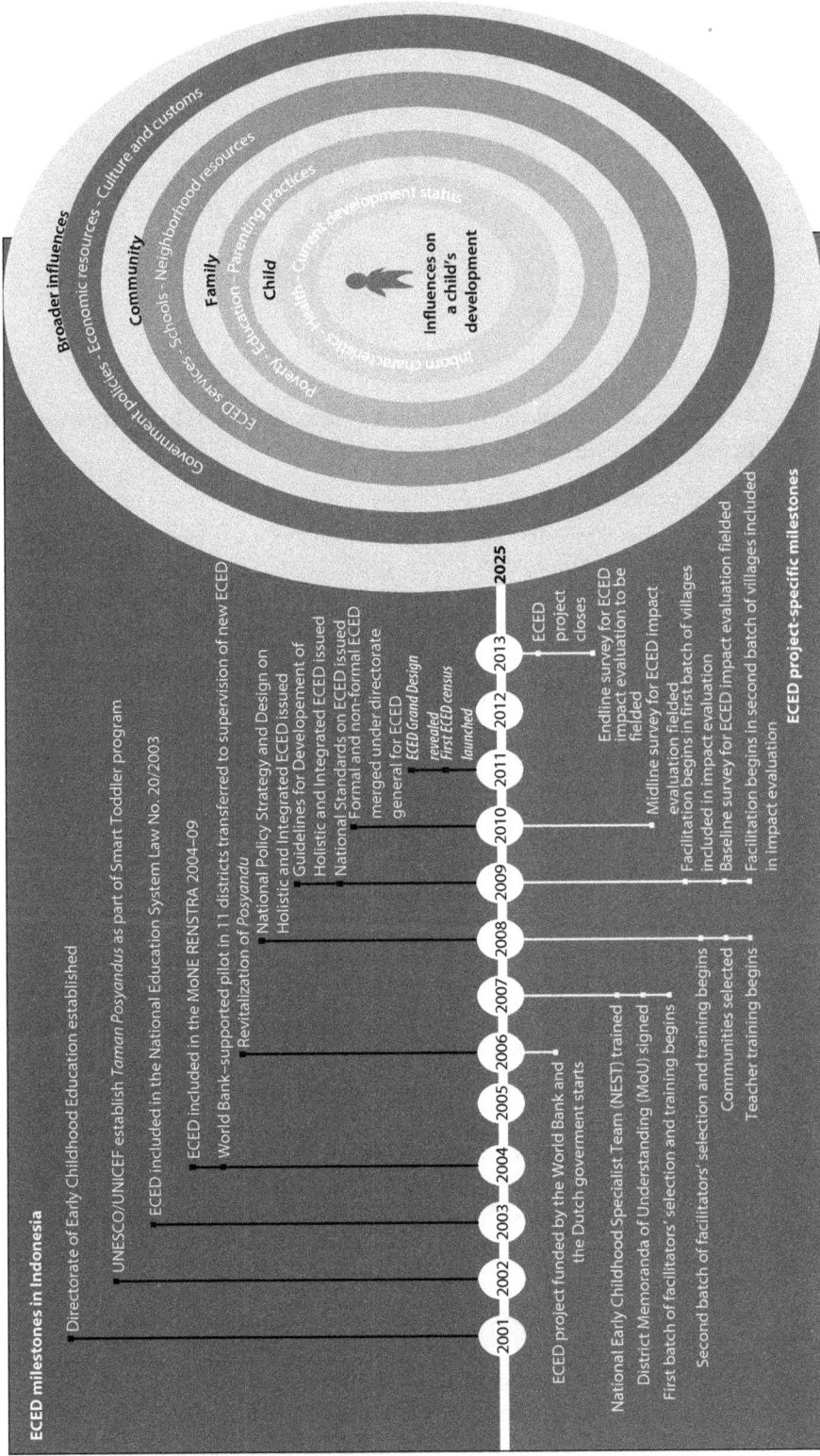

ECED milestones in Indonesia

- Directorate of Early Childhood Education established (2001)
- UNESCO/UNICEF establish *Taman Posyandus* as part of Smart Toddler program (2002)
- ECED included in the National Education System Law No. 20/2003 (2003)
- ECED included in the MoNE RENSTRA 2004–09 (2004)
- World Bank–supported pilot in 11 districts transferred to supervision of new ECED (2006)
- Revitalization of *Posyandu* (2008)
- National Policy Strategy and Design on Holistic and Integrated ECED issued (2009)
- Guidelines for Developement of Holistic and Integrated ECED issued (2010)
- National Standards on ECED issued (2010)
- Formal and non-formal ECED merged under directorate general for ECED (2011)
- *ECED Grand Design revealed* (2011)
- *First ECED census launched* (2012)

ECED project-specific milestones

- ECED project funded by the World Bank and the Dutch goverment starts (2003)
- National Early Childhood Specialist Team (NEST) trained (2004)
- District Memoranda of Understanding (MoU) signed (2006)
- First batch of facilitators' selection and training begins (2007)
- Communities selected (2007)
- Teacher training begins (2007)
- Second batch of facilitators' selection and training begins (2008)
- Baseline survey for ECED impact evaluation fielded (2009)
- Facilitation begins in first batch of villages included in impact evaluation (2009)
- Facilitation begins in second batch of villages included in impact evaluation (2010)
- Midline survey for ECED impact evaluation fielded (2010)
- Endline survey for ECED impact evaluation to be fielded (2012)
- ECED project closes (2013)

Timeline years: 2001 2002 2003 2004 2005 2006 2007 2008 2009 2010 2011 2012 2013 **2025**

Influences on a child's development

- **Child** — inborn characteristics · Health · Current development status
- **Family** — Poverty · Education · Parenting practices
- **Community** — ECED services · Schools · Neighborhood resources
- **Broader influences** — Government policies · Economic resources · Culture and customs

Note: ECED = early childhood education and development; MoNE = Ministry of National Education; UNESCO/UNICEF = United Nations Educational, Scientific, and Cultural Organization/United Nations Children's Fund.

139

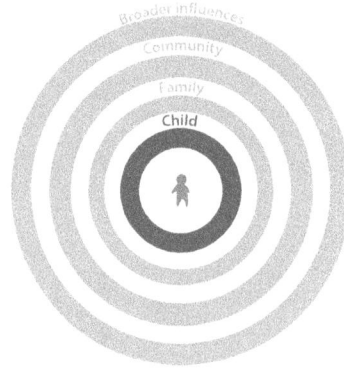

The Influence of Children's Current Characteristics: Insights from Data and Experiences in This Book

Before beginning any early childhood intervention, those who offer it must understand the characteristics, strengths, and needs of the potential beneficiaries. As seen in chapter 2, as part of this project extensive developmental data were collected on a sample of children in two age cohorts from low-income Indonesian villages, before implementing ECED services in some of these villages.

Knowing about children's current strengths—not just their vulnerabilities—can lead to better interventions. As noted in chapter 2, the Early Development Instrument (EDI) goes beyond identifying developmental delays or problems. Instead, it also yields information about children's strengths: domains of early childhood development in which groups of children may have particular competence, in comparison to other domains or in comparison to children in other countries.

In the sample of Indonesian children, for example, the EDI results identified strengths in the social and emotional domain as well as in basic communication and understanding of their everyday environment. Such information, whether in Indonesia or another country, helps us move away from a deficit approach to intervention to one that is based on strengths. If children have strong social skills, teachers can plan many socially interactive activities that will engage children while building competence in areas of developmental vulnerability.

If development is assessed across multiple domains, it is easier to identify areas of vulnerability that may otherwise be missed. Narrowly focused ECED interventions often collect data on only one aspect of development (such as cognitive outcomes). In this project, however, the use of a comprehensive set of assessments provided a wide window into children's development. The results of baseline assessments showed two distinct areas in which children, on average, were not developing well.

First, low-income Indonesian children are doing quite poorly on the EDI domain of language and cognitive development, which includes skills such as counting, identifying letters and words, and showing interest in books. Although these skills and motivational attributes are only one aspect of school readiness, they are important preparation for success in formal education. Knowing that Indonesian children are vulnerable in this dimension of their early development has implications for program planning. It does not suggest the need for teacher-dominated direct instruction in letters and numbers. Rather, programs may be encouraged to adopt playful learning strategies to further emphasize this aspect of development—as was done in the recent Indonesian Sesame Street (*Jalan Sesama*) outreach project—while also encouraging parents to increase their use of book-reading and storytelling. Together, these approaches are likely to improve outcomes in this domain.

Second, in a quite different domain, the assessments identified another area of serious concern: the continued prevalence of moderate to severe levels of stunted growth, confirming national patterns. Given the known relationship between stunted growth and cognitive and academic difficulties, it is possible that the overall high vulnerability scores on the EDI's language and cognitive development domain are related to the high prevalence of stunting in this sample. The implications of the stunting data are that prevention and very early intervention are essential, as catch-up becomes difficult if not impossible after age 2. It may be equally important to include this information in the professional development of teachers in programs for children ages 3–6, so that teachers know about stunting-related developmental difficulties and can learn how to modify curriculum and methods to maximize children's potential.

Together these findings illustrate the value of having background information on the strengths and vulnerabilities of groups that will be the focus of early intervention, using as broad and well-validated a set of measures as possible.

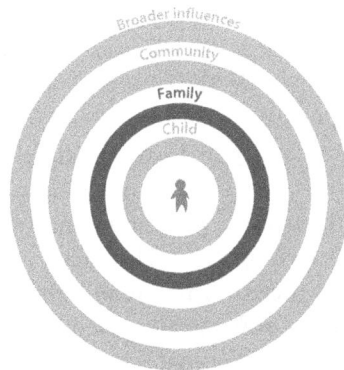

Family Influences: Insights from Data and Experiences in This Book

Accompanying the recognition that the earliest investments in ECED produce the best results—starting at birth if not before—is the recognition that families are in the best position to influence the development of their young children.

For this reason, family-focused ECED has been a theme in many countries' early childhood initiatives. The government of Indonesia has used international research on child development to show that families are indeed children's first teachers and that without strong family involvement in the early years, children may develop long-lasting difficulties with their development and learning. Building from a history of Mothers' Programs and monthly meetings of mothers and children at village health posts, the Early Childhood Directorate has recently given renewed emphasis to family-centered early childhood services.

Data from this project confirm international evidence of the importance of parenting for early development. The regression analyses reported in chapter 2 showed that parents' level of education and their use of positive parenting practices predicted better development for their children, even if their children were not enrolled in an ECED program. The reverse is also true: the lower a mother's education level and the less positive her parenting practices, the lower children's development scores were compared to the scores of other children the same age. These data provide strong justification for making parenting a focus of government policies and programs across ministries and ECED age groups.

Despite concerns about household environments and parenting practices, mothers and other family members in poor villages have strengths that can contribute to intervention. Interest in having ECED services in poor villages was motivated largely by mothers of young children. The mothers attended multiple community meetings, participated in village management teams, and eagerly enrolled their children in services (sometimes even when the child was technically too young or too old to attend). Many mothers accompanied their children to every playgroup session, until gently encouraged by teachers to separate from their children.

Although many of the parents in this sample were very poor, and on average did not generally provide children with a strong foundation for positive development, they possessed considerable individual strengths. Parenting practices, as assessed in this study, had a wide range, with many parents—even those living in great poverty and difficult circumstances—interacting with their children in warm, consistent ways and demonstrating a strong desire to support their children's development. This sincere motivation is a resource that can be tapped into as the government and others increase their efforts in this domain. Instead of a top-down prescription of what parents need to learn in parenting programs, another approach is to acknowledge the interest and motivation of families such as those in the ECED project, engaging them in considering their own needs and building on existing strengths, including parents who are models of "positive deviance" within villages (Save the Children 2004).

Impacts on parenting practices do not happen by chance, but rather require targeted family-focused interventions. At least at the time of the midline evaluation, no evidence was seen of an impact from project-supported

ECED services upon positive parenting practices. This result is not surprising. First, the time frame within which the evaluation was conducted was relatively short. A more likely explanation for the lack of parenting effects is that few of the village ECED programs included a strong emphasis on parent involvement and support, and teachers received little training on parenting issues.

There is some anecdotal evidence that mothers may be informally gaining knowledge of child development and parenting because many of them accompany their children to the ECED centers, where they see teacher-child interactions and converse with teachers and other parents. The recent distribution of block grants from the government to ECED programs to implement parenting services may contribute to more family-focused interventions in the future. For these efforts to be successful, however, more explicit guidance for ECED personnel about effective parenting services and more collaboration with other community providers of parenting services will be needed.

Decisions about the potential focus of future parenting interventions may be informed by research results about families' home environments and parenting practices. Data presented in the book show that in many poor communities parents are not providing many of the essentials of healthy, positive child development. Breastfeeding does not continue as long as recommended for sound nutrition; few parents in this sample read or tell stories to their young children because they do not own books and parents themselves may be illiterate; many children have limited opportunities to play at home or to draw pictures and scribble. This kind of information may help those who are implementing parenting interventions to determine what may be the most urgent areas on which to focus, while keeping in mind the wide range of practices found in the study and, as noted, using parents' sincere desire to help their children as a lever for change. For example, focused parenting sessions can help families extend into their homes what children are learning in ECED centers (Engle et al. 2011).

The data on the prevalence of stunting, combined with household environments data, create urgency about the need for parenting interventions to address risks to children's long-term development. As described in chapter 1, research shows strong connections between prenatal nutritional environments, low birth weight, early feeding practices, and a host of short- and longer-term deficits in health, cognitive development, and social development—including significant vulnerabilities for adult health problems such as heart disease, diabetes, and high blood pressure. Internationally, there is recognition that the first 1,000 days of life are critical to prevent stunting and its related risks. Targeting pregnant women and new parents, programs that provide supportive interactions with knowledgeable community members, especially those that combine an emphasis on nutrition and early stimulation, have the potential to address these risks in Indonesia as they have in other countries (Naudeau 2009).

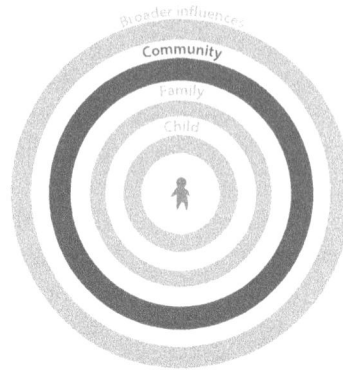

Community Influences and Community-Based ECED Services: Insights from Data and Experiences in This Book

Chapter 1 summarizes international research on the short- and longer-term benefits of ECED services, and subsequent chapters provide emerging evidence from the ECED project in Indonesia. Yet a recurring challenge in every country is the lack of services, especially for children and families living in poverty. Indonesia's investments in ECED are still modest, but it is remarkable that Indonesia has moved from a situation in which only 28 percent of 4- to 6-year-olds were enrolled in ECED services in 2004, to one in which approximately 47 percent are enrolled in 2010. Despite this growth, much still needs to be done to bring ECED services to those most in need. As Indonesia and other countries aim to expand service provision, the findings reported in this book provide encouragement, but also some cautions.

The benefits of ECED enrollment for the poorest children, and those not previously enrolled, suggest the value of targeting future interventions to these subgroups. Several findings presented in earlier chapters underscore the positive effect that participation in ECED services can have, even in the short run, and even if children live in very poor families. Another analysis emphasizes greater benefits for children who have never participated in any kind of ECED program than for other children, when new ECED services become available in the village. These kinds of findings point to the value of targeting the location, outreach, and recruitment of families to those most likely to benefit from enrollment.

There is much to learn from the various enrollment patterns found in this study. For example, it seems that enrollment patterns in Indonesian villages do not necessarily follow government guidelines about what age children should be enrolled in what categories of services. Rather, enrollment patterns are often a function of the alternatives that are available within villages, as well as parental preferences. If a playgroup teacher expects enrollment in her playgroup to be only 2- to 4-year-old children, as government regulations often do, and plans accordingly, then some features of the services offered in her playgroup may not match well with the learning needs of enrolled children who may be as old as 6 and who may need more of the focused literacy and math experiences that many playgroups seem to lack. These issues have implications not only for establishing centers, but also for anticipating what kinds of curriculums and teaching methods may best fit the local enrollment realities.

Well-facilitated community participation in setting up and managing ECED services can be further strengthened by involvement of village leadership. The participatory planning process used in the ECED project helped increase community knowledge of and commitment to ECED as a potential benefit for their children. In many ways, the process worked well. Facilitators' engagement with villages appeared to be a strong feature of the project; those selected for this position were dedicated and often went beyond their specified duties in productive ways. The use of a village management team also seemed to be a strength of project implementation. A formal role for the village head or similar key figure in other cultures would further enhance the visibility and sustainability of new or existing ECED services. Since 2011, district meetings to help project communities develop sustainability plans for their ECED services have for the first time invited village heads to be part of the teams. Their comments were evidence of their eagerness to be more centrally involved than in the past.

In contrast to earlier efforts, in the present ECED project a community mapping process helped locate ECED services in areas of the greatest need. Experiences with the pilot project that immediately preceded this project showed the risks of simply putting new services in any location where land is available. Lessons learned from that project showed a tendency for either under-enrollment—because families of young children could not get to the center—or enrollment primarily of better-off children, if the new services were located in a part of the village not populated by low-income families. In contrast, the present ECED project put less focus on new construction and more emphasis on using convenient spaces such as an existing village health post (*Posyandu*) or extra rooms in a village mosque. In other words, it put the new services where families are already likely to go.

In addition, this ECED project identified and trained teachers locally. It is feasible to identify and prepare people from the villages to be teachers in their own communities, but they need ongoing support. The ECED project had both practical and conceptual reasons to use community members as providers of ECED services. The rural and sometimes remote locations of project villages made it unlikely that teachers would relocate from other areas. But the process also revealed the strengths present in villages, where there was usually no lack of motivated candidates who were respected and endorsed by their fellow villagers. ECED teachers who were part of the fabric of the community seemed better able to perform functions such as connecting informally with families and engaging in outreach services. Some training providers found it difficult to work with trainees whose formal education was limited, but other trainers were able to create a match between training content and methods on the one hand, and the characteristics of the trainees on the other.

Because the initial training of the village teachers was relatively brief, the project aimed to provide continuing supervision with regular program visits from the master trainers, but difficulties related to travel and district budgets resulted in few such visits and an absence of follow-up training. If future ECED interventions aim to make the most of locally available staff, greater emphasis on continuing supervision and support will be needed.

It is difficult for ECED services to meet the developmental needs of children from birth to age 6 if services are delivered only in group- or center-based settings. The ECED project set out to address the needs of children in two age groups: birth to 3 and 3–6. Although facilitators presented villages with a range of service delivery options, for a variety of reasons, more than 90 percent opted to establish center-based or group programs, almost always playgroups. The majority of villages did not have any outreach services that might have provided home visiting or mother-child play-and-learn sessions to impact 0–3 child development through the parents. As a consequence, little attention was given to services for the youngest children in the villages. And as another consequence, there is also evidence that—perhaps given parents' interest in ECED and the absence of services specifically for the youngest children—some mothers of 1- and 2-year-olds may have enrolled their children in playgroups, services that had not been designed for young toddlers and for which teachers had not been well trained.

Posyandu may be the settings best positioned to promote the development of children 0–3, not by providing center-based programs for this age group but by helping mothers and other family caregivers observe and learn about how to promote their children's early development. In planning the project, the prohibition against new construction was intended in part to encourage collaboration with these kinds of existing ECED venues. Trusted in the community, *Posyandu* are promising home bases for ECED service provision that includes babies and toddlers, especially if volunteers receive additional training, if families are given additional resources, and if there are more frequent hours of service.

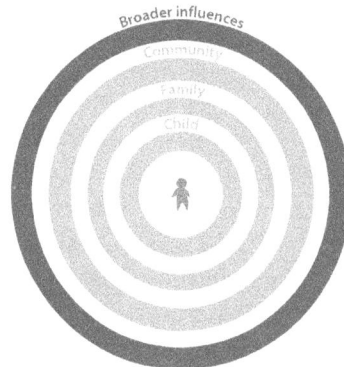

The Broader Influences of Policies, Systems, and Resources: Insights from Data and Experiences in This Book

Improved outcomes for young children will not be sustained by simply establishing a greater number of ECED services. Comprehensive policies, systems, and resources are needed to provide essential supports. In the initial plans for this project, the objective and key components went beyond service provision to address the need for ECED-specific policies, capacity-building efforts, quality assurance systems, and other resources. Although the primary focus of this book is on the evaluation of impact on children's development of the services themselves, a number of insights may be more broadly relevant.

Government commitment to, and institutionalization of, ECED is essential at all levels. Chapter 3 described a process in which districts qualified for participation not only on the basis of poverty, but also on their stated commitment to institutionalizing ECED within their districts. In line with this commitment, 90 percent of the 50 project districts now have a dedicated ECED office within their education departments, and more than 80 percent of districts have explicitly included ECED in their overall strategic planning documents.

The belief was that a basic level of local government capacity was essential, even if it meant that some of the very poorest districts were not able to be included in the project. In the future, the experience gained from implementing this project in only 10 percent of the districts in the country may produce better models and tools to further strengthen the potential of other, even poorer districts to move forward with their own ECED services.

Data on inequalities in children's development across and within districts have implications for targeting services. Analysis of children's EDI vulnerability scores by district shows that even though most children in this sample from poor areas are not developing well in some domains, certain districts have a much higher percentage of vulnerable children than others. Even if the ultimate goal is to have ECED services universally available, the magnitude of that task suggests that priorities—at least initially—might be given to those districts or areas within districts, that seem to have the greatest need for ECED interventions. Another problem is that at present the operational funds that Indonesia is providing in block grants to new ECED centers are not proportionately targeted toward centers that serve the poorest and most developmentally vulnerable children.

To provide services that address all developmental domains and all early childhood ages from birth to 6 requires supportive national policies with a holistic, cross-sectoral emphasis. Chapter 1 summarized international research about the features of ECED interventions that are most likely to produce positive outcomes for poor children and their families (Engle et al. 2007). The consensus is that services in the early years, especially for children at risk for poor development, (1) must include children from birth, or even before birth, to age 6; (2) must attend holistically or comprehensively to all aspects of young children's development—including health and nutrition, education, child protection, and family support; and (3) are best provided in an integrated fashion; that is, either at one site or with strong communication and coordination among service providers from different sectors.

Although the ECED project aimed to establish comprehensive services including education, health and nutrition, and parenting, across the 0–6 age range, in most cases the goals were not realized. Many countries, developed as well as developing, are struggling with how to ensure this kind of cross-sector

ECED in the context of multiple ministries with distinct missions, budgets, and bureaucracies, and often without a history of collaboration. Indonesia is no exception.

Future efforts may produce better outcomes, as Indonesia in 2008 formally established the concept of Holistic Integrated ECD (HI ECD) as a national policy strategy accompanied by guidelines. On the ground, implementation proves difficult. Solutions to facilitate cross-sector ECED in Indonesia or elsewhere are not easily found. Countries and states within the United States have tried various strategies, including establishing a separate cross-sector ECED office within the government but not under one ministry or by directing funds to a coordinating ECED unit. It does seem that coordination and communication are easier at the local than at the national level. Neither top-down nor bottom-up strategies seem completely successful, so perhaps a combination of approaches will best achieve the desired results.

A cost-effective, practical system of supports is needed for current and future ECED personnel. Although implementation of this project showed the benefits of recruiting and training local individuals as ECED personnel, the project's training system would be difficult to sustain and scale up. The initial training, although only 200 hours, was lengthy compared to other, nonproject training in Indonesia, including some models currently being implemented by the government. Project training was costly and required a commitment on the part of future teachers to be in residence at a training center for substantial blocks of time. Once project ECED personnel had received initial training, follow-up training and ongoing coaching/supervision were not part of the project's implementation. Because teachers were usually isolated in their villages, they had few opportunities to exchange knowledge with others beyond their own center or to receive supportive feedback. As the project moves toward its conclusion, the newly merged ECED directorate and the new teacher training directorate have been trying out a variety of innovative approaches, including short internships at exemplary ECED centers, monthly cluster meetings of teachers, and visits to centers by mentor teachers who provide supportive coaching.

As part of a larger effort across higher education, the government of Indonesia has also encouraged ECED teacher preparation programs to develop a common set of standards delineating what competencies graduates should possess and how they will attain them. Standards for ECED teachers were also part of the first-ever ECED standards approved by the National Education Standards Board (BSNP). Those standards go beyond academic credentials to describe professional and personal competencies that should be possessed by anyone who works with young children.

Anecdotally, the training provided in the ECED project was well received and, for some participants, transformational, because many had never experienced the kind of interactive, hands-on methods that were used. But the quality of the project's professional development and its influence on teachers' classroom practices were not evaluated, even though quality assurance systems for ECED are critical at all levels.

The benefits of having evaluation results are great, as the results can inform improvements to training designs and help explain variations in outcomes. But, except for basic annual monitoring, no system was in place to assess the quality of teachers' implementation of practices they had learned in training sessions. With national standards for ECED now in place, including standards for teachers, curriculum, and teaching practices, systematic approaches to quality assessment seem an essential next step. Such information would also help researchers better understand the presence or absence of positive child development outcomes as a result of the services that are provided. Assessment of classroom quality is planned for the endline evaluation in 2013; the results may inform future quality assurance efforts as the government scales up ECED services and teacher training systems.

Program evaluation designs need to be sensitive to program implementation realities. Based on the experiences documented in chapter 3, designs that are robust and immune to foreseeable changes in project implementation timelines are preferable to designs that are easily compromised by routine changes in implementation timelines. In hindsight, a simpler and more practical evaluation design could have taken advantage of the government's existing district and village selection mechanisms. These mechanisms relied on scores to determine whether a district or village was eligible for participation. These scores could have been used to evaluate the project instead of randomization.

Once agreed upon, designs must be adhered to if evaluation results are to be meaningful. A related lesson is that once an evaluation design has been agreed upon, project implementation should adhere to the design to ensure the quality of the evaluation. The point is a general one, but in the specific case of ECED interventions, how long a child was exposed to a particular intervention and how old the child was when the intervention started has significant consequences for the evaluation of results.

Conclusion

The evidence presented in this book reinforces that multiple influences affect children's development in the first years of life. Family poverty is an important mediator of the influence of community resources and children's innate abilities. Increased access to early childhood services can have positive effects on development outcomes, even in the short run. These services can buffer the effects of home environments that are not sufficiently stimulating and can encourage parents to increase their use of practices that will promote their children's development.

Policy makers and practitioners in Indonesia and countries around the world have made important progress in understanding the importance of these strong foundations for later success. As the next generation of development goals are considered, early childhood education and development is sure to be a central focus. Continued emphasis is needed on sustainable financing and ensuring quality as governments pursue agendas focused on the expansion of ECED services.

Bibliography

Bronfenbrenner, U. 1979. *The Ecology of Human Development*. Cambridge, MA: Harvard University Press.

Engle, P. L., M. M. Black, J. R. Behrman, M. Cabral de Mello, P. J. Gertler, L. Kapiriri, R. Martorell, and M. E. Young. 2007. Strategies to Avoid the Loss of Developmental Potential in More than 200 million Children in the Developing World. *The Lancet* 369 (9557): 229–42.

Engle, P. L., L. C. H. Fernald, H. Alderman, J. R. Behrman, C. O'Gara, A. Yousafzai, N. Ulkuer, I. Ertem, and S. Iltus. 2011. "Strategies for Reducing Inequalities and Improving Developmental Outcomes for Young Children in Low-income and Middle-income Countries." *The Lancet* 378 (9799): 1339–53.

Naudeau, S. 2009. "Supplementing Nutrition in the Early Years: The Role of Early Childhood Stimulation to Maximize Nutritional Inputs." *Children and Youth* 3 (1).

Save the Children U.S. 2004. "Positive Deviance: A Community Based Approach to Solving Community Problems." (Written in Bahasa Indonesia and English.) *Positive Deviance Bulletin* 1 (2) April.

Data Sources and Their Representativeness

To provide a complete picture of the opportunities for early child development in Indonesia, this book relies on a number of different data sources. Each source comes with its own scope of geographic coverage and degree of representativeness.

International Databases

World Bank Databases

The World Development Indicators (WDI) database is the World Bank's primary collection of development indicators. Compiled from officially recognized international sources, WDI aims to provide internationally comparable statistics about development and the quality of people's lives around the globe. These databases provide national data on 214 economies and are updated four times each year.

Nationally Representative Databases

Potensi Desa (PODES)

The Survey of Village Potential (PODES) provides information about village (*desa*) characteristics for all of Indonesia, with approximately 78,000 villages included in the most recent round. It is typically fielded in November, and since 2005 data have been available every 3 years. This study utilizes information from the 2003, 2005, 2008, and 2011 rounds of the PODES. Data are representative at the level of the village.

SUSENAS

The National Socioeconomic Household Survey (SUSENAS) is a large-scale multipurpose socioeconomic survey. Since 1993, SUSENAS have covered a nationally representative sample typically composed of 200,000 households. This book utilizes information from the 2004, 2007, 2009, and 2010 July rounds of the SUSENAS. The July rounds are representative at the level of the district.

PAUD (ECED) Census

Pendidikan Anak Usia Dini (PAUD) stands for education of children at an early age. Indonesia's first PAUD census was fielded in 2011 and collects information from all villages where Early Childhood Education And Development (ECED) services are offered. Often, a center may offer different types of ECED services, so that there are roughly 140,000 services offered at 100,000 centers across the country. Data allow for an analysis of the types of early childhood services offered in the country and include information on physical infrastructure and teacher qualifications. Data are meant to cover all villages with an ECED service, currently 90 percent of all Indonesian villages. The data available for this study are partial and preliminary as the census is ongoing.

Project Databases

Monitoring and Evaluation Data of the ECED Project

As part of the monitoring and evaluation (M and E) of the ECED project described in this book, since 2009 the World Bank has annually collected data on student enrollment, teachers, and facilities. The data cover the 6,000 project centers located in 3,000 villages across 50 districts. High poverty rates and low enrollment rates among children from birth to 6 years of age were among the criteria for including these districts in the project. The most recent available household survey (SUSENAS 2010) covers 497 districts in Indonesia. The most recent village census (PODES 2011) covers 9,900 villages in the 50 project districts. As such, the project M and E data cover roughly 10 percent of all districts in Indonesia and 30 percent of all villages within them.

Survey Data Collected for Impact Evaluation of the ECED Project

A sample of 310 villages was selected for the impact evaluation of the project; 217 of these villages participate in a randomized impact evaluation and receive the project over time. The remaining 93 villages have not received the project. Two rounds of data were collected from these villages in 2009 and in 2010.

The survey data collected include in-depth household surveys; interviews with village leaders, service providers, and caregivers; and assessment and observation of child development. Because the focus of the project was children up to the age of six, two cohorts of children have been followed since 2009. These cohorts were of children aged 1 and 4 years old in 2009. Approximately 3,000 1-year-olds and 3,000 4-year-olds were studied. These children reside in the 310 villages included in the impact evaluation of the project. It is for these children that we provide in-depth analyses on child development outcomes in chapters 2 and 3.

The Influence of Parenting Practices and ECED Involvement on Developmental Outcomes

Table A2.1 Influence of Parenting Practices and ECED Involvement in the Previous Month on Child Development Outcomes for 4-Year-Olds

	With no other controls		With all other controls	
	Parenting practices (1)	ECED involvement (2)	Parenting practices (3)	ECED involvement (4)
Early Development Instrument (EDI)				
Physical health and well-being	0.094***	0.014	0.103***	0.004
	(0.003)	(0.043)	(0.020)	(0.018)
Social competence	0.351***	0.297***	0.233***	0.193***
	(0.003)	(0.050)	(0.019)	(0.015)
Emotional maturity	0.302***	0.089***	0.278***	0.018
	(0.004)	(0.059)	(0.020)	(0.016)
Language and cognitive development	0.241***	0.286***	0.114***	0.183***
	(0.005)	(0.081)	(0.018)	(0.016)
Communication and general knowledge	0.138***	0.058**	0.113***	0.030*
	(0.003)	(0.043)	(0.021)	(0.016)
Strengths and Difficulties Questionnaire (SDQ)				
Emotional symptoms (−)	−0.188***	−0.079***	−0.147***	−0.0001
	(0.005)	(0.080)	(0.020)	(0.017)
Conduct problems (−)	−0.291***	−0.054***	−0.299***	0.009
	(0.004)	(0.074)	(0.020)	(0.016)
Hyperactivity/Inattention (−)	−0.169***	−0.083***	−0.148***	−0.039**
	(0.003)	(0.053)	(0.021)	(0.017)
Peer problems(−)	−0.172***	−0.083	−0.157***	−0.032**
	(0.004)	(0.059)	(0.020)	(0.016)
Prosocial behavior (reversed)	−0.311***	−0.089***	−0.239***	−0.061***
	(0.005)	(0.071)	(0.020)	(0.016)

table continues next page

Table A2.1 Influence of Parenting Practices and ECED Involvement in the Previous Month on Child Development Outcomes for 4-Year-Olds (continued)

	With no other controls		With all other controls	
	Parenting practices (1)	ECED involvement (2)	Parenting practices (3)	ECED involvement (4)
Total difficulties (−)	−0.314***	−0.110***	−0.289***	−0.018
	(0.010)	(0.176)	(0.019)	(0.015)
Other task measures				
Gross motor	0.047**	0.022	0.046**	0.030*
	(0.001)	(0.015)	(0.021)	(0.017)
Fine motor	0.025	0.050***	0.011	0.064***
	(0.001)	(0.011)	(0.019)	(0.017)
Language	0.007	0.084***	0.039**	0.072***
	(0.011)	(0.166)	(0.019)	(0.015)
Draw human	0.056***	0.093***	0.034*	0.064***
	(0.015)	(0.233)	(0.020)	(0.017)
Draw house	0.029	0.103***	−0.033	0.050***
	(0.009)	(0.152)	(0.020)	(0.018)
Executive function (DCCS card sort)	0.093***	0.124***	0.058***	0.087***
	(0.002)	(0.028)	(0.022)	(0.019)

Source: Calculations using ECED survey data.

Note: ECED = early childhood education and development. Beta values are shown with standard errors in parentheses. Each row represents the results of a separate regression. Each cell corresponds to a standardized coefficient on the variable in question. Columns 1 and 2 contain the results of regressions with only the indicated variable included. Columns 3 and 4 show the results from regressions where all other controls are included. The other controls are the child's sex, age, weight, and height; the household size; the highest education level completed by the mother; and household wealth.

* = 10 percent, ** = 5 percent, *** = 1 percent.

Table A2.2 Influence of Parenting Practices and ECED Involvement in the Previous Month on Child Development Outcomes for 1-Year-Olds

	With no other controls		With all other controls	
	Parenting practices (1)	ECED involvement (2)	Parenting practices (3)	ECED involvement (4)
Child tasks				
Language tasks	0.049***	0.058***	0.062***	0.121***
	(0.004)	(0.139)	(0.018)	(0.034)
Cognitive tasks	0.077***	0.054***	0.044**	0.048
	(0.004)	(0.135)	(0.020)	(0.037)
Gross motor tasks	0.020	0.048***	0.018	0.070**
	(0.011)	(0.367)	(0.018)	(0.035)
Fine motor tasks	0.073***	0.045***	0.047**	0.096***
	(0.006)	(0.216)	(0.020)	(0.036)
Socio-emotional tasks	−0.001	−0.049**	0.013	0.007
	(0.001)	(0.059)	(0.022)	(0.045)
Mother-rated child skills				
Receptive language skills	0.076***	0.048***	0.046**	0.074**
	(0.002)	(0.055)	(0.022)	(0.031)
Socio-emotional skills	0.135***	0.056***	0.114***	0.019
	(0.003)	(0.092)	(0.024)	(0.044)
Cognitive skills	0.081***	−0.003	0.062***	−0.015
	(0.002)	(0.069)	(0.021)	(0.042)

Source: Calculations using ECED survey data.
Note: ECED = early childhood education and development. Beta values are shown with standard errors in parentheses. Each row represents the results of a separate regression. Each cell corresponds to a standardized coefficient on the variable in question. Columns 1 and 2 contain the results of regressions with only the indicated variable included. Columns 3 and 4 show the results from regressions where all other controls are included. The other controls are the child's sex, age, weight, and height; the household size; the highest education level completed by the mother; and household wealth.
* = 10 percent, ** = 5 percent, *** = 1 percent.

APPENDIX 3

The Districts: Selecting and Gaining Commitment

District Selection Process

In selecting participating districts, two main considerations were observed, in line with the Project Development Objective: poverty and commitment to sustain the program.

In 2005, 111 districts were identified using a Poverty and Human Development Index developed by the Agency for National Development Planning Board (BAPPENAS), as being eligible to participate in the project. Considering the limited budget, the number of target districts was narrowed down using the following criteria: (1) district's commitment to Early Childhood Education and Development (ECED) programs; (2) district agreement on implementation arrangements and management procedures; and (3) districts with the poorest subdistricts (*kecamatan*).

District commitment is defined as current and future capacity to assign ECED responsibilities to existing staff or willingness to add staff, willingness to provide matching funds for teacher salaries (either at the beginning or in the 4th of the 5 years), willingness to supervise programs (monitoring and reporting functions), and willingness to be trained in ECED and the performance-based grants manual. The eligible districts were invited to a national workshop to receive this information.

In January 2006, 60 districts meeting the above criteria were invited to send their formal letter of commitment. In October 2006, 50 districts were selected, and the minister of National Education officially issued the decree to allow these districts to start allocating their local budget to support the program.

This commitment was formalized in the memorandum of understanding (MoU), signed by the director general of Non-Formal and Informal Education and the head of local government during an official ceremony hosted by the ministry.

Figure A3.1 District Selection Score

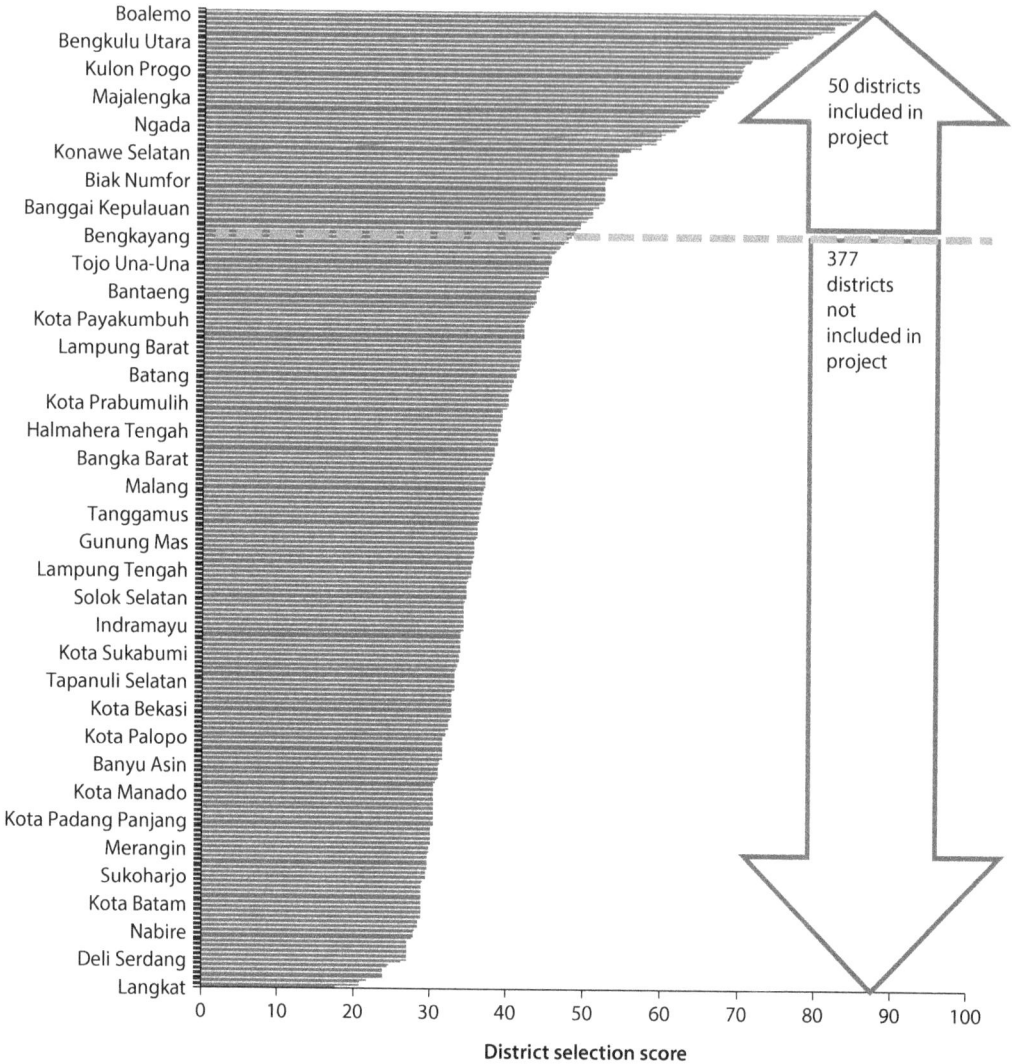

Lessons Learned and Recommendations

During the implementation, many district leaders were replaced through local elections, as were the local education staff. The existence of the formal MoU has proven to be a powerful instrument to track district compliance on the commitment with the new local administrators. Of particular importance is the establishment of a dedicated ECED unit in the local education structure, which allows for continued attention to technical issues to strengthen the districts' ECED agenda.

Table A3.1 Districts Included in the Project

No.	Province	District (Kabupaten)
1	Nanggroë Aceh Darussalam	Aceh Tenggara
2	Nanggroë Aceh Darussalam	Aceh Tengah
3	Sumut	Toba Samosir
4	Sumut	Tapanuli Tengah
5	Sumbar	Solok
6	Sumbar	Sawahlunto/Sijunjung
7	Sumbar	Pesisir Selatan
8	Jambi	Tanjung Jabung Timur
9	Jambi	Sarolangun
10	Sumsel	Ogan Komering Ilir
11	Bengkulu	Bengkulu Utara
12	Bengkulu	Bengkulu Selatan
13	Lampung	Lampung Timur
14	Lampung	Lampung Selatan
15	Jabar	Sumedang
16	Jabar	Sukabumi
17	Jabar	Subang
18	Jabar	Majalengka
19	Jabar	Garut
20	Kalbar	Sambas
21	Kalbar	Ketapang
22	Jateng	Wonogiri
23	Jateng	Rembang
24	Jateng	Cilacap
25	Jateng	Banjarnegara
26	Daerah Istimewa Yogyakarta	Kulon Progo
27	Daerah Istimewa Yogyakarta	Gunung Kidul
28	Jatim	Pacitan
29	Jatim	Madiun
30	Jatim	Bondowoso
31	Nusa Tenggara Barat	Sumbawa
32	Nusa Tenggara Barat	Lombok Tengah
33	Nusa Tenggara Barat	Dompu
34	Nusa Tenggara Timur	Timor Tengah Utara
35	Nusa Tenggara Timur	Sumba Barat
36	Sulut	Kepulauan Talaud
37	Sulut	Kepulauan Sangihe
38	Sulbar	Polewali Mandar
39	Sulbar	Mamuju
40	Sulsel	Wajo
41	Sulsel	Sinjai
42	Sulsel	Sidenreng Rappang
43	Sulsel	Jeneponto
44	Gorontalo	Gorontalo

table continues next page

Early Childhood Education and Development in Poor Villages of Indonesia •
http://dx.doi.org/10.1596/978-0-8213-9836-4

Table A3.1 Districts Included in the Project *(continued)*

No.	Province	District (Kabupaten)
45	Gorontalo	Boalemo
46	Malut	Halmahera Utara
47	Malut	Halmahera Selatan
48	Irjabar	Manokwari
49	Papua	Merauke
50	Papua	Jayapura

Village Scoring Indicators

Table A4.1 Weights Assigned to Village Scoring Indicators

Indicators	Value	Data source
Poverty index	42	Using statistics released by BPS (Bureau of Statistics) and PODES (Survey of Village Potential), village statistics issued by district statistic office
0–6 child population	39	Data generated from responsible district offices (population office, district development planning agency, statitistics bureau)
Total village population	9	Using statistics released by BPS
Community contribution	10	Includes expression of community interest (letters from village head, *Kepala Desa*), budget share to support the program (usually 2 percent of the total US$9,000 grants), as well as other types of community participation (labor, in-kind)

Table A4.2 Village Scoring Example

Village	Poverty rate		Young children		Population		Contributions		Total score	Ranking
Weight	42		39		9		10			
	Percent poor	Score	Number	Score	Number	Score	Number	Score	score	Ranking
[1]	[2]	[3]	[4]	[5]	[6]	[7]	[8]	[9]	[10]	[11]
Village A	12	16.8	300	29.3	5,000	4.5	1,000	5.0	55.6	6
Village B	16	22.4	275	26.8	7,500	6.8	2,000	10.0	66.0	5
Village C	22	30.8	400	39.0	10,000	9.0	1,000	5.0	83.8	1
Village D	21	29.4	350	34.1	5,000	4.5	900	4.5	72.5	4
Village E	18	25.2	375	36.6	10,000	9.0	800	4.0	74.8	3
Village F	30	42.0	250	24.4	7,500	6.8	1,200	6.0	79.1	2
Maximum score on the village long-list	30		400		10,000		2,000			

Formula:
[3] = [2]/(maximum % poor)*(poverty rate weight)
[5] = [4]/(maximum number of young children 0–6)*(young children weight)
[7] = [6]/(maximum population)*(population weight)
[9] = [8]/(maximum contribution)*(contribution weight)
[10] = [3] + [5] + [7] + [9]

Selecting Community Facilitators

Community facilitation was conducted by a team of village facilitators, consisting of four personnel (two from a community development background, one from an education background, and one from a health background). Each team was responsible for facilitating one batch, consisting of 20 villages. Each district had three batches of project-supported villages, allowing disbursement to be made in phases and allowing for facilitators to be properly trained and mobilized. The preferred qualifications and requirements for facilitators were bachelor degrees with some practical experience in community development.

The majority of the facilitators hired by the district were local residents for whom the project added to their knowledge and experience in local language, cultural, and community patterns, which were critical during project field execution. These facilitators were competitively selected by the District Education Office and intensively trained by a national team of community development specialists. Their 500 hours of intensive training included development of skills in community facilitation, participatory planning practical knowledge about early childhood education and development, and on-the-job experience in a real project village. Those who successfully completed the training were contracted by the central project implementing unit (Ministry of Education and Culture) for 3 years, starting in August 2008. This arrangement allowed for the preconditioning stage to start immediately and allowed the first payment or tranche of community block grants to be disbursed by the end of 2008, with village services beginning in early 2009.

APPENDIX 6

Participatory Planning Activities

Table A6.1 Planning Activities in Detail

Participatory activities	Information collected, decisions made
1. Focus group discussions	Parents' and communities' knowledge of early childhood education and development (ECED) Child rearing practices Local child development profile and history Venn diagram to indicate advantages of the program linked to different village sectors Seasonal calendar to indicate social and livelihood patterns Village social mapping to identify wealth classification, locations of public services, facilities, and other resources that can potentially support or disrupt ECED
2. Transect walk	Direct geographical observation Developing communities' awareness of potential child distribution and existing children's services, so that they could decide where they wanted to locate project services
3. Village meeting	To select speaker representatives to lead meetings To agree on the results of focus group discussion activities and transect walk, To clarify what was to be included in initial proposals: types of services, service location, duration and frequency, parents' contribution, supplementary feeding, health program, training program
4. Village plenum 1	To agree and decide what items were to be included in the proposal To elect members of an activities management team (a leader, a treasurer and a secretary) who were responsible for managing the block grant To elect village representatives who were able to serve as teachers and child development workers. Election was made transparently based on a set of criteria (among others, experience and skills appropriate for respective positions and dedication and commitment to early childhood education and development
5. Grant proposal writing	Facilitators assisted the newly selected village management team in developing and preparing a community proposal with budget estimates for 3-year implementation and in conducting price surveys
6. Village plenum 2	Activities management team (TPK) with village representatives agreed and approved their community grant proposal. Village head signed the proposal

APPENDIX 7

Tests of Evaluation Design

$$Y_{ij} = \beta_0 + \beta_1 I[Batch_2]_i + \beta_2 I[Batch_3]_i + \beta_3 I[Batch_5]_i + \sum_{k=2}^{9} \beta_k District_j + \varepsilon_{ij} \quad (1)$$

We test whether villages in Batches 2, 3 (control groups) and 5 (comparison group) are statistically different from those in Batch 1 (treatment group).

Each outcome that we test falls into one of five categories:

1. Environment
2. Population
3. Poverty
4. Service availability
5. Distance

Table A7.1 shows results from regression (1). The vast majority of estimated coefficients are not statistically significantly different from 0, indicating that the randomization worked well.

Table A7.1 Tests of Evaluation Design

Label	Batch 2 Coefficient	Batch 2 P-value	Batch 3 Coefficient	Batch 3 P-value	Batch 5 Coefficient	Batch 5 P-value	Constant Coefficient	Constant P-value	N
Distance									
Distance to hospitals	−3.408	0.177	−6.348	0.042	−4.350	0.192	17.418	0.000	295
Distance to maternity hospitals	−3.144	0.235	−5.291	0.093	−1.037	0.760	15.659	0.000	289
Distance to pharmacy (km)	−5.611	0.048	−6.230	0.050	−5.393	0.113	14.253	0.000	286
Distance to polyclinic (km)	0.456	0.855	1.605	0.634	2.833	0.399	9.849	0.000	280
Distance to drug store (km)	−5.208	0.055	−4.983	0.098	−4.717	0.148	15.229	0.000	272

table continues next page

Early Childhood Education and Development in Poor Villages of Indonesia ·
http://dx.doi.org/10.1596/978-0-8213-9836-4

Table A7.1 **Tests of Evaluation Design** (continued)

Label	Batch 2		Batch 3		Batch 5		Constant		N
	Coefficient	P-value	Coefficient	P-value	Coefficient	P-value	Coefficient	P-value	
Environment									
Natural disaster ever occurred in the past 3 years	−0.119	0.314	0.022	0.733	0.061	0.339	0.319	0.000	299
Fire disaster ever occurred in the past 3 years	0.011	0.100	0.021	0.145	0.010	0.359	−0.011	0.100	299
Epidemic ever occurred in the past 3 years	−0.025	0.823	−0.068	0.263	0.011	0.863	0.225	0.001	299
Cooking fuel: kerosene	0.193	0.103	0.007	0.903	−0.048	0.356	0.107	0.052	299
Population									
Number of population	−775.885	0.652	−664.805	0.332	−790.566	0.167	9,053.035	0.000	299
Number of families	143.924	0.529	26.434	0.736	−68.766	0.315	2,300.326	0.000	298
Number of families having electricity using PLN	220.253	0.435	7.980	0.927	−45.396	0.514	1,874.647	0.000	296
Number of families having electricity using non-PLN	37.092	0.545	−7.878	0.490	−4.785	0.628	37.408	0.020	296
Poverty									
Cooking fuel: wood	−0.204	0.085	−0.017	0.759	0.015	0.774	0.904	0.000	299
Family toilet: none	0.025	0.845	−0.020	0.749	−0.034	0.586	0.675	0.000	299
Waste disposal method: burning	0.007	0.957	0.088	0.156	0.061	0.348	0.493	0.000	299
Waste disposal method: other	−0.093	0.495	−0.102	0.061	−0.059	0.304	0.493	0.000	299
Family toilet: own	0.032	0.800	0.010	0.870	0.041	0.520	0.268	0.000	299
Number of family without electricity	−117.393	0.278	34.266	0.387	−14.422	0.654	392.243	0.000	295
Service availability									
Number of hospitals available in the village	−0.017	0.363	−0.000	0.987	0.013	0.508	0.017	0.363	299
Number of maternity hospitals available in the village	0.017	0.381	0.000	0.992	−0.013	0.631	1.983	0.000	299
Number of midwife facilities in the village	0.277	0.034	0.043	0.526	0.048	0.454	0.173	0.008	299
Number of senior secondary schools: public	0.066	0.620	0.002	0.976	−0.076	0.328	0.234	0.004	299

table continues next page

Table A7.1 Tests of Evaluation Design (continued)

Label	Batch 2		Batch 3		Batch 5		Constant		N
	Coefficient	P-value	Coefficient	P-value	Coefficient	P-value	Coefficient	P-value	
Number of senior secondary schools: private	0.235	0.543	0.085	0.476	0.055	0.628	1.115	0.000	299
Number of polyclinics available in the village	−0.092	0.039	−0.019	0.612	−0.024	0.496	0.092	0.039	299
Number of puskesmas facilities in the village	0.160	0.184	0.009	0.853	−0.020	0.680	0.140	0.018	299
Number of puskesmas pembantu facilities in the village	−0.045	0.721	0.001	0.987	−0.028	0.690	0.745	0.000	299
Number of doctor practice facilities in the village	0.254	0.055	0.017	0.753	−0.014	0.788	0.196	0.004	299
Number of pusat kesehatan desa in the village	−0.025	0.856	0.012	0.844	0.101	0.112	0.475	0.000	299
Number of polindes facilities in the village	−0.016	0.908	−0.048	0.467	−0.083	0.223	0.416	0.000	299
Number of pharmacy facilities in the village	−0.015	0.814	−0.031	0.351	−0.062	0.026	0.065	0.097	299
Number of drug store facilities in the village	0.055	0.306	0.009	0.820	0.008	0.842	−0.005	0.800	299
Number of primary school: public	0.785	0.189	0.019	0.921	−0.211	0.261	4.715	0.000	297
Number of kindergartens: private	−0.101	0.811	0.282	0.149	−0.079	0.643	2.259	0.000	275
Number of untrained traditional midwife (person) in the village	−0.872	0.605	0.132	0.756	0.880	0.185	9.322	0.000	275
Number of mantri kesehatan (person) in the village	0.342	0.301	0.220	0.269	0.123	0.521	1.221	0.000	265

Source: Calculations using PODES 2008.
Note: PLN = *Perusahaan Listrik Negara* (State Electricity Company) Sample is limited to the approximately 300 villages that are part of the impact evaluation study. District dummies are included. Reference category is Batch 1 villages. Minimum number of villages included = 265.

APPENDIX 8

Tests of Internal Validity

$$Y_{ij} = \beta_0 + \beta_1 I[Survey]_i + \sum_{k=2}^{49} \beta_k District_j + \varepsilon_{ij} \qquad (2)$$

Table A8.1 shows the results from regression (2).

Table A8.1 Tests of Internal Validity Including District Fixed Effects

Label	Survey Coefficient	Survey P-value	Constant Coefficient	Constant P-value	N
Distance					
Distance to drug store (km)	1.158	0.620	76.714	0.000	2,599
Distance to pharmacy (km)	−2.629	0.283	79.301	0.000	2,752
Distance to doctor practice (km)	−1.346	0.466	77.544	0.000	2,479
Distance to hospital	−2.878	0.232	73.382	0.000	2,843
Distance to market (km)	−0.709	0.741	60.254	0.000	2,205
Distance to maternity hospital	−2.956	0.231	75.328	0.000	2,838
Distance to polyclinic (km)	−2.865	0.250	76.499	0.000	2,677
Distance to praktek midwife (km)	−5.207	0.095	60.687	0.000	1,583
Distance to praktek polindes (km)	3.648	0.353	84.292	0.000	1,778
Distance to pusat kesehatan desa (km)	3.447	0.363	79.074	0.000	2,463
Distance to puskesmas (km)	−0.583	0.672	34.155	0.000	2,440
Distance to puskesmas pembantu (km)	−1.273	0.463	35.364	0.000	1,561
Environment					
Natural disaster ever occurred in the past 3 years	−0.062	0.148	0.037	0.080	2,872
Fire disaster ever occurred in the past 3 years	−0.005	0.712	0.024	0.156	2,872
Epidemic ever occurred in the past 3 years	−0.006	0.890	0.500	0.000	2,872
Cooking fuel: kerosene	−0.039	0.321	0.232	0.000	2,872
Population					
Number of families	−37.797	0.412	383.390	0.000	2,871
Number of population	−90.972	0.617	1,567.463	0.000	2,872
Number of families having electricity using PLN	−44.992	0.301	357.629	0.000	2,776
Number of families having electricity using non-PLN	−7.739	0.261	34.613	0.000	2,754

table continues next page

Table A8.1 Tests of Internal Validity Including District Fixed Effects (continued)

Label	Survey Coefficient	Survey P-value	Constant Coefficient	Constant P-value	N
Poverty					
Number of families without electricity	5.761	0.727	68.677	0.000	2,747
Cooking fuel: wood	0.045	0.255	0.768	0.000	2,872
Family toilet: none	−0.045	0.283	0.207	0.000	2,872
Waste disposal method: burning	0.049	0.221	0.866	0.000	2,872
Waste disposal method: other	−0.033	0.323	0.098	0.003	2,872
Family toilet: own	0.061	0.168	0.720	0.000	2,872
Service availability					
Number of doctor practice facilities in the village	−0.019	0.613	0.049	0.042	2,872
Number of drug store facilities in the village	−0.006	0.853	0.146	0.000	2,872
Number of hospitals available in the village	−0.004	0.681	0.037	0.080	2,872
Number of junior secondary schools: private	−0.033	0.655	0.857	0.000	1,820
Number of junior secondary schools: public	−0.012	0.858	0.920	0.000	1,975
Number of kindergartens: private	−0.192	0.144	1.297	0.000	2,267
Number of kindergartens: public	0.012	0.647	0.111	0.297	1,629
Number of mantri kesehatan (person) in the village	0.049	0.740	2.318	0.000	2,417
Number of maternity hospitals available in the village	0.001	0.965	1.976	0.000	2,872
Number of midwife (person) in the village	−0.337	0.107	3.080	0.000	1,913
Number of midwife facilities in the village	−0.027	0.570	0.134	0.000	2,872
Number of pharmacy facilities in the village	0.013	0.557	0.037	0.080	2,872
Number of polindes facilities in the village	0.076	0.092	0.073	0.012	2,872
Number of polyclinic available in the village	−0.006	0.812	0.049	0.042	2,872
Number of Posyandu facilities in the village	0.009	0.087	0.963	0.000	2,872
Number of primary schools: private	0.126	0.202	1.163	0.000	1,942
Number of primary schools: public	−0.069	0.587	1.224	0.000	2,692
Number of pusat kesehatan desa in the village	0.048	0.201	0.049	0.042	2,872
Number of puskesmas facilities in the village	−0.044	0.206	0.134	0.000	2,872
Number of puskesmas pembantu facilities in the village	0.014	0.768	0.732	0.000	2,872
Number of senior secondary schools: private	0.059	0.421	0.098	0.042	2,872
Number of senior secondary schools: public	0.050	0.371	0.220	0.000	2,872
Number of university/academy: private	0.012	0.614	0.500	0.005	1,563
Number of university/academy: public	0.027	0.340	0.125	0.293	1,543
Number of untrained traditional midwife (person) in the village	0.098	0.599	2.580	0.000	2,469

Source: Calculations using PODES 2008.

Note: Sample is limited to the approximately 3,000 villages that are part of the project. Survey indicates a dummy variable = 1 if villages are part of the impact evaluation study and 0 if villages are part of the project but not included in the project. District dummies are included. Minimum number of villages included = 1,543.

$$Y_{ij} = \beta_0 + \beta_1 I[Survey]_i + \varepsilon_{ij} \tag{3}$$

Table A8.2 shows the results from regression (3).

Table A8.2 Tests of Internal Validity Excluding District Fixed Effects

Label	Coefficient	P-value	Coefficient	P-value	N
Distance					
Distance to hospital	−9.972	0.000	33.186	0.000	2,843
Distance to maternity hospital	−23.192	0.000	46.696	0.000	2,838
Distance to polyclinic (km)	−14.875	0.000	37.034	0.000	2,677
Distance to puskesmas (km)	−1.490	0.100	8.826	0.000	2,440
Distance to puskesmas pembantu (km)	−4.024	0.001	8.610	0.000	1,561
Distance to doctor practice (km)	−9.904	0.000	19.134	0.000	2,479
Distance to praktek midwife (km)	−17.168	0.000	26.975	0.000	1,583
Distance to pusat kesehatan desa (km)	−16.719	0.000	42.734	0.000	2,463
Distance to praktek polindes (km)	−9.130	0.003	30.321	0.000	1,778
Distance to pharmacy (km)	−10.022	0.000	29.127	0.000	2,752
Distance to drug store (km)	−7.959	0.000	25.100	0.000	2,599
Distance to market (km)	−2.749	0.079	12.642	0.000	2,205
Environment					
Natural disaster ever occurred in the last 3 year	−0.078	0.031	0.501	0.000	2,872
Fire disaster ever occurred in the last 3 year	−0.010	0.195	0.019	0.000	2,872
Epidemic ever occurred in the last 3 year	−0.166	0.000	0.407	0.000	2,872
Cooking fuel: kerosene	−0.019	0.507	0.221	0.000	2,872
Population					
Number of family	470.752	0.000	812.100	0.000	2,871
Number of population	1,786.323	0.000	3,076.588	0.000	2,872
Number of family having electricity using PLN	412.667	0.000	641.969	0.000	2,776
Number of family having electricity using non-PLN	−9.419	0.275	35.687	0.000	2,754
Poverty					
Number of family without electricity	51.951	0.025	157.519	0.000	2,747
Cooking fuel: wood	0.034	0.251	0.759	0.000	2,872
Family toilet: none	−0.014	0.698	0.373	0.000	2,872
Waste disposal method: burning	0.019	0.569	0.691	0.000	2,872
Waste disposal method: other	−0.016	0.596	0.233	0.000	2,872
Family toilet: own	0.053	0.138	0.538	0.000	2,872
Service availability					
Number of doctor practice facility in the village	0.065	0.024	0.132	0.000	2,872
Number of drug store facility in the village	−0.012	0.548	0.096	0.000	2,872
Number of hospital available in the village	−0.006	0.293	0.010	0.000	2,872
Number of junior secondary school: private	0.587	0.000	0.444	0.000	1,820
Number of junior secondary school: public	0.011	0.818	0.518	0.000	1,975
Number of kindergarten: private	0.427	0.000	1.483	0.000	2,267
Number of kindergarten: public	−0.058	0.016	0.124	0.000	1,629
Number of mantri kesehatan (person) in village	−0.094	0.379	1.555	0.000	2,417
Number of maternity hospital available in the village	−0.019	0.114	1.990	0.000	2,872

table continues next page

Early Childhood Education and Development in Poor Villages of Indonesia •
http://dx.doi.org/10.1596/978-0-8213-9836-4

Table A8.2 Tests of Internal Validity Excluding District Fixed Effects *(continued)*

Label	Coefficient	P-value	Coefficient	P-value	N
Number of midwife (person) in the village	0.355	0.133	1.858	0.000	1,913
Number of midwife facility in the village	0.074	0.043	0.444	0.000	2,872
Number of pharmacy facility in the village	0.019	0.272	0.040	0.000	2,872
Number of polindes facility in the village	−0.002	0.961	0.381	0.000	2,872
Number of polyclinic available in the village	0.001	0.950	0.068	0.000	2,872
Number of posyandu facility in the village	0.033	0.000	0.967	0.000	2,872
Number of primary school: private	0.675	0.000	0.599	0.000	1,942
Number of primary school: public	0.695	0.000	2.359	0.000	2,692
Number of pusat kesehatan desa in the village	0.149	0.000	0.132	0.000	2,872
Number of puskesmas facility in the village	−0.003	0.913	0.151	0.000	2,872
Number of puskesmas pembantu facility in the village	0.102	0.005	0.449	0.000	2,872
Number of senior secondary school: private	0.367	0.000	0.165	0.000	2,872
Number of senior secondary school: public	0.055	0.161	0.147	0.000	2,872
Number of university/academy: private	0.051	0.109	0.055	0.000	1,563
Number of university/academy: public	0.014	0.493	0.018	0.002	1,543
Number of untrain traditional midwife (person) in village	1.324	0.000	3.270	0.000	2,469

Source: Calculations using PODES 2008.

Note: Sample is limited to 3,000 villages that are part of the project. Survey indicates a dummy variable = 1 if villages are part of the impact evaluation study and 0 if villages are part of the project but not included in the project. District dummies are not included. Minimum number of villages included = 1,543.

APPENDIX 9

Tests of External Validity

Test of external validity

$$Y_{ij} = \beta_0 + \beta_1 I[Project]_i + \sum_{k=2}^{466} \beta_k District_j + \varepsilon_{ij} \qquad (4)$$

Table A9.1 shows the results from regression (4).
Each outcome that we test falls into one of five categories:

1. Distance
2. Environment
3. Population
4. Poverty
5. Service availability

Table A9.1 Tests of External Validity

Label	Project		Constant		N
	Coefficient	P-value	Coefficient	P-value	
Distance					
Distance to hospital	−2.125	0.162	31.688	0.000	73,854
Distance to maternity hospital	−1.623	0.310	30.235	0.000	72,146
Distance to polyclinic (km)	−1.293	0.421	18.800	0.000	68,265
Distance to puskesmas (km)	0.116	0.903	5.791	0.000	66,840
Distance to puskesmas pembantu (km)	−0.887	0.436	4.999	0.000	52,247
Distance to doctor practice (km)	−1.445	0.221	8.937	0.000	63,119
Distance to praktek midwife (km)	−1.006	0.565	6.929	0.000	40,835
Distance to pusat kesehatan desa (km)	3.165	0.202	90.230	0.000	64,123
Distance to praktek polindes (km)	2.758	0.258	7.260	0.000	50,139
Distance to pharmacy (km)	−2.187	0.156	16.211	0.000	69,873
Distance to drug store (km)	−0.800	0.584	11.739	0.000	65,850
Distance to market (km)	−0.897	0.528	5.155	0.000	62,558

table continues next page

Table A9.1 Tests of External Validity *(continued)*

Label	Project		Constant		
	Coefficient	P-value	Coefficient	P-value	N
Environment					
Natural disaster ever occurred in the past 3 years	−0.006	0.836	0.572	0.000	75,410
Fire disaster ever occurred in the past 3 years	−0.012	0.123	0.005	0.046	75,410
Epidemic ever occurred in the past 3 years	−0.016	0.588	0.580	0.000	75,410
Cooking fuel: kerosene	−0.056	0.027	0.379	0.000	75,410
Population					
Number of families	98.670	0.004	153.018	0.000	75,408
Number of population	538.326	0.002	646.877	0.000	75,409
Number of families having electricity using PLN	66.081	0.063	119.697	0.000	70,503
Number of families having electricity using non-PLN	2.351	0.659	1.007	0.011	70,495
Poverty					
Number of families Without electricity	23.598	0.123	32.347	0.000	70,400
Cooking fuel: wood	0.053	0.039	0.613	0.000	75,410
Family toilet: none	−0.015	0.612	0.424	0.000	75,410
Waste disposal method: burning	0.031	0.276	0.885	0.000	75,410
Waste disposal method: other	0.004	0.880	0.081	0.000	75,410
Family toilet: own	0.047	0.116	0.485	0.000	75,410
Service availability					
Number of doctor practice facilities in the village	0.008	0.742	0.022	0.000	75,410
Number of drug store facilities in the village	−0.005	0.798	0.041	0.000	75,410
Number of junior secondary schools: private	0.158	0.008	0.919	0.000	46,277
Number of junior secondary schools: public	0.040	0.353	0.971	0.000	47,513
Number of kindergartens: private	0.047	0.582	1.095	0.000	59,041
Number of kindergartens: public	−0.030	0.227	0.872	0.000	42,267
Number of mantri kesehatan (person) in the village	0.065	0.520	1.690	0.000	58,856
Number of maternity hospitals available in the village	0.002	0.898	1.994	0.000	75,410
Number of midwife (person) in the village	−0.207	0.292	2.079	0.000	44,517
Number of midwife facilities in the village	0.021	0.499	0.096	0.000	75,410
Number of pharmacy facilities in the village	−0.010	0.478	0.021	0.000	75,410
Number of polindes facilities in the village	0.053	0.089	0.272	0.000	75,410
Number of polyclinic available in the village	0.010	0.537	0.022	0.000	75,410
Number of Posyandu facilities in the village	0.015	0.000	0.977	0.000	75,410
Number of primary schools: private	0.155	0.026	0.706	0.000	48,317
Number of primary schools: public	0.177	0.057	1.156	0.000	68,861
Number of puskesmas facilities in the village	0.013	0.566	0.032	0.000	75,410
Number of puskesmas pembantu facilities in the village	0.076	0.017	0.087	0.000	75,410
Number of senior secondary schools: private	0.129	0.018	0.022	0.000	75,410
Number of senior secondary schools: public	0.033	0.317	0.046	0.000	75,410
Number of untrained traditional midwife (person) in the village	0.326	0.104	1.446	0.000	59,953

Source: Calculations using PODES 2008.

Note: Sample includes all villages in PODES. Project is a dummy variable equal to 1 if village is part of the ECED project and 0 otherwise. District dummies are included. Minimum number of villages included = 39,959.

APPENDIX 10

Descriptive Statistics for the Younger Cohort

Table A10.1 **Means and Standard Deviations of Child Outcomes for the Younger Cohort (Age 1 at Baseline)**

	Treatment		Control		Comparison	
	Baseline	Midline	Baseline	Midline	Baseline	Midline
Enrollment						
Any ECED enrollment	0.151	0.369	0.031	0.352	0.052	0.182
	(0.358)	(0.483)	(0.172)	(0.478)	(0.222)	(0.386)
Child tasks						
Language tasks	2.921	4.716	2.931	4.778	3.011	4.759
	(1.434)	(0.561)	(1.497)	(0.480)	(1.433)	(0.510)
	1,027	981	1,121	1,042	908	866
Cognitive tasks	4.298	6.920	4.434	7.042	4.587	7.059
	(1.600)	(1.282)	(1.497)	(1.189)	(1.443)	(1.129)
	1,027	981	1,121	1,042	908	866
Gross motor tasks	13.382	17.873	13.613	18.132	14.206	18.062
	(4.648)	(1.680)	(4.682)	(1.449)	(4.387)	(1.544)
	1,031	978	1,122	1,041	913	854
Fine motor tasks	6.012	9.957	6.007	10.069	6.290	10.107
	(2.295)	(1.564)	(2.388)	(1.460)	(2.264)	(1.413)
	937	809	1,027	911	877	758
Socio-emotional tasks	1.595	1.469	1.676	1.465	1.619	1.422
	(0.550)	(0.499)	(0.527)	(0.499)	(0.549)	(0.494)
	1,037	988	1,136	1,060	922	874
Mother-rated child skills						
Receptive language skills	4.515	4.776	4.541	4.827	4.567	4.803
	(0.809)	(0.478)	(0.775)	(0.419)	(0.738)	(0.429)
	1,028	987	1,127	1,055	912	872
Socio-emotional skills	4.434	4.803	4.430	4.878	4.487	4.885
	(1.029)	(0.948)	(1.010)	(0.953)	(0.973)	(0.962)
	825	951	930	1,022	770	846

table continues next page

Table A10.1 **Means and Standard Deviations of Child Outcomes for the Younger Cohort (Age 1 at Baseline)**
(continued)

	Treatment		Control		Comparison	
	Baseline	*Midline*	*Baseline*	*Midline*	*Baseline*	*Midline*
Cognitive skills	5.435	5.946	5.502	5.962	5.516	5.951
	(0.752)	(0.226)	(0.728)	(0.191)	(0.669)	(0.217)
	1,020	*979*	*1,114*	*1,052*	*910*	*873*
Parenting practices						
Total parenting score	82.951	81.344	82.778	81.371	83.395	81.884
	(7.246)	(7.045)	(6.931)	(6.591)	(7.385)	(7.113)
	1,051	*995*	*1,151*	*1,072*	*932*	*886*
Nutritional outcomes						
Height for age Z score	−1.581	−1.348	−1.441	−1.460	−1.507	−1.499
	(1.59)	(1.54)	(1.76)	(1.48)	(1.56)	(1.42)
	993	*956*	*1,077*	*1,040*	*864*	*854*
Weight for age Z score	−1.657	−1.501	−1.670	−1.595	−1.689	−1.561
	(1.37)	(1.30)	(1.36)	(1.25)	(1.35)	(1.28)
	1,018	*973*	*1,119*	*1,050*	*899*	*866*
BMI Z score	−0.718	−0.677	−0.768	−0.735	−0.862	−0.658
	(1.75)	(1.64)	(1.79)	(1.52)	(1.74)	(1.56)
	979	*940*	*1,049*	*1,018*	*846*	*838*

Source: Calculations using ECED survey data.

Note: BMI = body mass index; ECED = early childhood education and development. Number of observations in italics; standard deviations in parentheses.

Descriptive Statistics for the Older Cohort

Table A11.1 Means and Standard Deviations of Child Outcomes, Older Cohort (Age 4 at Baseline)

	Treatment		Control		Comparison	
	Baseline	Midline	Baseline	Midline	Baseline	Midline
Ever enrolled						
Any ECED enrollment	0.61	0.90	0.34	0.82	0.36	0.73
	(0.49)	(0.30)	(0.47)	(0.39)	(0.48)	(0.44)
Early Development Instrument (EDI)						
Physical health and well-being	7.76	8.92	7.73	8.87	7.72	8.84
	(1.12)	(1.05)	(1.11)	(1.02)	(1.08)	(1.00)
Social competence	7.87	8.31	7.62	8.36	7.64	8.23
	(1.50)	(1.34)	(1.44)	(1.31)	(1.40)	(1.36)
Emotional maturity	6.62	7.03	6.53	6.98	6.54	6.9
	(1.54)	(1.45)	(1.49)	(1.49)	(1.55)	(1.51)
Language and cognitive development	3.19	5.75	3.06	5.75	3.17	5.62
	(2.10)	(2.65)	(1.97)	(2.67)	(2.07)	(2.68)
Communication and general knowledge	9.54	9.63	9.56	9.68	9.64	9.69
	(1.32)	(1.16)	(1.26)	(0.98)	(1.11)	(0.96)
Strengths and Difficulties Questionnaire (SDQ)						
Emotional symptoms (−)	3.59	3.49	3.78	3.59	3.73	3.57
	(2.06)	(1.99)	(2.02)	(2.09)	(2.04)	(1.98)
Conduct problems (−)	3.42	3.38	3.54	3.35	3.48	3.51
	(1.94)	(1.99)	(1.87)	(1.96)	(1.90)	(1.99)
Hyperactivity/inattention (−)	5.07	4.64	4.97	4.59	5.1	4.59
	(1.33)	(1.35)	(1.29)	(1.33)	(1.32)	(1.31)
Peer problems (−)	2.55	2.4	2.6	2.27	2.64	2.36
	(1.48)	(1.52)	(1.50)	(1.56)	(1.59)	(1.52)
Prosocial behavior (reversed) (−)	3.65	3.4	3.59	3.3	3.59	3.38
	(1.90)	(1.91)	(1.90)	(1.85)	(1.89)	(1.95)
Total difficulties (−)	14.63	13.92	14.88	13.8	14.95	14.03
	(4.46)	(4.45)	(4.45)	(4.70)	(4.67)	(4.48)

table continues next page

Table A11.1 Means and Standard Deviations of Child Outcomes, Older Cohort (Age 4 at Baseline) (continued)

	Treatment		Control		Comparison	
	Baseline	Midline	Baseline	Midline	Baseline	Midline
Other task measures						
Gross motor	4.88	4.95	4.91	4.96	4.91	4.97
	(0.47)	(0.24)	(0.38)	(0.21)	(0.38)	(0.19)
Fine motor	1.92	1.96	1.91	1.95	1.9	1.96
	(0.29)	(0.19)	(0.30)	(0.21)	(0.31)	(0.19)
Language	13.63	21.16	13.42	21.19	13.44	20.73
	(4.11)	(5.05)	(4.33)	(4.71)	(4.50)	(5.00)
Draw human	4.97	10.64	5.44	10.88	5.05	10.55
	(5.52)	(6.35)	(5.61)	(5.99)	(5.55)	(6.04)
Draw house	2.1	7.96	2.13	7.75	2.07	7.77
	(3.50)	(6.01)	(3.51)	(5.73)	(3.39)	(6.63)
DCCS card sort	0.64	0.86	0.64	0.89	0.68	0.89
	(0.48)	(0.34)	(0.48)	(0.32)	(0.47)	(0.31)
Parenting practices						
Total parenting score	80.656	79.741	80.254	79.719	80.397	79.915
	(7.376)	(7.306)	(7.008)	(6.773)	(7.135)	(7.318)
Nutritional outcomes						
Height for age Z score	−1.513	−1.506	−1.514	−1.517	−1.451	−1.539
	(1.224)	(1.085)	(1.155)	(1.081)	(1.212)	(1.066)
Weight for age Z score	−1.770	−1.671	−1.799	−1.756	−1.752	−1.684
	(1.151)	(1.192)	(1.205)	(1.234)	(1.276)	(1.267)
BMI Z score	−0.865	−0.870	−0.967	−0.933	−1.013	−0.862
	(1.462)	(1.353)	(1.474)	(1.376)	(1.411)	(1.328)

Source: Calculations using ECED survey data.

Note: BMI = body mass index; ECED = early childhood education and development. Standard deviations are in parentheses.

Estimates of Impacts of ECED Project

Table A12.1 Impacts for Younger Cohort

| | Experimental differences estimates | | | | | | Nonexperimental difference-in-difference estimates | | | | |
| | After 6 months of exposure | | | After 11 months of differential exposure | | | After 9 months of exposure | | | | |
	On average	Among females	Among children from poor families	On average	Among females	Among children from poor families	On average	Among females	Among children from poor families	Among children who were never enrolled at baseline	Among females who were never enrolled at baseline
Enrollment											
Any ECED enrollment	0.119***	0.129***	0.094***	−0.001	0.001	−0.033	0.189***	0.216***	0.185***	0.176***	0.213***
	(0.023)	(0.027)	(0.023)	(0.035)	(0.041)	(0.039)	(0.033)	(0.043)	(0.037)	(0.034)	(0.044)
Child tasks											
Language tasks	−0.045	−0.104	−0.072	−0.083**	−0.066	−0.109**	0.071	0.082	0.173	0.079	0.083
	(0.075)	(0.086)	(0.099)	(0.039)	(0.042)	(0.048)	(0.093)	(0.122)	(0.117)	(0.094)	(0.125)
Cognitive tasks	−0.135	−0.256**	−0.165	−0.145*	−0.156*	−0.144	0.124	0.137	0.269	0.132	0.151
	(0.099)	(0.105)	(0.136)	(0.082)	(0.093)	(0.094)	(0.126)	(0.152)	(0.173)	(0.130)	(0.156)
Gross motor tasks	−0.355	−0.688**	−0.600*	−0.292***	−0.251**	−0.426***	0.600**	0.484	0.990***	0.623**	0.528
	(0.229)	(0.293)	(0.350)	(0.093)	(0.114)	(0.141)	(0.259)	(0.355)	(0.374)	(0.263)	(0.355)
Fine motor tasks	−0.031	−0.056	0.038	−0.137	−0.119	−0.274*	0.241	0.190	0.505*	0.276	0.203
	(0.141)	(0.161)	(0.201)	(0.108)	(0.122)	(0.152)	(0.196)	(0.221)	(0.261)	(0.202)	(0.226)
Socio-emotional tasks	−0.074**	−0.062	−0.105**	−0.001	0.023	0.018	−0.022	−0.014	−0.059	−0.015	−0.018
	(0.035)	(0.041)	(0.046)	(0.030)	(0.037)	(0.040)	(0.052)	(0.057)	(0.067)	(0.053)	(0.059)
Mother-rated child skills											
Receptive language skills	−0.042	−0.016	−0.015	−0.056**	−0.077***	−0.068**	0.046	0.071	0.088	0.058	0.086
	(0.043)	(0.050)	(0.068)	(0.025)	(0.029)	(0.033)	(0.046)	(0.055)	(0.061)	(0.047)	(0.056)

table continues next page

Table A12.1 Impacts for Younger Cohort (continued)

| | Experimental differences estimates | | | | | | Nonexperimental difference-in-difference estimates | | | | |
| | After 6 months of exposure | | | After 11 months of differential exposure | | | After 9 months of exposure | | | | |
	On average	Among females	Among children from poor families	On average	Among females	Among children from poor families	On average	Among females	Among children from poor families	Among children who were never enrolled at baseline	Among females who were never enrolled at baseline
Socio-emotional skills	0.006	−0.058	−0.007	−0.068	−0.093	−0.074	0.044	0.075	0.102	0.038	0.082
	(0.064)	(0.083)	(0.087)	(0.057)	(0.069)	(0.072)	(0.092)	(0.113)	(0.106)	(0.093)	(0.113)
Cognitive skills	−0.058	−0.009	−0.080	−0.014	−0.011	−0.019	0.022	0.060	0.021	0.012	0.050
	(0.041)	(0.055)	(0.055)	(0.010)	(0.014)	(0.013)	(0.044)	(0.056)	(0.059)	(0.044)	(0.056)
Parenting practices											
Total parenting score	0.047	0.552	0.114	−0.088	0.243	0.308	0.066	−0.047	0.301	0.093	0.159
	(0.439)	(0.529)	(0.518)	(0.355)	(0.453)	(0.468)	(0.591)	(0.672)	(0.809)	(0.611)	(0.687)
Nutritional outcomes											
Height for age Z score	−0.143	−0.167	−0.174	0.124	0.103	0.186*	−0.030	0.018	0.027	−0.048	−0.003
	(0.090)	(0.121)	(0.118)	(0.091)	(0.110)	(0.102)	(0.109)	(0.142)	(0.142)	(0.112)	(0.148)
Weight for age Z score	−0.001	0.061	−0.012	0.083	0.136	0.123	−0.058	0.055	−0.086	−0.054	0.053
	(0.064)	(0.089)	(0.087)	(0.064)	(0.085)	(0.090)	(0.079)	(0.112)	(0.115)	(0.083)	(0.116)
BMI Z score	0.041	0.158	0.127	0.072	0.118	0.047	−0.166	−0.085	−0.107	−0.143	−0.057
	(0.099)	(0.126)	(0.126)	(0.079)	(0.116)	(0.104)	(0.130)	(0.172)	(0.171)	(0.135)	(0.180)

Source: Calculations using ECED survey data.

Note: BMI = body mass index; ECED = early childhood education and development. Significance levels: * = 10 percent, ** = 5 percent, *** = 1 percent. Each row corresponds to a different regression. Each cell is the point estimate assciated with the impact of the project for the sample specified in the column.

Table A12.2 Impacts for Older Cohort

| | Experimental difference estimates | | | | | | Nonexperimental difference-in-difference estimates | | | |
| | After 6 months of exposure | | | After 11 months of differential exposure | | | After 9 months of exposure | | | |
	On average	Among females	Among children from poor families	On average	Among females	Among children from poor families	On average	Among females	Among children from poor families	Among children who were never enrolled at baseline
Enrollment										
Ever enrolled	0.260***	0.291***	0.267***	0.068***	0.061**	0.091***	0.101***	0.129***	0.133***	0.135***
	(0.036)	(0.039)	(0.043)	(0.019)	(0.024)	(0.029)	(0.038)	(0.046)	(0.047)	(0.052)
Early Development Instrument										
Physical health and well-being	−0.002	0.111	0.031	−0.010	−0.006	0.073	0.043	0.080	0.127	0.018
	(0.061)	(0.078)	(0.071)	(0.053)	(0.058)	(0.073)	(0.070)	(0.096)	(0.099)	(0.087)
Social competence	0.199**	0.234**	0.319***	−0.105	−0.104	0.012	0.144	0.054	0.331**	0.186
	(0.082)	(0.098)	(0.114)	(0.068)	(0.076)	(0.085)	(0.112)	(0.131)	(0.149)	(0.132)
Emotional maturity	0.036	0.088	0.080	0.043	0.027	0.178*	0.122	0.113	0.155	0.147
	(0.083)	(0.092)	(0.108)	(0.075)	(0.105)	(0.104)	(0.112)	(0.148)	(0.158)	(0.128)
Language and cognitive development	0.105	0.232	0.148	−0.041	0.089	0.015	0.222	0.315*	0.454**	0.360**
	(0.120)	(0.154)	(0.143)	(0.162)	(0.195)	(0.210)	(0.143)	(0.186)	(0.186)	(0.160)
Communication and general knowledge	−0.048	−0.051	0.090	−0.097*	−0.072	−0.008	0.076	0.115	0.222*	0.076
	(0.072)	(0.075)	(0.101)	(0.056)	(0.066)	(0.066)	(0.088)	(0.095)	(0.125)	(0.122)
Strengths and Difficulties Questionnaire										
Emotional symptoms	−0.106	−0.035	−0.143	−0.065	−0.038	−0.123	−0.029	−0.034	−0.002	−0.013
	(0.113)	(0.144)	(0.140)	(0.110)	(0.141)	(0.159)	(0.141)	(0.190)	(0.200)	(0.153)

table continues next page

Table A12.2 Impacts for Older Cohort (continued)

| | Experimental difference estimates | | | | | | Nonexperimental difference-in-difference estimates | | | |
| | After 6 months of exposure | | | After 11 months of differential exposure | | | After 9 months of exposure | | | |
	On average	Among females	Among children from poor families	On average	Among females	Among children from poor families	On average	Among females	Among children from poor families	Among children who were never enrolled at baseline
Conduct problems	-0.092	-0.158	0.016	0.045	0.006	0.083	-0.262*	-0.220	-0.275	-0.290
	(0.104)	(0.127)	(0.138)	(0.097)	(0.128)	(0.128)	(0.149)	(0.191)	(0.194)	(0.183)
Hyperactivity/inattention	0.128*	0.114	0.165	0.034	-0.019	-0.029	0.125	0.133	0.063	0.085
	(0.077)	(0.095)	(0.101)	(0.068)	(0.091)	(0.091)	(0.103)	(0.128)	(0.130)	(0.118)
Peer problems	-0.036	-0.063	0.029	0.174*	0.168	0.157	-0.084	-0.189	-0.081	-0.105
	(0.088)	(0.108)	(0.109)	(0.093)	(0.113)	(0.127)	(0.115)	(0.145)	(0.150)	(0.134)
Prosocial behavior (reversed)	0.082	-0.041	0.007	0.130	0.184	0.087	-0.093	-0.068	-0.436*	-0.177
	(0.110)	(0.143)	(0.134)	(0.113)	(0.136)	(0.138)	(0.180)	(0.236)	(0.228)	(0.222)
Total difficulties	-0.109	-0.143	0.063	0.194	0.118	0.101	-0.255	-0.311	-0.302	-0.330
	(0.266)	(0.325)	(0.320)	(0.256)	(0.327)	(0.333)	(0.363)	(0.463)	(0.469)	(0.412)
Other task measures										
Gross motor tasks	-0.025	0.013	-0.032	-0.007	-0.004	-0.018	-0.014	0.019	-0.019	-0.018
	(0.020)	(0.029)	(0.030)	(0.010)	(0.014)	(0.017)	(0.022)	(0.031)	(0.035)	(0.029)
Fine motor tasks	0.008	0.011	0.028	0.010	0.007	0.018	-0.024	-0.035	-0.003	-0.026
	(0.014)	(0.018)	(0.023)	(0.011)	(0.011)	(0.016)	(0.022)	(0.031)	(0.029)	(0.026)
Language tasks	0.323	0.346	0.670	-0.137	-0.247	-0.342	0.556	0.414	0.475	0.629
	(0.364)	(0.420)	(0.434)	(0.275)	(0.347)	(0.439)	(0.434)	(0.519)	(0.592)	(0.522)
Draw human	-0.341	0.034	-0.328	-0.054	-0.065	0.187	-0.079	0.258	-0.281	0.231
	(0.371)	(0.469)	(0.466)	(0.350)	(0.438)	(0.488)	(0.484)	(0.605)	(0.629)	(0.569)

table continues next page

Table A12.2 Impacts for Older Cohort (continued)

	Experimental difference estimates						Nonexperimental difference-in-difference estimates			
	After 6 months of exposure			After 11 months of differential exposure			After 9 months of exposure			
	On average	Among females	Among children from poor families	On average	Among females	Among children from poor families	On average	Among females	Among children from poor families	Among children who were never enrolled at baseline
Draw house	0.059	−0.000	0.100	0.283	0.632	0.193	−0.204	−0.560	0.192	0.029
	(0.230)	(0.285)	(0.254)	(0.358)	(0.463)	(0.438)	(0.439)	(0.583)	(0.492)	(0.506)
DCCS card sort	−0.006	0.041	−0.013	−0.022	−0.029	−0.019	0.037	0.070*	0.072*	0.046
	(0.027)	(0.034)	(0.037)	(0.016)	(0.020)	(0.025)	(0.033)	(0.041)	(0.042)	(0.041)
Parenting practices										
Total parenting score	0.067	0.416	0.406	−0.241	−0.025	−0.384	−0.088	−0.066	0.832	−0.070
	(0.444)	(0.506)	(0.561)	(0.376)	(0.441)	(0.522)	(0.548)	(0.740)	(0.749)	(0.647)
Child nutrition										
Height for age Z score	0.016	0.047	0.001	0.036	0.128*	0.047	0.089	0.055	0.101	0.108
	(0.063)	(0.076)	(0.083)	(0.053)	(0.077)	(0.064)	(0.060)	(0.079)	(0.082)	(0.076)
Weight for age Z score	0.018	0.039	0.073	0.092	0.191**	0.110	−0.015	−0.007	0.014	0.061
	(0.057)	(0.081)	(0.069)	(0.059)	(0.080)	(0.072)	(0.058)	(0.075)	(0.080)	(0.069)
BMI for age Z score	0.073	0.049	0.137	0.051	0.110	0.092	−0.119	−0.049	−0.122	−0.119
	(0.077)	(0.104)	(0.102)	(0.070)	(0.089)	(0.092)	(0.095)	(0.118)	(0.129)	(0.121)

Source: Calculations using ECED survey data.

Note: BMI = body mass index. Significance level: * = 10 percent; ** = 5 percent; *** = 1 percent. Each row corresponds to a different regression. Each cell is the point estimate assciated with the impact of the project for the sample specified in the column.

186

Additional Reading

Ackerman, D. J. 2004. "Getting Teachers from Here to There: Examining Issues Related to an Early Care and Education Teach Policy." *Early Childhood Research and Practice* 7 (1). http://ecrp.uiuc.edu/v7n1/ackerman.html.

Behrman, J. R., E. M. King, G. Armecin, P. Duazo, S. Ghuman, S. Gultiano, and N. Lee. 2006. "Early Childhood Development through an Integrated Program: Evidence from the Philippines." Policy Research Working Paper 3922, World Bank, Washington, DC. doi: 10.1596/1813-9450-3922.

Behrman, J. R., E. M. King, and L. Laigo. 2004. *A Better Start in life: The Early Childhood Development Program in the Philippines*. Washington, DC: World Bank.

Binswanger-Mkhize, H. P., J. de Regt, and S. Spector. 2010. *Scaling Up Local and Community Driven Development (LCDD): A Real World Guide to Its Theory and Practice*. http://siteresources.worldbank.org/EXTSOCIALDEVELOPMENT/Resour ces/244362-1237844546330/5949218-1237844567860/Scaling_Up_LCDD_Book_ rfillesize.pdf.

Blair, M., S. Stewart-Brown, T. Waterson, and R. Crowther. 2010. *Child Public Health*. 2nd ed. New York: Oxford University Press.

Evans, D. K., and K. Kosec. 2012. *Early Child Education: Making Programs Work for Brazil's Most Important Generation*. Washington, DC: World Bank.

Gabbard, C. 2008. *Lifelong Motor Development*. 5th ed. San Francisco, CA: Benjamin Cummings.

Gertler, P. J. and L. C. Fernald. 2004. *The Medium Term Impact of Oportunidades on Child Development in Rural Areas*. Southern Africa Regional Poverty Network. Final report (fourth draft). http://sarpn.octoplus.co.za/documents/d0001264/P1498-Child_dev_ terminado_1dic04.pdf.

Goodman. R. 2005. "Strengths and Difficulties Questionnaire—Indonesian translation." http://www.sdqinfo.org/py/doc/b3.py?language=Indonesian.

Grantham-McGregor, S. M., S. P. Walker, S. M. Chang, and C. A. Powell. 1997. "Effects of Early Childhood Supplementation with and without Stimulation on Later Development in Stunted Jamaican Children." *American Journal of Clinical Nutrition* 66 (2): 247–53.

Harris, D. B. 1963. *Children's Drawings as Measures of Intellectual Maturity: A Revision and Extension of the Goodenough Draw-a-Man Test*. New York: Harcourt, Brace, and World.

Heaver, R. A., and J. M. Hunt. 1995. *Improving Early Childhood Development: An Integrated Program for the Philippines.* Washington, DC: World Bank and Asian Development Bank.

Heckman, J. J., R. J. Lalonde, and J. A. Smith. 1999. "The Economics and Econometrics of Active Labor Market Programs." In *Handbook of Labor Economics (Vol. 3),* edited by Orley C. Ashenfelter and David E. Card, 1865–2097. Vol. 3. Elsevier B.V.

Huttly, S. R., S. S. Morris, and V. Pisani. 1997. "Prevention of Diarrhoea in Young Children in Developing Countries." *Bulletin of the World Health Organization* 75 (2): 163–74.

Kluyskens, J., R. Rawlinson, and A. Ragatz. 2007. *Improving Efficiency and Equity in Teacher Employment and Deployment.* Jakarta: World Bank.

Little, A. 2006. *Education for All and Multi-Grade Teaching: Challenges and Opportunities.* London: Springer.

Lynch, J. W., C. Law, S. Brinkman, C. Chittleborough, and M. Sawyer. 2010. "Inequalities in Child Healthy Development: Some Challenges for Effective Implementation." *Social Science and Medicine* 71 (7): 1219–374.

Manhart, J. J., and R. A. Forsyth. 1999. "Mathematics Achievement in the Middle School Years: IEA's Third International Mathematics and Science Study (TIMSS)." *Journal of Educational Measurement* 36 (1): 79–85.

McKenzie, P., and P. Santiago. 2005. *Teachers Matter: Attracting, Developing and Retaining Effective Teachers.* Paris: Organisation for Economic Co-operation and Development.

Meisels, S. J. 1989. "Can Developmental Screening Tests Identify Children Who Are Developmentally at Risk?" *Pediatrics* 83 (4): 578–85.

———. 1998. *Assessing Readiness.* Center for the Improvement of Early Reading Achievement Report 3-002, Ann Arbor, MI.

Melhuish, E. 2011. "Preschool Matters." *Science* 333 (6040): 299–300.

Moskowitz, J. H., and M. Stephens. 1997. *From Students of Teaching to Teachers of Students: Teacher Induction around the Pacific Rim.* Washington, DC: U.S. Department of Education.

Naudeau, S., S. Martinez, P. Premand, and D. Filmer. 2011. "Cognitive Development among Young Children in Low-Income Countries." In *No Small Matter: The Impact of Poverty, Shocks, and Human Capital Investments in Early Childhood Development,* edited by H. Alderman. Washington, DC: World Bank.

Newberry, J. 2010. "The Global Child and Nongovernmental Governance of the Family in Post-Suharto Indonesia." *Economy and Society* 39 (3): 403–26.

Pradhan, M., S. A. Brinkman, A. Beatty, A. Maika, E. Satriawan, J. DeRee, and A. Hasan, 2012. "Study protocol for the evaluation of a community based early childhood education and development program in Indonesia: A pragmatic cluster randomized controlled trial with supplementary matched control group." Trials under review.

Schady, N. 2006. *Early Childhood Development in Latin America and the Caribbean.* Washington, DC: World Bank.

United Nations. 2011. *The Millennium Development Goals Report.* New York: United Nations.

UNESCO (United Nations Educational, Scientific and Cultural Organization). 2006. *Strong Foundations: Early Childhood Care and Education.* Education for All, Global Monitoring Report. Paris. http://unesdoc.unesco.org/images/0014/001477/147785E.pdf.

WHO (World Health Organization). 2011. "Exclusive Breastfeeding for Six Months Best for Babies Everywhere." Statement, WHO, Geneva. http://www.who.int/mediacentre/news/statements/2011/breastfeeding_20110115/en/index.html.

Wu, K. B., M. E. Young, and J. Cai. 2012. *Early Child Development in China: Breaking the Cycle of Poverty and Improving Future Competitiveness.* Washington, DC: World Bank.

Young, M. E. 1996. *Early Childhood Development: Investing in the Future.* Washington, DC: World Bank.

Environmental Benefits Statement

The World Bank is committed to reducing its environmental footprint. In support of this commitment, the Office of the Publisher leverages electronic publishing options and print-on-demand technology, which is located in regional hubs worldwide. Together, these initiatives enable print runs to be lowered and shipping distances decreased, resulting in reduced paper consumption, chemical use, greenhouse gas emissions, and waste.

The Office of the Publisher follows the recommended standards for paper use set by the Green Press Initiative. Whenever possible, books are printed on 50% to 100% postconsumer recycled paper, and at least 50% of the fiber in our book paper is either unbleached or bleached using Totally Chlorine Free (TCF), Processed Chlorine Free (PCF), or Enhanced Elemental Chlorine Free (EECF) processes.

More information about the Bank's environmental philosophy can be found at http://crinfo.worldbank.org/crinfo/environmental_responsibility/index.html.

www.ingramcontent.com/pod-product-compliance
Lightning Source LLC
Chambersburg PA
CBHW080610270326
41928CB00016B/2998